Education in Ethiopia

Education in Ethiopia
Prospect and Retrospect

Teshome G. Wagaw

Ann Arbor   The University of Michigan Press

Library of Congress Cataloging in Publication Data

Teshome G Wagaw, 1930–
   Education in Ethiopia.

  Bibliography: p.
  Includes index.
  1. Education—Ethiopia—History. I. Title.
LA1516.T47   370'.963   79-274
ISBN 0-472-08945-5

To Menelik, Fikirte, and Seble-Hiwot

Foreword

Not much has been written or published on the development of modern education in Ethiopia. The situation is even worse when it comes to the very elaborate traditional church education which has been operating for centuries in several regions of the country. The few books that exist have been written predominately by non-Ethiopians. In this respect, Dr. Teshome Wagaw's book—a comprehensive documentary exposition and analysis of education in Ethiopia—is a significant contribution. It is not only the first book of its kind to appear dealing with education, but also the first to be authored by an Ethiopian. His book could not have come at a more appropriate time to provide the historical setting and perspective necessary and useful as serious questions and questionings are taking place in and about the country in the political, social, and cultural spheres.

I commend it not only to those involved in the development of education in Ethiopia and Africa, but also to those interested in the fields of comparative education and the development of education in developing societies.

Aklilu Habte

Preface

Today in Ethiopia as everywhere else in Africa the demand for "modern" education by parents and children alike is unprecedented. The demand for and commitment to the expansion of public education is primarily a post–World War II phenomenon. The prevailing belief among most segments of the society is that education holds the key to social mobility, personal success, and national development. The national government, which controls and maintains public education throughout the country, has been under strong pressure to expand the system of education vertically as well as horizontally for a greater number of the children and youth of the nation, yet often insufficient thought has been given to the nature and relevancy of programs and, indeed, to whether the heavy investment of scarce resources would yield proportionate qualitative results.

Contrary to what is frequently written, Ethiopia, a sub–Sahara African state, maintained a highly structured, organized system of church education from at least the sixth century of the Christian era. The Ethiopian Orthodox church with the cooperation of the country's rulers had historically assumed this responsibility for children and adults alike. This program covered a wide range—from primary school to higher education—and was, quite naturally, oriented around religious themes and principles. Until recent times the church remained the sole reservoir from which the literate military, civil, and religious leaders, as well as scribes and scholars, were drawn. With the progress of time, unfortunately, the church's approach to education became increasingly rigid, to the point of ossification. At the same time, the emergence of Ethiopia as a modern state with a growing need for people trained in statecraft, diplomacy, commerce, and industry necessitated the redirection and secularization of education. Thus at the turn of this century a timid effort was made to initiate a secular system of education independent of church influence, an effort which required the importation of new ideas, philosophies, personnel, and methodology from abroad. As was to be expected, the indignation of the church leadership was aroused. Gradually, over the past forty years much of the opposition has been overcome, and today most of Ethiopia's young people prefer to attend public schools rather than those of the church.

This book then is an expository analysis of the development of education in Ethiopia from the early part of the Christian era to the present. The work does not purport to be a definitive treatise on socioeconomic development problems. As the title suggests, it is a treatise primarily dealing with major issues affecting the development of education and educational institutions in the context of one of the world's most ancient, traditionally conservative, and developing states. Analysis of the general socioeconomic as well as political issues is brought to bear to the extent that these are factors directly affecting education or are affected by it at critical junctures of its development.

Attempting to deal with so many major issues of Ethiopian education under one cover presented a number of formidable problems, for example, what to incorporate or leave out and which aspects of the issues to analyze in depth. I am cognizant of the fact that the student of educational development may not always agree with the choices and analytical emphasis of certain issues over others. For illustrative purposes let us take a few of the major issues persistently confronted by Ethiopian policymakers which have been treated in the present book with varying degrees of emphasis. One fundamental concern is whether to continue the use of Amharic as a language of instruction at all levels (Amharic is the national language and thus has a well-developed linguistic and literary tradition, but is politically tinted by its association with a certain ethnic group), or try to develop and use the many other local languages with the attendant risk of diverting scarce resources to the development of additional instructional materials and personnel and its uncertain implication for national cohesion or unity. Other issues include: the maldistribution of educational opportunity among urban and rural dwellers, males and females, Christians and non-Christians; the "scourge of illiteracy," which affects more than 80 percent of the school-age population and more than 90 percent of the adult population, and is growing; the philosophy, quality, and effect of the national examinations; the quality and relevance of the content of education; and the vexing problem of underemployment or unemployment of school leavers and graduates. These are some of the critical issues examined throughout the book and summarized in chapter 9, together with some implications for long-term policies and programs. The extent of analytical treatment or emphasis of the issues, however, varies in accordance to my values and in relation to many other issues competing for equal treatment and within the constraints mandated by space limitation. I hope I have achieved acceptable balance.

The work is organized chronologically and by eras. I found this convenient for my purpose, but I also realize that it could have been done in a number of other ways without diminishing much of its effectiveness.

As the only one of its kind in the market, this book may be of scholarly interest as well as serving as a useful text or reference work for colleges, teacher-training institutes, and other governmental and nongovernmental departments and institutions that play a role in the development of Ethiopian education. Overseas universities and governmental and international agencies may find it useful for their understanding of and participation in Ethiopia's developmental efforts.

After studying and working for twelve years overseas, I returned to Ethiopia in the summer of 1966 eager to make a contribution to its development. One of the first things of which I became painfully aware was the absence of research in all aspects of Ethiopian life—particularly in education and human development. It was my decision to engage in research in both these areas simultaneously. My first assignment at the Addis Ababa University, then known as Haile Selassie I University, as leader of the Ethiopian University Service (EUS), took me to the most remote parts of the country where I was able to make systematic observations of the problems of the educational system and lay the foundation for this book. Further administrative responsibilities at that university delayed additional research work until 1969. The original version of the work was written between 1969 and 1973 and has since been abridged and updated.

As I went about gathering material, I encountered far more

formidable problems than I had expected even in my most pessimistic moments. This had to do in part with the absence of reliable coherent information and in part with the difficulty of gaining access to primary sources such as reports that had been generated by various commissions, as well as by governmental and international agencies. Most of these documents, produced at great expense to the public, were locked up by government archivists who obviously believed in the archaic axiom that he who controls information controls power. I hope in the future to see a national law giving serious scholars access to government studies and reports. The lack of available data and the conflicting nature of that which was available were additional problems, particularly in the first decade of the postwar era. In many cases, I had to spend days and weeks gathering, piecing together, and evaluating bits of information from various sources to achieve a complete presentation. When conflicting information was encountered predetermined internal criteria were followed.

When I first began to formulate the strategy for the unabridged version of this book, I solicited various friends and colleagues for their opinions. One well-meaning colleague remarked, "Why don't you take a bite you can swallow?," meaning that under existing political and social conditions the undertaking was a formidable one. Others who were enthusiastic about the idea itself feared that the dearth of accurate data and the vastness of the project might prove to be overwhelming. On the other hand, there were colleagues whose confidence, optimism, and moral and material support were of constant inspiration throughout the project, and to them I owe a debt of gratitude. Among them I would like to mention Dr. Aklilu Habte, then president of the national university, who not only saw the great need for the book but provided the initial funds for its development; later he took time to read some of the early draft chapters and made valuable comments. Drs. Germa Amare and Mulugeta Wodajo read most of the early version of the manuscript and provided helpful comments. Ato Alemu Begashaw, as university registrar, provided access to the early files of the University College. Mr. Colin Darch, as university librarian, was helpful in reading the earlier version of the entire manuscript and suggesting valuable technical improvements. I'd like to express my gratitude to Mrs. Alice Gibson for doing a very good editorial job in helping me muster enough courage to reduce the size of the manuscript and to Jan Kralovec for typing parts of the manuscript. Addis Ababa University and the Agency for International Development (AID) Ethiopia, in the latter case through the enlightened encouragement of Dr. William P. Saunders, then chief of education of the agency, collaborated in providing means from the university trust fund for part of the writing of the book. The Center for Afroamerican and African Studies of the University of Michigan provided some resources toward the production of the final manuscript. I am grateful for their tangible support.

Throughout the book I have tried to give credit to authors and publishers from whose work I have drawn and to whom I am deeply indebted. Although these individuals and institutions have given me great assistance in the production of this work, any errors in fact or judgment are strictly my own responsibility.

My wife Tsehai Wolde–Tsadik has been of constant moral support to me. She and our children sacrificed without complaint many evenings, holidays, and weekends so that I could carry on the work of writing this book. Without their understanding and moral support it would not have been completed.

Teshome G. Wagaw

Contents

1   Introduction

Chapter

10   1. The Beginnings: Traditional Church Education

22   2. Foundations of Modern Education

41   3. The Italian Occupation

54   4. The Reconstruction Era, 1941–51: Needs and Objectives

79   5. The Reconstruction Era, 1941–51: Patterns of Growth, Management, and Legislation

95   6. The Territory of Eritrea, 1941–62

103   7. Consolidation and Planned Expansion, 1951–61

147   8. The Decade of Africa, 1962–72

183   9. Toward the Year 2000

199   Notes

217   Bibliography

253   Index

Explanatory Notes

Abun(a)	The head of the Ethiopian Church
Abyssinia	Another name for Ethiopia
Aleqa or Aleka	Chief; head of a parish or head teacher
Debtera	A deacon or cantor of the church
E.C.	Ethiopian Calendar; the Ethiopian year (Julian Calendar) consists of thirteen months; each of the twelve months has thirty days; Pagumen, the thirteenth month, has five days (six in leap year). The year begins on September 11 and ends in August. From September through February it is seven years behind; from January through August, eight years behind the Gregorian Calendar. The months of the year and their Gregorian equivalent are as follows:

Maskerem	September
Tikimt	October
Hidar	November
Tahisas	December
Tir	January
Yekatit	February
Megabit	March
Miazia	April
Ginbot	May
Sene	June
Hamile	July
Nehasse	August
Pagumen	

Eth.$ (Birr)	Ethiopian dollar equivalent to U.S.$0.40 (in the text, all monetary transactions are stated in Eth.$ unless otherwise specified)

G.C.	Gregorian Calendar
Ge'ez	The ancient language of Ethiopia still in use in Church services
Hakim	Physician; doctor of medicine
Lij	Literally, child; used with a proper noun it signifies a title of courtesy given to a person of noble birth or rank; the equivalent of esquire
Liq	Scholar; one who excels in any branch of scholarly endeavor
Liqe-Siltanat	Full professor; chief scholar, or one who excels over other scholars

Note that in the Bibliography names of Ethiopian authors appear first name first as is the custom in that country. Thus this author's name is listed as Teshome Wagaw, not as Wagaw, Teshome.

Ethiopia

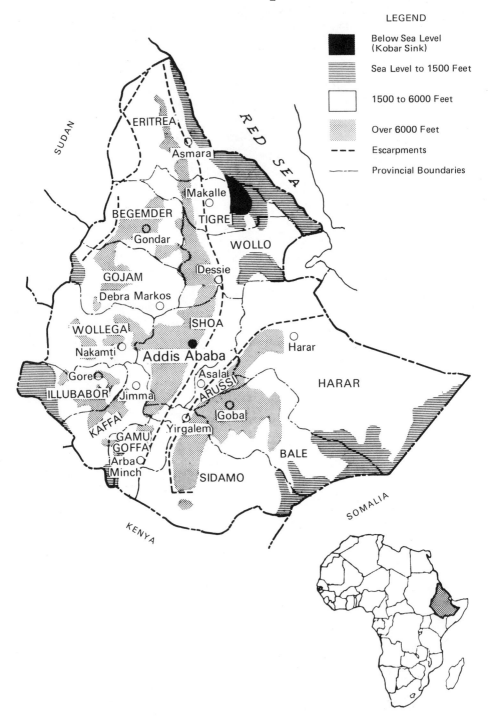

LEGEND

Below Sea Level (Kobar Sink)

Sea Level to 1500 Feet

1500 to 6000 Feet

Over 6000 Feet

---- Escarpments

---·- Provincial Boundaries

RED SEA

SUDAN

ERITREA

Asmara

Makalle

BEGEMDER

TIGRE

Gondar

WOLLO

GOJAM

Dessie

Debra Markos

SHOA

WOLLEGA

Harar

Nakamti

Addis Ababa

Gore

Asalal

HARAR

ILLUBABOR

Jimma

ARUSSI

KAFFA

Goba

GAMU

Yirgalem

GOFFA

Arba

BALE

Minch

SIDAMO

KENYA

SOMALIA

Introduction

Ethiopia is a large country, as large as Spain and France together. The terrain, which has served the nation as a natural fortress against external enemies, is beautiful but rugged. It contains mountain ranges rising to 14,000 feet, vast fertile highlands, hot desert country, and tropical rain forest. The varied countryside is inhabited by Ethiopians of many ethnic groups and traditions. There are three major religions in the country and a great many languages are spoken. A road system linking the different regions of Ethiopia is a relatively recent phenomenon. The capitals and urban centers in each province are now connected with Addis Ababa by Ethiopian Airlines and a few highways. Nevertheless, easy communication from one region of the country to another is still lacking.

Diversity in language, religion, and culture provides Ethiopia's rich and unique characteristics, which have tended to challenge national unity. In the past, unity was maintained by the two most important institutions in the country, the church and the monarchy. In recent years national integration has been encouraged by the growing use of the official national language, Amharic. Amharic is taught as a subject at all levels of education, and is the medium of instruction in primary schools. It is being further developed for communication in science, technology, and commerce.

In 1972, Ethiopia was a nation of approximately 25 million people, according to estimates supplied by the Central Statistical Office in the absence of an official census. Population increase was estimated at 2.5 percent per annum. An estimated 90 percent lived in rural areas, and 10 percent in urban areas, defined as settlements of more than two thousand. Income per capita for the rural population in 1969 was estimated at $109, of which only one-third was monetary, while the urban population had an average per capita income of $680, of which 95 percent was monetary.

Ethiopia is not overpopulated. The total area of the country is 1,221,900 square kilometers. Present mean density is thus about twenty people per square kilometer. If estimates are realized, the total population in the year 2000 will be more than 52 million, with two-thirds living in rural areas and one-third in urban centers.[1]

The first glimpse of Ethiopian history shows the Cushitic peoples in full occupation of the country. The Egyptians were probably the first foreigners to establish relations with them. Around the first millennium B.C. the Sabeans of southwestern Arabia brought an advanced material and intellectual culture across the Red Sea and settled in the highlands of Eritrea in the north. They must have noticed many similarities to the country they had just come from: a hot, arid, and narrow coastal strip of land leading up to highlands which enjoy regular rainfall sufficient for agricultural development. They spoke a language that we call Sabean, whose written form is closely related to Phoenician, and from which Ge'ez, the ancient Ethiopic language, is descended. Ge'ez became the dominant language. Most early manuscripts are in Ge'ez and it is still the liturgical language of Ethiopia. They founded the civilization of Aksum, a mixture of their own culture with the indigenous Cushitic culture. The legend of the Queen of Sheba may have had its origin in this early period of Sabean migration to Africa.

The civilization of Aksum was a sophisticated one. The rulers constructed impressive palaces, temples, and tombs, as well as obelisks or stelae beautifully carved out of single pieces of stone. We find stone inscriptions from this period written in Sabean, Ge'ez, and Greek, describing military campaigns and the victories of kings. We know that the Aksumites had commercial relations with Arabia, Egypt, Syria, Greece, and India, and gold, silver, and copper coins were minted for their trade.

In the fourth century, during King Ezana's reign, Aksum reached the zenith of its power. Ezana was a great ruler, whose reputation rests not only on successful military campaigns and his conversion to Christianity, but on his proclamation of Christianity as the state religion. He also built the great series of obelisks at Aksum, the largest of which exceeds thirty-three meters in height.

With the death of Ezana, the Aksumite kingdom began to decline, and near the end of the sixth century Christian rule in south Arabia came to an end with the Persian occupation. Persian influence soon gave way, however, to the onslaught of emergent Islam. With the coming of Islam neither conquest nor trade was possible with that region and the Ethiopians retreated into cultural and commercial isolation, which was to last until the appearance of King Zara Yakob in 1434. Of this remarkable man it is said, "He was unquestionably the greatest ruler Ethiopia had seen since Ezana . . . and none of his successors on the throne—except only the Emperors Menelik II and Haile Selassie I—can be compared to him."[2] He not only waged successful war against intruders and extended the frontiers of the empire but also introduced religious and administrative reforms. He became a genuine patron of literature, and some of the oldest extant Ge'ez manuscripts date back to his reign.

With his death in 1468 the great expansion of the Middle Ages came to an end, and his successors were unable to control his vast empire. Within fifty years, in spite of Portuguese aid, the country was overrun by Islam.

In about 1528 a forceful commander named Ahmed ibn Ibrahim (Gran, the Left-handed) began to menace the foothills of Ethiopia. Two years later he invaded the entire country, looting and destroying churches and monasteries and forcibly converting Christians to Islam. The holocaust enveloped most parts of Ethiopia and brought in its train misery and murder, ruin and devastation. Much of the literary and intellectual heritage of Ethiopia was irretrievably lost.[3] In 1541 Gran was defeated and slain in a hard–fought engagement near Lake Tana.

With the death of Gran, Ethiopia was left prostrate and exhausted. Many of the treasure houses of culture and religion were no more; the people were frightened and demoralized. In addition, a new threat was coming from another quarter. The Oromo migration from the south and southeast, beginning in the sixteenth century, was to remain the dominant influence for the next three centuries.

For the rest of the seventeenth century until the beginning of the nineteenth, Ethiopia "remained hidden and concealed, brooding and sullen. Leaderless, it floated like a rudderless ship in a sea of uncertainty."[4] At last, in 1632, Emperor Fasiladas emerged as a strong ruler. He built the great Gondar castles which still stand and reconstructed Aksum's cathedral which had been in ruins since the days of Gran. His grandson Iyasu I (the Great), who reigned from 1682 to 1706, can be counted among the notable rulers of Ethiopian history. He arrested temporarily the decline of state and monarchy, expanded the frontier southwards, and introduced tax reform throughout the country.

The expansion of the Oromos into Ethiopia proper meanwhile continued unchecked. Egyptian policy reawakened fears of Moslem expansion, and the European powers had begun to make their presence felt on African soil. The combined result was to be confronted by the Emperor Tewodros II whose rule (1855–68) marked the emergence of modern Ethiopia.

One of the first acts of Tewodros II was to eliminate the power of the local chiefs and to concentrate it in his own hands, reaffirming the authority of the crown. A police service was initiated; some attempts were made to regulate the administration of justice. For the defense of the empire, Tewodros proposed a regular army. He also turned his attention to social welfare and progress, and was the first to regard these as a function of the state. Adopting the motto, "Turn the swords and the spears into ploughs," he encouraged the people to return to agriculture, handicrafts, and trades. His high hopes, however, were shattered by the power of regional chiefs and by clerical disaffection, and the national unity he so ardently sought did not survive to the end of his reign.

Emperor Yohannes IV (1871–89) attempted to impose national unity through religious conformity, but Menelik II (1889–1913), a wise and courageous monarch, picked up and pursued the centralizing policies of Emperor Tewodros, constructing roads, establishing centers for public health, encouraging small industries, and interesting himself in education. In 1908 he created nine ministries to take charge of the various aspects of internal and external affairs. It is said that Menelik also planned a Ministry of Education, but that the Abun Matewos (head of the Ethiopian Orthodox Church) persuaded him that education came within the province of the church. The Ministry of Education was not in fact established until after Menelik's death, during the brief period of power enjoyed by Lij Iyasu,[5] his grandson. Lij Iyasu was never crowned emperor, and ruled for only three restive years before Menelik's daughter, Weyzero Zewditu, succeeded him. Ras Tafari Makonnen, later Emperor Haile Selassie I, was declared prince regent and heir to the throne.[6]

During this period, a number of progressive steps were taken. Slavery was suppressed, more schools and hospitals were established, Ethiopia joined the League of Nations in 1923, and military power was consolidated in the person of the regent. On the death of the Empress, the prince regent ascended the throne as Haile Selassie I, emperor of Ethiopia. The modernization initiated by Tewodros and continued by Menelik was now to be reactivated and expanded.

Ethiopia's first constitution appeared in 1931. It dealt first with the power and prerogatives of the emperor. A number of civil rights were recognized, though provisions for freedom of speech, religion, and association, contained in its Japanese model, were left out. A truly democratic or liberal constitution could not at that time have been implemented, but at least it could be claimed that a start had been made. It has been said that the constitution's sole direct result was the foundation of the parliament, although there was no legal or administrative machinery available to implement it. The power of the emperor over the provinces was expanded by a gradual process rather than by constitutional provision; and relations between the emperor and the parliament were left undefined in the constitution.[7]

At the opening of the first parliament in November 1932, Haile Selassie stated:

> Our basic intention is to renew our country; our purpose is to guide our people toward the advantages that modern times can bring; it is not to destroy the customs of our fathers that have come down to us from ancient times, traditions that have lasted for thousands of years. . . . Later on, when our people's knowledge is adequate, they will be able of themselves to choose members for this Chamber and send them to us; and these, once they know how to use properly the power we grant them, will become principal assistants of our government.[8]

Thus, the parliament created by the constitution of 1931 was not one in the Western sense; it was the first step towards an

ideal situation where all adult citizens would be ready to participate fully in the election of representatives.

Occupation and Restoration

On 3 October 1935, under Benito Mussolini's instructions and
without any declaration of war, three of his army corps crossed
the Ethiopian frontier, while Italian planes bombed Adwa and
Adigrat.[9] In a matter of seven months the formal war was concluded in Italy's favor, and in May 1936 Mussolini proclaimed
the establishment of an Italian empire in East Africa. The king of
Italy was invested with the title of Emperor.[10] The emperor of
Ethiopia went into exile in England, while many of his nobles and
their families found refuge in neighboring African countries and
in Jerusalem.

During the years of occupation (1936–41), the Italians tried
to impose a system of government designed to serve the purposes of Rome. Among other things, they created six major
administrative divisions or "governments" in Italian East Africa
along allegedly logical racial and ethnic lines. The division was
created by Italian propagandists to foment strife among the
peoples of Ethiopia, but to all intents and purposes such conflict
never took place.

On 5 May 1941, exactly five years after he left, the emperor
returned to the capital. To those who were aware of the magnitude of the task ahead—the reconstruction of the political, social,
and economic life of the country—the joys of military and diplomatic victory must have been mixed with apprehension. Ethiopia
had to disentangle the political and military web with Britain, her
leading partner in the fight for liberation. An immense program
of constitutional construction and social reform had to be carried
out, without destroying the essential character of the social fab-
ric. The two formidable tasks of centralization and modernization
loomed large, and the church and the nobility had to be handled
diplomatically if a new order was to be peacefully set in motion.

Since the war continued in Ethiopia and elsewhere, and the
British insisted on using materials and facilities in Ethiopia, some
form of administrative arrangement had to be made which would
meet both British requirements and those of the emperor. Nine
administrative areas were established, each to be as self-
contained as possible, and to include medical, agricultural, and

financial services. British officers were to "guide and direct" the local authority. It was made clear from London that while the reappearance of an independent Ethiopian state was welcome the advice of the British military authorities was to be strictly adhered to by the emperor as long as the existing military situation continued.[11]

Eventually, after involved and lengthy negotiations, the Anglo-Ethiopian Treaty and the Anglo-Ethiopian Agreement of 1942, dealing with the political and military relations between the two countries were concluded.[12] After the signing of the treaty the British withdrawal began at once;[13] by August 1942 the last British forces had left.[14]

When the 1942 Agreement expired, Ethiopia and the United Kingdom negotiated another treaty. The war was still going on, and the treaty promised Ethiopian resources for its prosecution; otherwise it fully recognized the sovereignty of Ethiopia.[15] The 1944 Agreement was the last of its kind. Ethiopia began to look around for other allies, not military but economic, and found one in the United States.

After 1941, Ethiopian administration expanded and improved. The Constitution of 1931 was reactivated, and in its 1955 revised form it made two great steps forward. For the first time the Chamber of Deputies was elected by universal adult suffrage, and the power of the parliament was increased. Its previous role had been primarily advisory, but now it could veto or amend legislation (in theory at least) and was independent of the other branches of government. This constitution was further defined as "the 'supreme law' of the Empire of Ethiopia . . . binding on the whole area 'under the sovereignty of the Ethiopian Crown' and on all people and organizations within that area."[16]

Successive laws clarified the duties and relationships of the Council of Ministers, set up under the chairmanship of the emperor or prime minister, but its character was changed by the replacement of older members by younger educated people. In 1948 only three of the ten ministers had a university education; twenty years later, sixteen of the twenty cabinet members were university graduates, five of them having graduated overseas since the occupation. Furthermore, these graduates rose to high office primarily through loyalty to the emperor.

After 1958 increased responsibilities were assigned to the

prime minister, who became responsible for legislation and relations with the Parliament and for mediation between ministers. By 1973 there were Ministries of Agriculture; Commerce; Industry and Tourism; Communications; Education and Fine Arts; Finance; Foreign Affairs; Imperial Court; Information; Interior; Justice; Land Reform and Administration; Mines; National Community Development and Social Affairs; National Defense; Pen, Posts, Telegraphs, and Telephones; Public Health; and Public Works. The head of the Central Personnel and Pensions Commission was also a member of the Council of Ministers.

Specialized agencies were established to deal with a number of technical and commercial activities, including the Ethiopian Airlines, the Imperial Highway Authority, the Awash Valley Authority, the National Bank of Ethiopia, and the Commercial Bank of Ethiopia.[17] These agencies have on the whole been more efficient and less open to political pressure than the ministries.

Reunion of Eritrea

Eritrea was an Italian colony from 1890 to 1941. After 1941 it was under British military administration, until the General Assembly of the United Nations resolved in 1950 that Eritrea should be federated with Ethiopia as an "autonomous unit under the sovereignty of the Ethiopian Crown." The steps to federation were complicated, but in 1952, the Eritrean Assembly unanimously adopted the prepared federal constitution, and the Act of Federation was ratified the same year.[18] After nearly sixty-two years of separation Eritrea was reunited with Ethiopia. It is interesting to note that the 1952 Constitution guaranteed the *right to education* to citizens of Eritrea. This responsibility was transferred to the Addis Ababa government ten years later, when the Eritrean Assembly voted for the abolition of the federation and for integration into the empire of Ethiopia.[19]

The Revolution

At this writing Ethiopia is once again undergoing vast social and political changes. The revolution that was precipitated in February 1974 is still in progress. In the process dramatic changes have already occurred. In September 1974 the emperor was dethroned and the monarchy was subsequently abolished. The constitution was suspended, the Parliament dissolved, and rural and urban lands, as well as major industries and commercial establishments, taken over by the state. A Marxist military government has been declared. Since that time much unnecessary destruction of human lives and property has been inflicted upon the country. Partly as a reaction to this cruelty and wanton destruction, internal armed resistance and external pressures are mounting, and the continued survival of Ethiopia as a political entity is now seriously questioned. This social and political turmoil has badly disrupted the schooling system. The implication of this fomentation and change for the future progress of education cannot be fully assessed or clearly predicted, but it is bound to be profound.

Chapter 1

The Beginnings: Traditional Church Education

Christianity, Islam, Judaism, and paganism have coexisted in Ethiopia for centuries, and all have founded schools for their adherents' children. Christianity is predominant in the northern, northwestern, and central regions, while Islam is dominant in the east, south, and west. Judaism is largely limited to Lake Tana and the region of the province of Begemder and Semien. Paganism is mainly confined to the southern, eastern, and western regions, including parts of the central plateau. Any account of Ethiopian education must recognize the contributions made by these different religious, linguistic, and cultural communities.[1] The most important of these has been, and continues to be, the Ethiopian Orthodox church.

Philosophy and Structure

We cannot date the beginnings of church education exactly. It might have originated in the Aksumite kingdom when Christianity was introduced at the court of King Ezana in the fourth century.[2] Expansion and modification continued until the golden age of church education, from 1200 to 1500. From the seventeenth century on, the pattern of education changed very little.[3] Nonetheless, it is true that: "In the course of their long history of Christianity, the Ethiopians evolved their own peculiar system of education. Like church education in other parts of Christendom, it was designed primarily for the training of the priesthood, but served also to diffuse and preserve all aspects of Christian culture."[4]

Church education, then, aimed to prepare priests, monks, *debtera* (deacons or cantors, who are often better educated than the priests but serve under them), and teachers to serve in the church's programs. Church education also produced civil ser-

10

vants, however, such as judges, governors, scribes, treasurers, and general administrators. There was no other source of trained personnel, and most civil servants shouldered the dual responsibility of serving both church and state. Some rulers, such as Zara Yakob, were actually priest-kings. In more recent times, the Constitutions of 1931 and 1955 stipulated that the emperor not only must confess the Orthodox faith but was also to be "defender of the faith."[5]

Iyasu the Great made the city of Gondar the center not only of religious activities but of secular learning and culture, and during his reign more than five hundred scholars lived in Gojam. The Church of Debre Berhan Selassie in Gondar had a famous library, with a collection of nearly a thousand religious books and manuscripts. The learned King Gelawdewos spent 3,000 ounces of gold on the collection of Ge'ez manuscripts, sponsored translations from Arabic into Ge'ez, and himself wrote the *Confessions of Faith*.[6]

Church education was a prescribed and traditional process. The age of admission to a church school was between seven and twelve years, and the time spent before graduation depended on health, intelligence, and motivation, as well as on the type of program followed. A pupil who planned to go on to higher education would first be required to learn the following:

Reading, writing, oral learning, until the Psalms of David
   (*Dawit Medgem*) are read—two years
Singing (*kum zema*)—four years
Advanced singing (*msaewait zema*)—one year
Liturgical dancing and sistern holding (*mergad*)—three years
Poetry (*qine*) and law—five years
Interpretation of Old and New Testaments—four years
Interpretation of the works of learned fathers and monks—
   three years
Book of the Blind (*merha euoor*)—six months
History—one year
Handicrafts, writing, parchment making, preparing writing
   stones, bookbinding, drawing, and so forth—four years

The full curriculum consisted of the Ge'ez and Amharic languages and literature, poetry, church music, world history, mathematics, philosophy, Biblical exegesis and history, doctrine, history of the church, liturgics, civil and canon law, Christian ethics, and pastoral theology.[7] Not every student completed the course, and those who did had to specialize in certain fields. The two preliminary stages were divided into the elementary and the secondary.

There were four stages in the elementary school, and in principle all of them were open to girls as well as to boys. In practice, only those boys whose parents were members of the Orthodox church were admitted. Church schools did not serve the whole nation, therefore, and so cannot be considered impartial or democratic. At the age of five or so, the child was taken by his parents to school, usually in or near his village, and presented to the master, who would hereafter stand in loco parentis.[8] The pupil first mastered the Amharic syllabary of 265 characters until he could identify them in any sequence.[9] In the second stage, he proceeded to the *Fidele Hawariya* (Epistle of St. John). In the third stage he began to read *Gebre Hawariya* (Acts of the Apostles), and the reading of Ge'ez was introduced.[10] The student had to memorize numerous religious works. Only those pupils who had progressed to straight fluent reading of Ge'ez texts were qualified to join the memorizing classes, which as a rule were held in the evening. At about nine o'clock a stone bell rang and the class recited the Lord's Prayer in Ge'ez. Then the pupils said good night to the master, kissed the ground, and went home. Some of them lived on the school premises where they ate dinner in groups and studied again before retiring. Meanwhile the master concluded his private prayers, ate dinner, and retired to his simple quarters. The routine continued day after day. On holidays there were no classes, but on Sundays senior pupils were expected to assist in church services, as a form of in-service training.

Handwriting skills during the last century or so were taught during the senior year of primary education or early in the secondary stage. The pupil learned to prepare his own ink and to fashion his pen from a reed. For three or four months he practiced on bone or wooden "slates" or cheap parchment until he had complete calligraphic command.

It usually took two years to graduate from the "House of Reading" or primary school. The term *Dawit degeme* ("He read the Psalms") announced the completion of elementary education. This was the terminal point for the vast majority of pupils and might qualify them for a career in the church or in civil service. When the good news of graduation reached the pupil's family, a big feast was prepared. The master was invited, as were members of the family, relatives, and friends. The master might ask the pupil to recite passages from the Psalms, then gifts were given to the master and pupil by the parents.[11] From then on the young man was a member of an intellectual elite.

The more ambitious student could now proceed to the school of *zema,* or church music. Entry was much sought after because here a pupil could prepare for a career in the church or in music composition. It was also important for those who would pursue advanced fields of study.[12] An additional advantage of the school of *zema* was that land grants were often related to service in the church, and this naturally provided a strong incentive for the young people to go and for the parents to send their children to the advanced schools.

The study of *zema* was divided into distinct stages. For about four and a half years, the students studied fundamental books of religious music composed by Yared (the legendary founder of Ethiopian church music) in the sixth century A.D. The study of the more refined and complex music (funeral music) then took one year, and was followed by a three-year course in *aqwaqwam* (religious dancing accompanied by drum and sistrum).[13]

The chief book of hymns, the *Digwa,* was divided into hymns addressed to specific persons or things and to hymns more general in character. Small signs or letters were written above and below the lines to indicate how the piece was to be recited or sung. The student had to memorize an immense corpus of religious music.[14] Thirty to forty students usually attended the *zema* classes and were joined by celibate monks in the vicinity who might wish to attend.

Classes began immediately after early morning service. When the stone bell rang or at the clapping of hands, the students assembled around the master, who was seated on a sheepskin or goatskin spread on a slightly elevated earthen dais. After communal prayers the students in turn recited directly to the master. In the late afternoon the students were released to eat or to search for firewood, although a few remained behind to take part in evening prayers conducted by the master. The evening session lasted for three or four hours. Then the students retired for some four or five hours' sleep. At cockcrow the cycle of activities was resumed.

Halfway through the *zema* school, the students could choose either to complete the course to go on to the school of *qine* (poetry), or to attend both schools at once. In the latter case, he had to find a center where there were qualified masters. The city of Gondar was the foremost center of learning for *aqwaqwam*. City life was distracting, however, and it was difficult to live there by begging, which was the most common way for students to earn a living. Surrounding centers such as Azezo, Chilga, Dembiya, and Wogara often met students' needs better. They offered only the rudiments of *aqwaqwam,* however, and the student still had to proceed to Gondar to finish. When this became necessary, the wise student brought enough food to last him at least a year. Depending on his intelligence, motivation, and background, it would take him between one and ten years to complete his studies.

By this time the student had begun to acquire a higher social status. In many respects he was a master in his own right and was treated as such by his peers and masters. He was no longer expectd to run errands, fetch firewood or water for the master, wash the feet of guests, or call the master *Yeneta* (My Lord). He now had more leisure than ever before in his life. He studied in the various departments under different masters, and the method of instruction began to reflect the student's maturity. Life in the school of *zema* had been rigorous; it had taken him between fourteen and twenty years to complete the course. If he was successful, and if his health was still good, he might want to proceed to the school of *qine,* the most challenging stage of all.

There were a number of centers for *qine* in Chilga, Fogara, and Wogara in Begemder and Semien province, Wadla and Lasta in Wollo province, and certain places in the provinces of Gojam and Tigre. The centers in Gojam were the best known. Before the student decided which school to attend, he again made inquiries regarding the qualifications, character, and reputation of his prospective teachers and determined whether or not he would be able to earn enough to support himself. After making his decision the student took leave of the *zema* school. He might even disappear without a word, perhaps fearing that his relatives might exert pressure on him to stop his program of schooling and to come home and settle down instead.

At the center of his choice, the student was first questioned by the master concerning his background for further study. If the responses were satisfactory, he was given formal permission to join the school and was assigned to an assistant (usually a senior student) who would introduce him to the institution and the surrounding community. The assistant would also help him to learn the rudiments of Ge'ez vocabulary and to analyze and memorize the classical poems. This might take from seven to ten days. The student then began to read *Gubae Qanna* (Congregation of Qanna) before his master. This is the original *qine,* believed to have originated in Qanna, Amara Sayint, in northern Shoa. For the first time he began to understand what he was singing or reading in Ge'ez. Soon he was composing simple couplets in Ge'ez and proceeded to advanced forms of composition in traditional styles.

As a rule, a student of *qine* got up early and went to the neighboring woods or hills to compose his poem for the day. In the evening he recited his composition aloud to the master in the presence of other students. In this way, each student compiled his own book of poetry. Occasionally the master read a composition of his own, encouraging and challenging his students to emulate his style of composition and recitation. An Ethiopian scholar, Germa Amare, has observed:

> The study of *Kine* [sic] derives its significance from the fact that this is the most highly refined expression of Ethiopian culture, which, it is said, is characterized by ambiguity, vagueness and secretiveness. *Kine* may be defined as the art of detecting others' ambiguities [in communications] while increasing the subtleties of one's own. This art is acquired through the mastery of two types of poetry, *Semena-Work* (Wax and Gold) and *Wusta Waira* (Inside the Olive Tree).[15]

Students studied *qine* from one to five years; after this, they began to specialize.[16]

The question has been raised from time to time as to whether Ethiopian church education was equivalent to that of other ancient cultures, especially with regard to higher education. Mulugeta Wodajo[17] thinks it was not necessarily always so, while Germa Amare disagrees. It is clear, however, that the concept of higher education did exist and still exists in the church. One aspect of the problem is whether to include the school of *qine,* the advanced forms of *aqwaqwam,* and other branches of the *zema* school under this description. It is not easy to provide an answer. For our purposes, however, we will consider that higher education began at the end of the school of *qine.* By this time, the student was a mature and serious scholar. The choice of whether or not to enter the next stage, the *metsahift bet* (House of Books), was entirely his, but if he did so he declared his intention of reaching the educational summit.

Here he again found that the major centers were Gojam and Begemder. The teachers might be married clergy, or they might be monks and hermits, who supported themselves on small payments from the students or through alms from the community. Scholars who reached this level were comparatively few, but those few were treated with great respect and the master himself might think of them as his peers. As a student of the Scriptures, the scholar might defray his expenses by working part of the time in the local church, or he might choose to make handicrafts to sell in the local market. Students who entered *metsahift bet* might specialize in the Old Testament, the New Testament, church dogma and philosophy, or astronomy. Although they were expected to specialize, and most did, some scholars excelled in all four areas and were called *Arat–Ayna* or "four–eyed ones."[18] These were few in number, perhaps only three or four in each generation.

After completing his Old or New Testament studies, the student still faced a long curriculum that would include familiarity with the *Fitha Negest* (Judgment of the Kings), the Ethiopian traditional code of law, the rules and spiritual discipline governing the life of monks, and the computation of the Ethiopian church calendar which afforded mathematical training. To graduate might take thirteen years or more, but the long, arduous journey was now over. The scholar, now some thirty-five years of age, was henceforth permitted to teach at advanced levels in churches or monasteries.

The study of history might also be undertaken as part of the advanced program. There were no organized schools for this discipline but for a year or more, the scholar might visit historical sites, churches, and monasteries.[19] Study of the sciences and of astronomy was minimal. Science was represented by two works written in the eighteenth century, possibly derived from Arab and Syrian sources. There is evidence that they have been modified; for example, prescription for the treatment of hair, skin, and eye diseases seem to be Ethiopian. The astronomical works probably originated from similar sources, again with adaptations to suit local conditions. Apart from these, scientific studies were apparently never pursued—perhaps because "works of science do not exist in Abyssinian literature. As the heavens and the earth are ruled by God all enquiries into the working of the heavenly bodies and the laws of nature were and are regarded as sinful."[20]

As Liqe Siltanat Habte Maryam notes, the art of Ethiopian calligraphy has always been taken seriously, though its origin (probably in the twelfth century) and the development of different styles are obscure. The goal was to facilitate certification of authenticity at a time when printing was unknown. The first books to be copied in the standard form were the Holy Books, followed by works of religion, philosophy, and history. The work was tedious and time-consuming; it took a year to copy a book of average size, in addition to preparing inks and parchments. In this way the monasteries and churches became the centers of religious, philosophical, and scientific investigation and production.[21]

Study of fine arts was part of the curriculum, though it was not compulsory. There is some evidence that in pre-Christian times paintings were exported to Egypt, but there is little information about their character. After the introduction of Christianity, Byzantine and Syrian influences become apparent, but Ethiopian traditional art has developed along its own lines.

Critics of Ethiopian literature and painting complain that it is too stereotyped, allowing little scope for individuality. They object to the fact that subject matter was narrowly circumscribed "by the force of tradition." As one writer put it: "The effect of this literature has served rather to buttress conformity, by rekindling identification with the sacred symbols of the society. Ethiopian religious literature does not invite introspection; it is a corpus to be venerated and solemnly rehearsed."[22] It is true that the

primary creative urge was religious rather than esthetic for patrons and artists alike. Anonymity was essential. For a writer or
painter to display his name was considered most immodest. Most
early paintings have religious themes, and painting has acquired
over the centuries a stifling, repetitive, and rigid quality. One
convention out of many will serve as an example. By tradition
any figure painted in profile, with only one eye showing, was
evil—Satan, the Jews demanding Christ's crucifixion, and so on.
Saints, angels, the Virgin, or Christ himself were always shown
full-face, with both eyes visible. The order in which the lines
were drawn and the figures painted, as well as the colors used,
was dictated by strict rules. Even the position of a painting within
the church was prescribed. Pictures of the life of the Virgin were
always hung on the south wall, pictures of Christ and the apostles
in the east corner.[23] Nevertheless, great masterpieces of Ethiopian art were produced in the sixteenth century by painters
working meticulously within the established conventions.

The preparation of brushes, parchments, and colors was a
complex and skilled business and took considerable time. For
example, a certain black ink was made from a mixture of soot
and nine herbal ingredients which had to be fermented for at
least three months. Parchment was made from sheepskin or goatskin and involved making and using at least ten different tools.[24]
It was possible to buy prepared materials, but most students
underwent extensive training in the techniques of mixing and
preferred to use their own materials. The fact that many ancient
paintings are still fresh and unfaded is a testimony to the students' patience and care. Professional artists commanded respect,
both at court and in the community at large, and rewards were
generous. Public recognition, respect, and the opportunity to
gain material possessions were strong incentives for the student
to persist in his lengthy period of training.[25]

Most students earned their living by begging, as we have
said. The community assumed responsibility for the student and
responded generously to his distinctive chanting, designating him
as a "guest of God." But as each student progressed he had to
begin to pay his way by working. He learned to make ink by
mixing soot, roasted wheat, leaves, and gum in precise quantities.
He prepared parchment for use in carrying medicines or for
paintings and holy writings. A bright student could tutor pri-

vately or he could sell drugs prepared from various herbs. He could make parasols, umbrellas, or mats from reeds, prepare coffins, and tailor clothes. He was taught how to make every kind of pouch and bag for food, books, or anything else that had to be transported. In fact, he would make almost anything for which there was a demand so that he might ensure his academic survival.[26]

Teaching

Requirements and rewards for teaching at different levels of the church system of education varied from one region to the next. A teacher at any level had to be a well-educated man of upright character, to ensure a high standard of instruction and the moral well-being of his students. He might be a monk, a hermit, an *aleka* (head of a parish), or a priest. Hermits and monks had to be celibate and to devote their lives to the welfare of others, for teachers rendered many services to the church and to the sick and poor in their communities. Most were proficient in *zema,* and quite a few were masters of scriptural interpretation, philosophy, history, and the arts.[27]

Those who conducted classes in the fundamentals of reading, writing, and religion were not expected to be especially learned, and certification of their teaching ability was not required. At the *zema bet* level, however, teachers had to have certificates, for which they worked for seven years. At this level they were and are crucial to the system, since they teach not only writing and reading at an advanced level, but also the practice of church services and *zema.*

Qine was considered the gateway to Ge'ez and hence to the mysteries. It was the criterion of an able mind in a crowded field. It is reported that some who taught *qine* were not eager to reveal their knowledge to their students and that they thrived on challenging colleagues to debate subtle points of learning. At the same time these teachers, as well as their students, knew that mastery of *qine* led to the ability to read and interpret the Holy Books and to understand the hymns, prayers, and rituals of the church. Anyone serving in the church who did not know *qine* and Ge'ez was open to humiliation.

Teachers in the School of Books were a class apart. They were wise men, the most respected members of the community of scholars. Even their disciples commanded respect in the community.[28] The *Metsahift Bet* was in essence a university where the whole approach to learning, including the qualifications of the professors, methods of teaching and learning, and the popular attitude toward the leadership of the community of scholars, reflected maturity of mind and the ideal of democracy in action.

Some church teachers received remuneration in kind or in cash, others received none at all. Furthermore, the teacher did not always know whom to charge. He could not ask the church, because there was no central administration to supervise his work or to accept responsibility for operating costs. He could not charge his students, because they lived at subsistence level on what they were given, and when they were through with their education would often disappear without even saying good-bye. The master had to look elsewhere to find means of support. He might exercise a craft or cultivate a piece of land, in which case students would lend a hand during planting and harvesting. In some cases he might receive a stipend from the national treasury, from the king's private purse, or from a wealthy man's private coffer. Other teachers wandered from place to place, begging for their meals.[29] Sometimes the essentials of life were acquired by begging or provided unasked by laymen of the community. Still others of the teachers were hired by wealthy lords to teach in their private compounds, and so provided with room and board and an adequate salary.[30] After 1939 E.C.,[31] the emperor paid the salaries of the occupants of the traditional chairs in Gondar, who led comfortable lives in contrast to their colleagues elsewhere.[32]

At lower levels the teacher priest was often married, with a family to support. In the *Metsahift Bet* most teachers were celibate monks and hermits, demanding no remuneration from any quarter. They undertook handicrafts, wrote parchments and manuscripts, bound books, or carved the *Tselat* (Holy Tablet) for modest fees and thus were able to contribute to the upkeep of a needy student. Most teachers indeed followed the divine injunction, "What you have received freely, give freely."

Results

What were the results of the church system of education? Church leaders, here as elsewhere, were conservative in thought and deed, and the philosophy behind their whole approach to education reflects their attitudes. A child was supposed to be quiet, polite, shy, unquestioningly obedient and uncomplaining, and respectful toward the church, government officials, and his elders. If he disobeyed or absented himself from class, he was beaten severely.[33] Donald Levine has observed that: "the atmosphere of the schools where reading is taught is harsh and primitive. Pedagogy at all levels of instruction is based on repetition and memorization, with strict adherence to the conventions preferred by the teacher. . . . [Traditional formal education] in no wise seeks to cultivate the individual, but aims solely to prepare cultural specialists who will be able to perform the rituals and perpetuate the teachings of the Ethiopian church."[34] Germa Amare elaborated: "The purpose of church education is not to extend man's understanding of the world, but rather to lead men to accepting the existing order of things as it is, to preserve whatever has been handed down through the years, and in turn to pass it on unchanged to the next generation."[35]

It may be true that such education has tended to stifle healthy curiosity and independent thinking. From the school of *Qine* through the School of Books, however, the student's personality was not so harshly repressed as in the lower grades, although his restrictive experience there may already have done lasting damage.

The next chapter will deal with the dawn of the "modern" system of education under the auspices of the state. As we shall see, this new venture created determined opposition from the church and from many of the traditional political leaders.

Chapter 2

Foundations of Modern Education

As we have seen, education in Ethiopia was for centuries in the hands of private institutions, primarily the Ethiopian Orthodox church. Although the church guarded its responsibilities with jealousy and vigor, it cannot be said that it dominated education entirely. Influential men prided themselves on being patrons of education, the arts, and literature. Some of them promoted the production of books and paintings, albeit from religious motives; others supported a teacher or two to conduct classes for children of the village or community. Resident teachers were employed to teach children of the wealthy landlords as well as the offspring of their dependents. Never once, however, until the beginning of the present century, had any ruler sought to establish a secular program of education. Had one tried, he would perhaps have aroused the indignation of the church, as Emperors Menelik and Haile Selassie did later; or perhaps, isolated from Europe and the world, these earlier emperors lacked any sense of the importance of secular education. Again, knowing the power of the church and what it could do politically, they may have had no wish to antagonize it.

At any rate, the church system of education, more than sixteen hundred years old, persisted, meeting in a limited way the manpower and intellectual needs of church and state alike. It is true that in the sixteenth century, when the Jesuit missionaries entered Ethiopia, the enterprising Pero Paez organized a small school for Ethiopian boys. A Lutheran missionary is said to have organized lessons in Hebrew and Greek for boys in 1634. These schools were set up primarily for proselytizing purposes, however, and left no lasting mark on the country.

In the 1830s, the missionaries Isenberg and Krapf ran a school in Shoa. A generation or so later, during the reign of Tewodros, Martin Flad ran a small school at Awra and later at

22

Magdala. One of the most important of the missionary organizations, the Swedish Evangelical Mission, entered Massawa in 1866 and established a school in Monkullu. Another was opened in Asmara in 1897, and a girls' school at Belessa in 1890. Similar schools followed in other parts of Eritrea. By 1905 there were 100 students in these schools, 88 men and 12 women in retreats, and 144 other people in contact with mission stations.

Study Abroad

In the middle of the nineteenth century, individuals began to go abroad through the sponsorship of private or foreign missions. Two brothers who had studied abroad became prominent during the reign of Emperor Tewodros II. One of them was Mahdere Qal, who served as interpreter for the emperor and is reported to have been at Magdala during the fighting with the British forces. Mahdere Qal was first taken by a private traveler to Paris, where he studied at the College de Henri IV. He later transferred to a Protestant college in Malta and from there went on to England. He returned to Ethiopia by way of Egypt in 1856, just after the coronation of Emperor Tewodros. The young man served the emperor faithfully, and later performed several important missions for his successor, Emperor Yohannes IV. Mercha Werqu, son of an Armenian blacksmith and an Ethiopian mother, studied in a missionary institution in Bombay and returned to found a short-lived school for Ethiopian boys with funds obtained in Bombay. Mercha served both Tewodros and Yohannes as interpreter for diplomatic missions and was sent to England on a mission for the latter.

In the late 1860s several young Ethiopians went abroad to study. In 1869 it was reported that there were eight boys in two missionary schools in Jerusalem and several more at schools in Switzerland. The students in Switzerland included several converted Felashas (Ethiopian Jews) who had been at Bishop Gobat's school in Jerusalem. All of them were under the general guardianship of Martin Flad, who had taught them German at his home in southern Germany.

The most important of the mission-educated boys of this time was Gebru Desta, a Christian youth of Begemder who had been with the Protestant mission to the Felashas. After the battle of Magdala, the missionaries took him to Bishop Gobat's school in Jerusalem. In 1873 he went to Basle. On completing his studies there he returned to Gobat's school as a teacher, then joined a group of missionaries in Zanzibar, where he was instrumental in securing the release of some Ethiopian slaves. Later he joined a British medical mission in Aden. On learning of the Italian occupation of Massawa in 1885, he returned home, but was received coolly by Emperor Yohannes, who was suspicious of missionaries. Gebru finally won his confidence and was charged with several important commissions. He was appointed by the missionaries to run a school near Lake Tana and was then asked by Negus Tekle Haymanot, governor of the region of Guduru, to transfer his activities there.

After Yohannes's death, Aleqa Gebru went to Harar to distribute Bible tracts on behalf of the British and Foreign Bible Society. Soon Emperor Menelik summoned him to court and made use of his services for many years thereafter. He is reported to have accompanied the emperor to the battle of Adwa in 1896 and to have been made responsible for the Italian prisoners of war. He pointed out to Menelik the diplomatic benefits to be gained by humane treatment of war prisoners. In 1898, Gebru was appointed mayor of Gondar. For a time he was imprisoned and his property confiscated. This period of confinement he passed in literary and scholarly pursuits, and later he became interpreter at the German Legation. On the promulgation of the first constitution in 1931, Mayor Gebru was appointed vice-president of the senate. After the Italian occupation in 1936, he went to Gore in an attempt to organize guerrilla resistance.

It is of interest to note at this juncture that foreign-educated youths returning home often met with a cool or even hostile reception. One such incident is reported by Pankhurst: "The critical attitude with which these early returned students were regarded is apparent from an incident, recalled by Flad, when the Emperor Yohannes dismissed Aregawi and Agaje from his presence, commenting unfavourably on the fact that they had adopted the European fashion of wearing shoes. 'If you appear again before me . . . come barefoot. We Ethiopians do not have shoes; dress yourselves according to the custom of the land.' "[1] After the long isolation following the civil strife and the expulsion of the Jesuit mission from the country, this suspicious attitude toward things foreign is perhaps understandable.

A remarkable young man who was taken to England at the end of the battle of Magdala was Werqneh Ishete, known as Dr. Charles Martin to Europeans. Born in Gondar in 1863, he accompanied his parents to Magdala where they were taken by Tewodros. The British soldiers carried him off to England. From England he went to India, where he graduated from medical school. Later again in England, he did additional work in surgery, working afterwards in Burma as a medical officer and civil surgeon. Some thirty-two years later he came back to Ethiopia and worked for Emperor Menelik, then for Ras Makonnen in Harar. In 1902 he returned to Burma, but came back to Ethiopia to work in the British Legation. He went once again to Burma, but while there he heard of Menelik's death and the subsequent accession of Ras Tafari to the throne. In 1919 he resigned and returned to Ethiopia for good, having spent twenty-eight years in British service. In Ethiopia, the fifty-six-year-old physician, "zealous as ever to assist his country, undertook medical work, ran farms and flour mills. . . . He persuaded the Regent to open a new school, the Tafari Makonnen Lycée . . . and acted as its director . . . until 1930. He also himself started a school for girls."[2] Later he became governor of Chercher where he initiated the "package" approach to community development, and thereafter was appointed ambassador to London.

Foreign missionary organizations were also active in sending students abroad. Monseigneur De Jacobis took twenty-three Ethiopians to Rome as early as 1841, while in 1869 eight young men were installed in and around a Capuchin institution, St. Michael's College, near Marseille. The Swedish Evangelical Mission also educated a few students overseas. One of the first was Nesib, who was rescued from the hands of slave-traders and who later became very active in the work of the mission in Ethiopia and took part in the translation of the Bible into Afan Oromo (Galligna). Four Eritreans were also sent to Sweden.[3]

This is only a partial list of the young people who went abroad to study during the nineteenth century. In all likelihood their training consisted for the most part of religious education. On their return home, they were expected either to teach in the mission schools or to propagate their faith on behalf of the sponsoring organization. Others worked full-time for their emperors. At any rate, the initial momentum had been created.

From now on, there was only one direction for Ethiopian education: forward.

The reign of Menelik and the establishment of Addis Ababa as the capital of Ethiopia toward the end of the nineteenth century offered opportunities not only for the expansion of education but for its modernization. Menelik had set himself objectives that included the centralization of the government, the reform of administrative apparatus, and the improvement of social conditions for the people. The value of education was not lost on the emperor: "We need educated people in order to ensure our peace, to reconstruct our country and to enable it to exist as a great nation in the face of the European powers."[4] When asked about the possibility of sending students to America, the emperor replied: "Yes, that will come; our young men must be educated."[5]

For the time being at least, Menelik decided to educate students abroad. In 1894, two years before the battle of Adwa, he arranged to send three young people to Switzerland with his Swiss adviser, Alfred Ilg. One of them, Afewerq Gebre Yesus, studied literature and painting, and on one occasion incurred the wrath of Empress Taytu for being "too European" in manner. He married first a Swiss and later an Italian, and became known for his writings in Amharic, Italian, and French.

Soon after, a group of students were sent to Russia. Two of them, Gizaw and Dagne by name, studied medicine; Azmach Genno and Semu Nigus studied literature; and Tekle Hawaryat, sent by Ras Makonnen, studied military science, specializing in engineering. On returning home Gizaw and Dagne became well-known doctors and helped to establish the Menelik II Hospital. Tekle Hawaryat joined the Mikhailovskaia Artillery School in Saint Petersburg and was given the rank of colonel, an unusual honor for a foreigner. After seventeen years in Russia, he came home to work for the Franco–Ethiopian Railway Company and was responsible for development work in the Chercher area of Harar province. In personal interviews with this author in 1954 and 1967, *Bejrond* (treasurer) Tekle Hawaryat said that he found the court in Addis Ababa full of self-seekers and that he was glad to be sent to France and England by Ras Tafari to study agriculture, on which he published a book in Amharic. Later he was instrumental in drafting the first constitution of 1931, was minister of finance, and later the Ethiopian ambassador in Paris and delegate to the League of Nations.[6]

Toward the end of the nineteenth century, while Menelik was sending a number of Ethiopians overseas for their education, his endeavors began to be supplemented from other sources. The British and Sudanese governments arranged for the admission of about a dozen students to Gordon College in Khartoum. An international Jewish organization, the Alliance Israelite Universelle, sponsored students in Italy, France, and Germany.

Other Ethiopians went abroad during this period to do research and to teach in the fields of Ethiopian languages, history, and ecclesiastical affairs.[7] The influence of the foreign educated in the times of Emperors Tewodros, Yohannes, and even Menelik was not so significant as one would expect. Perhaps they were objects of suspicion because of their affiliation with foreign missions, foreign ideas, or foreign religions. Such suspicions were real and difficult to overcome. In any event, many of these men undoubtedly made major contributions to the well–being of their country.

Progress at Home

Meanwhile, developments in education were taking place within Ethiopia itself. After the first quarter of the nineteenth century, Protestant and Catholic missionaries who had been expelled during the previous century began to repenetrate the country and to operate a few schools of somewhat limited conception. An appraisal prior to the 1935 Fascist invasion noted: "The various missions do a certain amount of education work, but not a great deal; their curriculum is suitable only for training youths to be interpreters, and thus their contribution to the problem of the education of the masses is not as yet of much value. . . . Unfortunately dogmatic religion rather than useful education seems to be the aim of at least some of them."[8] A recent writer has added that "Christian missionaries were not as important in founding secular education in Ethiopia as in other African countries."[9] While this may be true, the contribution of the missionary societies should not be underestimated. Emperor Menelik was tolerant enough of missionaries to encourage some of them to operate schools and hospitals. Emperor Haile Selassie I tacitly encouraged their educational activities. Nevertheless, fear and suspicion of foreigners, including missionaries, was never entirely absent among the general population nor among the clergy of the Orthodox church.

The Catholic Mission had also been reopened. By 1872 it had established a seminary at Keren, Eritrea; by 1880 there was also a day school. There were problems of placement for children reared and educated in the missions, however. "Outcast from their own people and unable to find employment among Mussulman authorities (i.e., under Egyptian rule) they are thrown on their own resources, which proves more fatal to the women than to the men."[10]

The activities of the missionaries were interrupted for a time when the Dervishes invaded the area in 1885. The teaching personnel had to leave temporarily, but were soon back at their posts. With the arrival of the Italians in Eritrea, the young people who had been trained in printing, carpentry, metalwork, agriculture, needlework, and languages, as well as in religion, readily found employment. The coming of the Italians, however, marked the end for the French Lazarists. On 13 September 1895, the pope transferred the work to the Capuchins, and in January of the following year the Italian government banished the Lazarist Fathers and Sisters of Charity on the pretext that they tended to reduce the prestige of the Italian government in Eritrea. As we shall see, similar action was taken following the 1935 invasion of Ethiopia. The Lazarists, however, continued to run schools in other parts of Ethiopia.

The Italian presence in Eritrea affected educational activity there significantly, as we shall see in the next chapter, for now education had to be provided as well for the children of Italian soldiers, administrators, and settlers. A contemporary report mentions fifty-eight "native" schools, presumably traditional Ethiopian church schools, scattered over the area. In addition, the military authorities established schools for the *ascari,* or local soldiers. The curriculum included rudimentary courses in Italian, Arabic, and Amharic, as well as a little arithmetic and geography.[11]

We now enter an even more significant stage in the history of education in Ethiopia, for a secular state system of education was to be operated within the country itself. By 1905 Emperor Menelik had already started a school in the palace, primarily for the sons of the nobility.[12] Young Ethiopians working in various capacities in the country suggested to him that no progress could be made without educated manpower, and in 1905 he issued the following proclamation on the importance of support for education: "In other countries, not only do they learn, even more they make new things. Therefore, from now on after reaching the age of six, boys and girls must be sent to school. As for parents who would not send their children to school, when the former die, their wealth, instead of reverting to their children, will be transferred to the Government. My Government will prepare the schools and the teachers."[13]

Accordingly, in 1906, he arranged with the Abun Matewos, the head of the Ethiopian Church, to hire teachers from Egypt. Some ten Coptic teachers arrived and, with a few Ethiopian teachers, were stationed in Addis Ababa, Harar, Ankober, and Dessie, where schools were established under the general direction of one of their number, Professor Hanna Saleh Bey. The curriculum included French, English, Arabic, Italian, Amharic, Ge'ez, mathematics, science, physical training, and sports.[14] Board and tuition were free.

Fortunately for Menelik and for the cause of education, the political ground for such an undertaking had been prepared beforehand. At the end of the nineteenth century and in the first few years of the twentieth, both the emperor and Empress Taytu had been active in building new churches or rebuilding old ones. They ordered governors and military officers to do likewise in their respective provinces: "The foundation of religion and the sign of Christianity is the construction of churches."[15] Menelik's credentials as a staunch supporter of the Orthodox faith were therefore unassailable. They served him in good stead, since even for a ruler of Menelik's stature the decision to open and maintain schools that were independent of the church required deliberation and caution. By this time, in addition, the emperor had suffered a series of strokes and was not physically able to mount an open confrontation with church leaders. As a result, when the decision was made in 1907 to appoint some ten ministers responsible for various departments of government, the emperor, though well aware that education should properly be a function of the state, left this responsibilty in the hands of the church. In schools that taught modern subjects, the Ministry of Health would assist the church. This seems to have satisfied the claims of Abun Matewos, who had insisted on church responsibility for matters pertaining to education.[16]

In 1909 Professor Hanna Saleh Bey was appointed director of education. The following proclamation was issued in 1908: "Religious matters shall fall under the Abun. He is the Head of religion. . . . The Ministry of Religion shall serve as liaison between the Abun and the Government . . . [its] main function . . . shall be to look after the interests of the church and the clergy. . . . The Ministry of Religion shall look after the schools."[17] Thus the Abun was left as head of the schools, but the emperor set aside a time every week to receive progress reports on education.[18]

One problem that needed urgent action was the negative attitude of most Ethiopians toward skilled manual labor. Menelik wanted to change this self-defeating point of view by setting a positive example himself, as well as through legislation. Thus the emperor could be seen engaging in any manual work that happened to be at hand, whether it was cutting grass or carrying stones for church construction. Furthermore, he set up a number of royal workshops near his palace where he could constantly supervise them.[19] In 1908 the emperor issued a proclamation which said, "Let those who insult the worker on account of his labour cease to do so." He added that heretofore the Ethiopian people had discriminated against the blacksmith, the weaver, the traditional doctor, and the scribe, and went on to say:

> Discrimination is the result of ignorance. God said to Adam: "In the sweat of thy brow shalt thou eat bread." If we do not carry out this injunction, if everyone is idle, there will be neither government nor country. In European countries when people undertake new kinds of work and make cannon, guns, trains and other things . . . they are praised and given more assistants, not insulted on account of their craft. But you by your insults are going to leave my country without people who can make the plough; the land will thus become barren and destitute. Hereafter anyone who insults these people is insulting me. From this time forth anyone found insulting another on account of his work will be punished by a year's imprisonment. If officials find it difficult to imprison such persons for a year let the former be arrested and sent before me.[20]

Thus the emperor hoped to minimize actual and potential opposition on the part of those who had much to gain by maintaining the status quo and much to lose by programs of modernization.

The thinking of the general public in respect to modern practices was vividly described to this author by a day student who attended the Menelik II School in Addis Ababa in 1924:

> The reason the Copts were chosen as teachers was to minimize the fear that foreign teachers might engage in religious propaganda. Furthermore, even though these teachers were of the Orthodox faith, they were forbidden to give religious instruction in classes. . . . Although the school was opened primarily for the children of the big people, little by little most of the students in the school were children of the poor families. . . . Education was considered fit only for the children of the poor who would not have any other means of self-support. For education was considered primarily as a means of earning a livelihood, hence unnecessary for the children of the rich.[21]

The public had no concept of educaton outside the church; sending one's children to a modern school was tantamount to being anti-Ethiopian. Since the teachers were mostly foreigners associated in the public mind with Catholics, attending a modern school seemed like an acceptance of Catholicism—a betrayal of one's honor and religion—or a willingness to become instruments in the hands of aliens. By encouraging such attitudes, the leaders of the organized church seriously hampered the government plans to expand learning throughout the land.

The Menelik II School is important therefore not only because it provided education in line with the demands of its time, but because it ushered in a new era of modern thinking. People of wealth and influence began to talk of the importance of education for the progress of the nation, and politicians soon began to capitalize on this concept.

From 1906 to 1908, Emperor Menelik suffered the series of strokes menioned above, and until his death in 1913 further progress in education was limited. He was succeeded by his grandson Lij Iyasu, a young man lacking in experience. Education received little attention except for his appointment of the first minister of education, Melake Tsehay Isdros, whose functions were never defined vis-a-vis the Ministry of Religion.[22]

Lij Iyasu was succeeded in 1916 by Empress Zewditu Menelik, daughter of the Emperor Menelik, and Dejazmach Tafari Makonnen became Ras Tafari and prince regent of the Ethiopian throne. Empress Zewditu was a devout, religious woman but no politician. Perhaps she was unable to grasp what was going on around her, surrounded as she was by the power struggle among the old politicians from the days of the great Menelik II. In 1921 (E.C.), however, Zewditu did make the following announcement:

> Every parent is hereby required to teach his child reading and writing through which the child may learn to tell the difference between evil and good; the fear of God and Emperor. Any parent refusing to do so will be fined fifty dollars, which money will go to churches to be used to feed and clothe the poor.
>
> Every Soul-Father [father priest] is hereby urged to advise all your confessants [charges] to teach their children. After having advised them two or three times, if they still refuse to heed to your advice, notify the local Government representative that they are transgressors of law.
>
> Those of you who are leaders of parishes in rural as well as urban areas, in addition to your regular responsibilities in the churches, teach the children of your respective communities how to read and write. . . . If you fail to teach, you will be deprived of your positions entrusted to you.
>
> Every parent, after you have taught your child how to read and write, make him attend your choice of any of the local trade schools of our country, lest your child will be faced with difficulty in earning his livelihood. If you fail to do so, you will be considered as one who has deprived another of limbs, and accordingly you will be fined fifty dollars, which money will be used for the education of the poor. This proclamation applies to those between the ages of seven and twenty-one years. A parent will not be held responsible for any child of his who is over twenty-one years old.[23]

We have no record of the impact of this progressive legislation, but it has continued significance for Ethiopia even in the 1970s.

Among the more important schools run by missionary societies and not by the government at this time was one established in Addis Ababa in 1907 by Félix de Nole on behalf of the French community. In 1921, the Ecole Française was opened there, also run by the Brothers of Saint Gabriel under the guidance of a local committee composed of Ethiopians, Greeks, Armenians, and Lebanese, as well as Frenchmen. The first students included Ethiopian, French, Greek, and Armenian children. By 1924 enrollment was 150, and 1,400 students had graduated. They came from all social classes and entrance to the school was free. In Eritrea the Missione dei Minori Cappuccini established a school of arts and crafts at Segeneyti in 1914.[24]

The opening of schools such as that of the Ecole Française aroused interest among progressives. An anonymous Ethiopian commentator remarks:

> The construction of schools is more important than anything else. Learning means the foundation of civilization, of wealth, of honour, of purity, of good character. If we examine the history of former times we will ascertain that a learned man is more honoured than unlettered one. Our evidence for this is the Holy Bible. . . . It is indeed a useful work. My [dear] sirs, I beg you to aid in their work those who after much thought have commenced to construct for us this school, so that many schools may be built in our country, and learning everywhere increase. With the exception of learning, everything when it became abundant becomes cheap, but learning increases in value. . . .
>
> Do you think it ignorance which has constructed for man's advantage cannon, aeroplanes, telegraphs, railways, submarines, and which has extracted from wood and earth [that is, organic and inorganic substances] the different kinds of drugs there are in the world! Or is it ignorance which has extracted from the bowels of the earth all these things that are useful to mankind! No!
>
> Now, why should we be the last of all introducing knowledge [in our midst], and what is it that prevents us from sending our children to school? If we do, and if this does not suffice, let us continue to open many schools, so that after a short time we may see youths who cause their

fathers to be praised for their [the children's] knowledge. So that he may boast saying: 'I have sown one fertile seed and gathered ten-thousand-fold!' And now may learning last forever and science reign! Let us say: 'May God lengthen the days of the people who assist learning!'[25]

Mention has also been made of the work of the Swedish Mission. Arriving in Addis Ababa in 1904, the missionary Cederqvist reported home that he had met with no opposition from the emperor. The mission opened an English school in Addis Ababa. Students were at first reluctant to apply, but Emperor Menelik's proclamation of 1905 encouraged many to attend.[26]

By 1922 the only modern school in Ethiopia was Menelik II School in Addis Ababa. The others that had been started at Ankober, Dessie, and Harar had disappeared. Even Menelik School was by now declining, perhaps from lack of leadership after the emperor's death and the ensuing political instability. Mosley observes, "There was already one school in Addis Ababa [the institution, founded by Menelik, which Tafari had attended for a time] but it was now directed entirely by priests and its educational standards were low."[27] Another measure of the school's weakness was its staff: by 1929 there was only one teacher for each of the courses offered—Ge'ez and Amharic, French, English, fine arts, and gymnastics and drill formation—a far lower number than when the school had opened two decades before.[28] However weak the school may have become, it had considerable influence both as a precedent and as an active contributor.

As a boy, Ras Tafari Makonnen, the future Emperor Haile Selassie I, first studied under the direction of a priest and then received instruction from one of the French fathers at Harar. Later he attended Menelik II School. In 1922 Tafari Makonnen, now regent, ordered the construction of a new school. In 1924, on a state visit to Europe, he arranged for the purchase of books and equipment, but upon his return met with severe opposition from the directors of the Menelik School, who saw the new institution as a dangerous rival. Indeed, they went to the empress and charged that its establishment was an attempt to force Ethiopian children to abandon their own religion in favor of Catholicism.[29]

In fact the school was erected, and at a cost of some 130,000 Ethiopian dollars. The campus covered twenty-five hectares of land enclosed by stone walls on all sides. The principal and teachers were French, and the administrator was the indefatigable and versatile Hakim Werqneh Ishete. The courses taught included French, Arabic, mathematics, chemistry, history, geography, gymnastics, and sports, as well as Amharic. The school was spacious, with "many large well-lit classrooms, a library, a laboratory, refectories, dormitories, ample gardens and recreation grounds."[30] Most students were boarders.

On Easter Monday, 27 April 1925, the regent visited the Tafari Makonnen Lyceum to inspect it for an afternoon gala. The guests, including cabinet ministers, nobles, and the diplomatic corps, were treated to an open-air display put on by the children. Later the Regent delivered a memorable speech:

> Of Ethiopia's greatness and antiquity, and especially of the long years when, surrounded by pagans, she struggled for her faith and her freedom, we ourselves, her own children, can indeed bear witness. Moreover we hear people of foreign lands the world over declaring, in speech and writings, the beauty of her terrain and the grandeur of her history. But it is not what she was that can profit Ethiopia, but what she may become. . . . Knowledge must be sought and found whereby Ethiopia too, an African state which has preserved her independence, may be led towards progress and may attain political stability and the well-being of her people. Now, therefore, anyone who says he is a friend to his country Ethiopia has the duty to show the token of his love by helping schools—by getting schools built so far as lies in his power, and by having his own children educated. It may be said that all who do this truly display their love of country. . . . To be able to say we have 100,000 scholars, we must start with one; to say we have 20,000 schools, we must start with one. It is certain that you are taking your place in the numerical series of scholars and schools in Ethiopia.[31]

After the regent's speech, Administrator Hakim Werqneh Ishete concluded his own speech with pertinent moral guidelines.[32]

A foreign observer who visited the new school commented that "the small though very admirable beginning made by Ras Tafari is a step in the right direction," but he doubted that this kind of venture could be undertaken on a large scale until the government had "put their financial house in order, a proceeding which would involve the reform and reorganization of the whole of the central and local administration." He went on:

> The big chiefs do not want their sons to be educated; . . . And the sons themselves . . . are the least keen of all the boys at Ras Tafari's school. . . . They have their fathers' lands to inherit and to rule, and ample wealth at their disposal, what more do they want? Whereas their less fortunately endowed brothers at the school, having more incentive, acquire more, and when they grow up and realize that theirs is the knowledge, but that the power is in the hands of others, less capable and more reactionary, . . . one of two alternatives may well eventuate. Either a serious social upheaval will take place, with the attendant risk to Abyssinian independence of civil war, or reaction will so assert itself that a collision with the outside world becomes inevitable.[33]

The French teachers found that the subjects the children were really enthusiastic about were languages, English and French, and that they learned these with amazing rapidity. They were also "learning history, geography, and arithmetic, and trying football, about which I am bound to say they seemed to have confused ideas. Unfortunately, they would take no interest in gardening or crafts, which seem a great pity."[34] Courses in arts and crafts were added later, however.

The school was much more French oriented than the old Menelik School. The medium of instruction was French; there was a succession of French principals, and teachers came from French Lebanon. The four Ethiopian teachers on the staff taught Amharic and elementary French. The pupils sat for an annual examination at the French Legation for the French government's Certificate of Competence in Primary Studies.[35] Initially 50 students were enrolled, but later in the year the number increased to 184, and in 1928–29 had reached 200. In April 1936 the country was occupied by the Fascist enemy, and the school closed.

Initially it had cost some $130,000 (in the currency known at the time as Maria Theresa) to build and equip the Tafari

Makonnen School. During the ensuing years, expansion and operating costs required a significant amount of money. To meet the mounting costs, nine months after the establishment of the school a special education tax of 6 percent was imposed on all imports and exports. The tax was expected to yield $240,000 a year, perhaps three times as much as the annual expenses of the school.[36]

The first official financial report available, one given by Dr. Werqneh at the end of June 1927, shows that income from all sources for the two-year period since the school became operational was $128,348. After expenses, a favorable balance of $33,118 remained. Following the report, donations were made by some of the wealthy people present.[37] The financial report for the following year showed another impressive budget surplus of $32,905.[38] Unfortunately, detailed information does not continue up to 1935, but apparently the school continued to operate on a sound financial basis, drawing support from the regent, the state treasury, and voluntary contributions.

Knowing the obstacles in the way, and to drive his points home, the regent continued to deliver supportive speeches. At the prize-giving ceremony at Menelik II School in 1927, he stressed local education:

> Further, as there is a great profit in being taught in Ge'ez and Amharic, the learning of our country, it will be necessary for all the governors to provide this education by setting up in their respective provinces schools for reading and writing; only when the pupils have received enough education to prepare them for foreign studies should they come hither. My reason for establishing this rule is that any one of us who proposes to study foreign knowledge without being versed in the learning of our country is like a man who builds a house on loose gravel.[39]

A year later, at Tafari Makonnen School, the regent pointed out once more the need for greater participation by nobles and wealthy people in the advancement of education. He also mentioned the possibility of establishing a national university on Ethiopian soil at some future date. As we will see, this desire was not to be satisfied until some twenty-three years later, in 1951.

The ground for general participation had been prepared with care, and now the public in Addis Ababa began to clamor for education. An examination of local newspapers of the 1920s and 1930s shows unmistakably that many had begun to see its value for national development. An article in 1928 urged the people to ask the regent for a law governing compulsory school attendance.[40] An earlier article, in 1927, had suggested reform of the curriculum and appealed to the empress, the cabinet ministers, and administrators, as well as to the prince regent, to require the teaching of Amharic and Ethiopian geography; in the Menelik II School, to appoint a minister of education who would have the schools evaluated each year; and to ensure that teaching take place within the country rather than abroad.[41] The attitude toward education was changing fast.[42]

In spite of opposition from traditionalists the regent continued to send the most promising boys overseas, most of them at his own expense. Students were sent to Europe, the Middle East, other parts of Africa, and North America. Many Ethiopians went to Egypt and Lebanon, but a number of these later transferred to Europe or the United States. The largest group of the 1920s and 1930s went to France, where a score of them studied political science, law, or economics. At that time French was Ethiopia's principal foreign language. Many of these young people were killed during the Fascist occupation, but the few that escaped became prominent in the civil service and in literature, among them a prime minister, Aklilu Habte Wold. Other young people studied in England, Germany, Switzerland, Belgium, and Italy. Although Eritrea was still an Italian colony, a number of Eritrea youths were also able to take part in scholarship ventures.[43]

Inevitably, education for women was slow in developing. Princess Tsehai Haile Selassie and a few others studied French in Switzerland. Senedu Gebru, who studied in Lausanne, joined the resistance forces during the Italian invasion of Ethiopia and was subsequently imprisoned in Italy. She later became the director of Itegue Menen Schools for girls, which was founded in 1930 by the Empress Menen, and eventually became the first Ethiopian woman member of Parliament.[44]

In the meantime, education at home continued to expand. The nongovernment schools, run mostly by foreign missionary societies, expanded faster than the state-supported schools. Despite historical opposition and the limitations of their curricula, the missions made progress. The Swedish Evangelical Mission was in Eritrea by 1886, and in Addis Ababa by 1905. By 1924 it had established eight schools and was also working in several centers in northern Ethiopia. The *Bibeltrogña Vanner* (Friends of the Bible) Mission came to Eritrea in 1912 and to Addis Ababa in 1921, where it maintained three schools with a total of 125 pupils. The Seventh-Day Adventist Mission, established in Eritrea in 1907, opened a school in Addis Ababa in 1923, and another at Addis Alem. The United Presbyterian church of North America opened a school at Sayo in 1922 with eighty-three pupils, all boys, who were taught in Galligna.[45] The French and Italian Catholic Missions also continued to operate schools, primarily in Eritrea. With the opportunity provided by a more tolerant social climate, the educational efforts of the missionaries thus began to be felt in Ethiopia.

With the accession to the throne of Haile Selassie I in 1930, the tempo of educational progress quickened, and education was coordinated under the guidance of a central Ministry of Education and Fine Arts. In addition to the education tax, the ministry now received 2 percent of the national treasury revenue. Zervos has pointed out that the administrative structure was similar to that in Britain or Italy;[46] this was not the case in grade structure. Ernest Work, an American brought in in 1930 to advise the government, suggested that the educational system should be "neither French, Italian, English nor American," but Ethiopian. He recommended first that Amharic be used as the medium of instruction, but felt the language needed some modification and simplification to make it more suitable for instruction and book production. Second, the curriculum should be relevant: "Ethiopian boys and girls should be educated in their own languages, learn about their own country and men and interesting things, as well as the world in general." As soon as possible, the teachers should be Ethiopians. A definite plan of education was essential, providing for six years of elementary education for all and for industrial and trade schools, including agriculture and homemaking. Five or six additional years should be available for those who desired to go into business and the professional world. Finally, a university was needed, to be established if possible with foreign private aid; one of its branches should be a college for teacher education.[47] These were far-sighted proposals, and in fact they describe what we found ourselves trying to do forty-one years later.

The state schools now began to expand faster. By the outbreak of the Fascist war in 1935, there were eight or nine schools in operation. Menelik II School gave primary and secondary instruction in French, English, and Italian; Tafari Makonnen School offered elementary and secondary instruction; the Itegue Menen School for girls offered primary and secondary instruction in French. In all three schools the pupils took an annual examination for the French Certificate in Primary Studies. Haile Selassie I School was founded in 1930 by the emperor, and gave technical and linguistic training in French. There were in addition several elementary schools in Addis Ababa, founded between 1929 and 1935.

In the provinces, there were two primary schools in Harar, one established by Emperor Menelik II in 1908 and the other by Emperor Haile Selassie I in 1930; in 1933 they united as Ras Makonnen School. The Dire Dawa Elementary School was opened in 1929, and the Weyzero Sihine School in Dessie in 1928. The Tafari Makonnen Elementary School in Gore appeared in 1928. All these schools taught in French. The Tafari Makonnen School in Jijiga, built in 1929, used English as the medium of instruction. The Haile Selassie Elementary School in Nakamti, Wollega, was built in the same year and also used English. The Asbe Tafari Elementary School in Asbe Tafari, Harar province, and the Haile Selassie I Elementary School built in 1932 in Jimma, Kaffa, used French; the Gojam Elementary School in Debra Markos used English, as did the Gondar Elementary School, both established in 1934; the Sellale school used French. The Adwa and Makalle schools of the same year both used English as a language of instruction.[48] With some exaggeration a resident of Addis Ababa commented on the general literacy: "It was remarkable to the resident of many year's [sic] standing that whereas in 1920 the boy on his household staff who could read and write was a notable exception, in 1935 among the same society there were few young men and boys who had not mastered the elementary processes of reading and writing the Amharic script."[49] There were twenty-one government schools functioning in the empire with a total enrollment of 4,200 students, and a number of others were studying abroad or in church and mission schools.[50] At this point the Fascists struck.

Chapter 3

The Italian Occupation

Italy first gained a foothold on Ethiopian soil in 1869, when an Italian Lazarist missionary, acting as agent for the Rubatline Shipping Company, bought the port of Assab. This transaction had the tacit approval of the Italian government, which in 1882 bought the port from the company. In the same year France annexed Tunisia which Italy had coveted for herself, a move viewed with disapproval by the Italian public who were interested in the Mediterranean, not in the Red Sea. Mancini, then foreign minister, pointed out that the Red Sea might provide the key to the Mediterranean. In 1885, Italy, with British encouragement, took possession of Massawa, and by 1890 had gained enough territory in the area to "justify" the establishment of the colony of Eritrea.

Italy did not confine herself to the Red Sea. In 1891 she extended her protection to the sultanates of Obbia and Miguirtini in northern Somaliland and to the coastal stretches of southern Somaliland. By military occupation and by the trade agreements of 1892 and 1905 with the sultanate of Zanzibar, Italy established the colony of Somaliland, further strengthening her position in the Indian Ocean.

In the meantime Italy tried to expand southward. Eritrea was no longer considered a key to the Mediterranean but a stepping-stone to the colonization of Ethiopia itself. Ethiopia had concluded a treaty with Italy by which Ethiopia might use the mediation of Italy in dealing with foreign powers, a clause that Italy took to mean that Ethiopia was obliged to use Italy's good offices in overseas transactions. This misunderstanding, deliberate or not, led to the battle of Adwa in 1896. Italy sustained a crushing defeat, while Ethiopia won international respect, but the humiliation of Italy planted seeds of trouble that were to bear fruit thirty–nine years later.

After Adwa, the British and French were granted favors at the court of Emperor Menelik II, while Italy was completely ignored. In 1906, however, the emperor suffered his first stroke, and, fearing civil war in Ethiopia, Britain invited France and Italy to take common action with her after the emperor's death. By the tripartite agreement of December 1906, each was given distinct "spheres of influence" in Ethiopia. Italy's colonial appetite was reviving.

In 1919 Italy suggested to Britain a consultation in respect to interests in Ethiopia, and in 1925 an Anglo-Italian agreement confirming Italy's exclusive right to the exploitation of western Ethiopia and to the construction of a railway across the country connecting Eritrea and Somaliland was concluded. The two imperialist powers did not see fit to consult Ethiopia. When the agreement was published, Ethiopia protested vigorously to the League of Nations, an action which resulted in the nullification of the treaty. In 1928 Italy concluded a treaty of friendship, conciliation, and arbitration with Ethiopia; when the economic gains anticipated by Italy did not materialize, however, she resorted to aggression. In October 1935 open war broke out and Ethiopia again appealed to the League of Nations, this time without success. The war was over within seven months; Italy with her modern weapons, machines, and poison gas, gained the victory, and Marshal Badoglio entered Addis Ababa on 5 May 1936. On 9 May, Mussolini announced the annexation of Ethiopia to Italy and the foundation of the Fascist empire. By royal decree, Eritrea, Italian Somaliland, and Ethiopia were merged into Italian East Africa, which was subdivided into the six regions of Eritrea, Somalia, Amhara, Galla and Sidama, Harar, and Addis Ababa, with a combined population of nearly eight million people.[1]

Colonial Administrative Structure

When Fascist Italy invaded Ethiopia in 1936, there were at least twenty-one government schools in Ethiopia, three of which, in the capital, held secondary classes. Although Eritrea had been a colony since the turn of the century, some Eritreans had been able to cross into Ethiopia for education and later became prominent national figures. The infrastructure of modern education was already securely laid in Ethiopia by the time the occupation took place. Unfortunately, and perhaps understandably, the kind of education provided by a national government for its free citizens was not to be reconciled with the plans of an imperialist government for its subject people. To understand this sudden shift of direction, it is necessary to look at what had been happening in Eritrea.

After 1912 all Italian colonial education services were put under the direction of the minister of colonies, assisted by the ministers of national education and of finance. In the Ministry of Colonies the particular office charged with the direction of colonial education was the Inspectorate of Schools and Archaeological Services, located in Italy. The chief inspector was concerned with general policy matters regarding colonial educational institutions both public and private, budgetary matters, and youth organizations. Colonial education for East Africa in particular was administered by the six colonial governments through the Office of the Superintendent located in the capital cities.[2]

Education for colonial peoples was regulated by various decrees and laws. The decree of 1921 represented a pre–Fascist attempt to organize native education in Eritrea. The law of 1924, although intended only for Libya, was significant in that it presaged the reorganization of education in the colonies along Fascist lines. The educational decree of 1931 was yet another attempt to systematize government education for Eritrea, but it was considerably modified in practice. The Fundamental Law of 1936 made it mandatory to use the local language as the medium of instruction in each of the regions of Italian East Africa. Finally, the 1936 educational ordinance was the first to apply to education throughout Italian Africa.

Since Eritrea had not shared the educational experience of the rest of Ethiopia, Italian colonization there brought with it the need to provide education. Richard Pankhurst states that a 1905 census showed that there were already 754 Europeans under the age of fifteen in the colony. Two years later, four main types of schools were founded in the territory: government schools for Italian children, missionary schools for Italian children, traditional Christian and Muslim schools run by the local people, and Catholic or Protestant schools for the colonial subjects.[3] This dual system of education, always of lower quality for the Eritreans, was to persist, not only in government schools but to a large extent in the missionary schools as well.

This, of course, was part of a deliberate policy. As Jasper-dean has pointed out, Italy's aims in Eritrea were first to secure and organize it, then to develop its natural resources for a European population to exploit, and lastly to use it as a base for further expansion and conquest in Africa. From the start, then, Italy wanted direct and complete political control and so initiated a policy of assimilation and adaptation. Assimilation never meant the granting of political rights to Eritreans. A. Malvezzi de Medici, a professor of colonial law, said that assimilation "can only take place gradually, while absolute cultural equality with the Italians would breed in them [the Eritreans] aspirations and pretensions compatible neither with their true situation nor with the actual conditions of the colonies. . . . The Italian government proposes to extend to the most advanced natives the opportunity to acquire an education developed in terms of their own traditional culture, which . . . permits them to know and appreciate the superior character of our methods and culture."[4]

Accordingly, separate schools were established in Eritrea not only for Italian children but for the different ethnic and religious groups: natives, Catholics, Moslems, and Coptic Christians. This segregated approach was allegedly in the interests of the different groups, but the true intent was, of course, political. According to the report of Colosimo, the minister of colonies, there were in 1918 four government schools for Eritreans in the colony. By 1926 the Victor Emanuel II School with boarding facilities was partially operational, and by 1933 there were seven schools in operation. After 1935 Eritrean education was reorganized and expanded; twenty-six schools were established within a few months. They were hastily organized in private homes, old buildings, tents, and huts to impress the Eritreans and the outside world with Italy's "civilizing mission."[5] Education for the local people was elementary and circumscribed; not a single secondary school was established for them.

Although entrance requirements to government schools were simple, the Eritreans were far from eager to compete for places, even though graduation from any of them meant a chance of securing menial government employment. The two years of supplementary schooling offered at Victor Emanuel II School were designed simply to buy the loyalty of the children and their parents. The pupils here were of "proven worth," a phrase, of course, used not to mean individuals of scholastic competence so much as obedient, loyal sycophants. Graduates of the school at Asmara served as government colonial clerks and teacher assistants,[6] but "under Fascism, all trades and crafts were closed to Eritreans. . . . The surplus of Italian labour was so great that Europeans were employed on stone breaking on the roads. The only occupations open to the Eritreans outside their own community were those of office messenger, porter, stevedore, house or outdoor servant, odd job man, and, of course, soldier in the colonial forces. It was, in fact, illegal to employ an Eritrean without special written authorization from the Governor."[7]

Eritrean youths could join various militaristic organizations where they donned uniforms and took part in flamboyant Fascist-style parades. As an additional inducement, free board and lodging were provided.[8] Eritrean attendance at middle school was negligible,[9] though theoretically possible.

Private and semiprivate schools were maintained by different religious societies and local groups. They were under strict surveillance by the colonial authorities who had the right to close any school that dared to operate on "principles contrary to public order."[10] Apparently the Fascist regime found that some of the private and religious organizations did not strictly subscribe to the dogma of the day. In 1932 the Swedish and American Protestant Missions were closed, and a member of the Swedish Mission complained that "in December 1935, all its missionaries were expelled and the properties of the mission taken by the Italian government for their own use."[11] Education in Eritrea was more closely under Fascist control than ever before. The reasons offered for the limitation of educational opportunity included the varied character of the Eritrean population, consisting of Copts, Moslems, Catholics, and Protestants at all different levels of "civilization"; the difficulty of securing teachers; the aversion of many Eritreans to manual trades; and religious divisions among the population.[12] The colonial authorities were not frank enough to admit that the root of the problem was a lack of Eritrean confidence in the education provided by Italy. De Marco observed: "The difficulty experienced by Italy in convincing natives of Eritrea that instruction in agriculture and in arts and crafts was the best type of training for them demonstrated that Eritreans as a whole would be slow to patronize Italian schools."[13] And Andrea Festa, the director of elementary education, stated that the program aimed to make the native child a "conscious propagandist" of Italian civilization and so to proselytize the parents; to make the native child a "conscious militia man" under the Italian flag; and to give him a knowledge of hygiene, geography, and history. Festa added that schools run on these lines had already produced effective "soldiers of Italy."[14]

The Fascist government made no important changes in colonial education in Eritrea until 1931, when the various schools were reorganized into elementary and arts and crafts schools. A Central Office of Primary Education was established, along with final criteria for the schools. Many primary schools, operated by various Roman Catholic orders on behalf of the government, were not entrusted exclusively to Catholic sisters. The schools were divided into four-year elementary schools, arts and crafts schools offering four years of elementary and four years of practical instruction, and two-year complementary schools to integrate and complete the information acquired at the elementary level.

After the Ethio-Italian War, military chaplains, officers, blackshirts, and soldiers, as well as some local people and priests and nuns, served as assistant teachers under the supervision of qualified Italians. The teaching load was heavy: four thousand pupils were instructed by ninety-seven teachers (twenty-six Eritreans and seventy-one Italians, of whom fifty-five belonged to religious orders). Teachers, regarded as sentinels of Italy's interests in the colonies, were expected to impress Italian values upon their pupils. They were also responsible for school furnishings, which had to include portraits of the royal family and Il Duce, and for distributing food and school supplies to the pupils. Salaries, except for those of the Eritrean assistant teachers, were equal to those in Italy, plus hardship allowances.[15]

Discriminatory Racial Policies
While the facilities and curriculum for Italian children corresponded to those in Italy, only second-rate programs were provided for Eritreans. Emphasis was on military drill and elementary training, a policy designed to make the schools a base for pre-*ascari* training and to prevent the creation of an educated elite who would compete for jobs with the Italians in the colony.

Underlying these policies was official racial discrimination, although no such attitude was apparent between the Italian and Ethiopian populations. The Four Power Investigation Committee clearly stated that "curricula in these Italian schools were established in accordance with the instructions of the Ministry of Education in Rome." The report adds: "Under the Italian Government the Italian schools were in practice not open to natives." In the indigenous schools, according to reports made by Eritrean teachers, only about one out of five students remained until the end of the school year, and "no education higher than elementary was available for the natives."[16]

A British government report states:

Under the Italians, native education served a political purpose. All instruction in the government schools was given in Italian, and such mission schools as were not repressed in 1932 survived only by agreeing to limit their teaching of Tigrinya and Ge'ez to religious instruction. The textbooks . . . glorified the Duce on almost every page. Military service was lauded. Boys were encouraged to become "little soldiers of the Duce," the Fascist salute was compulsory, and at the morning hoisting of the flag Italian songs were sung.[17]

This discrimination sent some of the more gifted youths across the Mereb to highland Ethiopia or abroad for further studies. Many served Ethiopia with distinction on their return.[18]

In Ethiopia proper the occupation lasted from 1936 to 1941. "As soon as the Italians occupied Addis Ababa in 1936," observed a foreign writer recently, "the task of building the new Ethiopian government school system was stopped for seven years."[19] Sylvia Pankhurst commented: "During the Italian occupation the schools of Ethiopia were closed and all genuine education for the Ethiopian people terminated."[20] In 1946 the Ethiopian delegation to the Peace Conference in Paris said: "The educational system suffered a terrible setback as a result of the Italian occupation when every attempt was made by the aggressors to stamp out from the previously established system of education then on a firm footing."[21]

It was not lost upon the Fascists that educated minds are the best shield a country can have. On one pretext or another all the educated youngsters were hounded and many were murdered. Only a few managed to leave the country.[22] When an attempt was made on the life of Marshal Graziani on 19 February 1937, a massacre followed. For the next three days, any Ethiopian in sight was shot, bayoneted, or locked in a house and burned to death. At least 3,000 Ethiopians perished. Educated men and women were hunted down and killed in cold blood, and at least 125 of those known to have met their deaths were people educated abroad at great expense and sacrifice who had returned to Ethiopia to modernize their country. Two hundred ninety-seven monks and 129 deacons of the Debre Libanos monastery were put to death in an orgy of merciless destruction. In all, it is estimated that about 75 percent of those who had some modern education were wiped out during the years of occupation.[23] Mosley noted that "in one month the cream of Ethiopia's educated youth was destroyed. That year [1937] altogether 3,000 Ethiopians went before Italian firing squads." Sylvia Pankhurst added that 75 percent of the young graduates, young intellectuals who were to have been the administrators and technicians of modern Ethiopia, were murdered.[24]

Italian educational objectives during the occupation of Ethiopia were identical to those applied up to 1935 to Eritrea alone. It has been contended that Italy's stay in Ethiopia was too brief and insecure for the development of education, but our argument is concerned less with the extent of education than with policy. The excuses given by Fascist officials for the subjugation of Ethiopia were mere window dressing. Mussolini asked an audience of mothers and widows of fallen soldiers what crime Italy was committing except "to carry civilization to backward countries, to construct schools and roads." Marshal Pietro Badoglio, duce of Addis Ababa, declared, "We shall construct school buildings and, besides educating the natives and their sons, we shall seek to carry prosperity everywhere." Viceroy Graziani, the man responsible for the massacre of February 1937, is reported to have said: "We shall open schools in order that the Ethiopian people may come out of its secular ignorance and go towards the light of truth."[25]

Colonial educational policy was actually designed to Italianize the African as much as possible, to produce soldiers for Italy, and to create a reserve of menial laborers. The colonial schools, in keeping with most European schools of the time, were expected to teach respect for authority, obedience, and discipline.[26] Colonial schools were used also for indoctrination, however, to make the people accept their inferior status without analysis of the true conditions of their life under the totalitarian regime.

Policies of racism, discrimination, and inequality were stated time and again by Mussolini and his subordinates. Mussolini declared in 1938 that "to maintain prestige we must have a strict and clear racial consciousness, which will stabilize not only the difference of race but also our absolute superiority."[27] Marshal Badoglio added sycophantically:

> To the solution of the racial problem expounded with unequivocal clarity by the Duce, the destiny of our Empire is united. The sooner the full application of the wise decision already made is realized, the sooner our prestige, already clearly affirmed by the power and glory of the army, will be profoundly felt by all the innumerable people for whom we intend to develop an era of civilization and beneficence under the invincible sign of the King and the Roman Lictors. Prestige means Roman solidarity within the Empire.

The editor of this publication, Giuseppe Fabbri, tried to substantiate Fascist policy with historical evidence by citing the "mistake" made by ancient Rome when she educated the native chiefs of Britain, who eventually brought about her downfall.[28]

Further insights are gained by reading some of the confidential letters of high officials in the government. One, by General Gugliemo Nasi, governor of Harar, advised in 1938:

> I continue to notice that Commissions and Residents have above all an ambition to extend elementary education for natives, and to teach our language to as many children as possible. This is a fundamental political mistake that tends to put individuals out of their class who, solely because they possess a veneer of education, will refuse to work in the fields, as we know by our own colonial experience and by that of other countries. They are attracted to the towns, ask for government employment, compete with the nationals in trades that should be reserved to the latter, forming a class

of discontented or, even worse, of rebellious people. We should reserve the strictly necessary education for the sons of chiefs and more important notabilities only, because these can later on succeed to the duties of their fathers, serve us as interpreters and hold modest positions in offices. However, while for obvious reasons we cannot altogether close the door of public education to the youth of the lower social classes, we can and we ought to close tightly the door to special courses, e.g., those for interpreters; and in general we should avoid propaganda and, still worse, pressure on families to send their sons to the Italian schools.

This principle, which can be absolute in the country, ought of course for obvious reasons to be subject to many exceptions in the larger towns [Harar and Dire Dawa]. It is superfluous to add that the present directive is of a very secret character, and should be applied without divulging the real motives.[29]

A year later, on 26 October 1939, the governor-general of Italian East Africa, the duke of Aosta, wrote: "The schools of all kinds established for the subject peoples of Italian East Africa ought above all to aim at this goal: to train the pupils in the cultivation of the soil or to become qualified workers (not specialized) in order to create gradually native skilled craftsmanship for all fields of labour where, for reasons of climate, surroundings or race prestige, the use of Italian labour is not admissable or convenient and for the purpose of reducing the cost of labour and production in general by making use of native labour."[30]

Curriculum

Complete enrollment data for the five-year period are lacking, but available figures show that by 1937 there were sixty-one schools and 5,057 pupils in the six administrative regions. It is interesting to note here that if we subtract the figures for Eritrea, which had been under Italian rule for nearly fifty years, we are left with only 1,460 pupils for the rest of Ethiopia, in sharp contrast to the 4,000 enrolled students just before the invasion took place. When inferior instruction and the nature of the courses are taken into account it can readily be seen how severely education for Ethiopians had regressed in only three years.

As far as programs of study were concerned, the Eritrean

pattern of 1932 was followed in Ethiopia proper. Some textbooks used there had been used first in Libya and Eritrea. Others
had been written especially for Ethiopian children, although textbooks for Italian colonies were not fully developed until 1936.
These were in the nature of "didactic aids adapted to the attitude
and capacity of the natives," aimed at imbuing the native child
with "patriotic devotion and love for Italy and her leaders."
Three primers produced in 1936 for Libyan children contained
such phrases as "Italy governs her colonies wisely. . . . Italy is
one of the greatest nations of Europe. It is rich and powerful. . . ." Then, printed in large type, was the following: "Italy
does not conquer colonies to exploit them or to oppress them,
but to give them the benefit of civilization. . . . Benito Mussolini,
the Head of the Government and Leader of Italy, works without
rest not only for the greatness of his country but also for the
good of Italian Africa."[31]

Most of these phrases and concepts were later adopted in
Eritrea, Somaliland, and Ethiopia. Usually the vocabulary sections of the textbooks were written either in Italian and Arabic,
Italian and Tigrinya, or Italian and Amharic, and were illustrated
with photographs of Mussolini, the king of Italy, Marshal Badoglio, and Marshal Graziani. One section on Somalia declared:
"All Italian and Somalis wish Benito Mussolini well because his
words are just, his hands are strong and his heart is large. The
Duce founded the Empire of Ethiopia."

The second-year textbook was specially written for East African children and contained the usual slogans regarding Italy and
the flag and extolling the leaders' virtues, and were amply illustrated with photographs. King Victor Emanuel was depicted as
"very good, educated and wise." Mussolini was described as a
scholar who studied many books when he was a schoolboy.

The same primer also contained useful information about
the sun, the moon, the planets, forests, trees, flowers, animals,
insects, and a section on certain occupations, among them the
farmer and the herdsman. There were other chapters on Italy
and the Italian Empire, with photographs of ancient Rome and
the modern Italian colonies, as well as references to modern
Italy, described as rich, strong, and one of the greatest powers in
Europe. Emphasis was laid on obedience and loyalty. "Be always
obedient children"; "Love . . . your teachers who teach you to
love Italy, the common mother."

The section on the *fascio* (the symbol of Fascism) declared: "O children of Ethiopia, you must feel proud to belong to the great Italian nation and to work under the insignia of the lictors' fascio."[32] In another primer, produced for Libyan children but also used in East Africa, "subjects of academic interest were subordinated to fables, descriptions of Libyan life, and undisguised fascist propaganda." Since the children were nearing the time when they were to join the Italian army, a section praised the joys of serving Italy as a soldier.[33]

Despite all this emphasis on Italianization, one thing was purposely omitted from Italian history. On the orders of the director of elementary schools, Andrea Festa, textbooks intended for indigenous children were to omit references to the political history of Italy in 1848 and to the revolutionary motives and ideas which came before and after that period. The clear instruction to the textbook production committee was that the African child "must know nothing about conspiracy and revolution."[34]

The Italian teacher in the colonies was credited with performing "a valorous duty and with carrying out a high mission." He knew the local language, but used it with the children only when strictly necessary. He was expected to be capable of "penetrating the minds of colonial subjects and inculcating in them a love for their new Fatherland." Other qualifications included membership in the Fascist party and a knowledge of the "Fascist interpretation of education and of Fascist culture." Italy indeed desired its colonial teachers to "do more than impart formal education."[35]

Provisions for Religious Groups

As indicated above, during the Fascist period some education was provided for the various religious groups represented in Ethiopia—Catholics, Ethiopian Orthodox, and Moslems. There was always a suspicion among non-Catholics that the Vatican would use the umbrella of the Fascist conquest to impose Roman Catholicism. An article written in England in 1935 declared:

> The Italians intend to maintain only two kinds of schools in Ethiopia, and these have already started working. The first type of school is for spreading Roman Catholicism, the second for teaching Ethiopian youth the duties of a Fascist soldier. It is not astonishing that the Roman Catholic priests

should get permission to force their religion upon the people of Ethiopia, after having given their Church crosses and contributed money to the Italian treasury, in order that more arms and ammunition might be sent for the conquest of Ethiopia. It is not astonishing also that the Fascist schools have decided to ban all useful subjects from their curriculum and to bring up young Ethiopians as instruments of Fascism only; what is really astonishing is that in the twentieth century, the civilized nations of the world sit by unmoved while the Roman barbarians are exterminating an ancient Christian people in the name of civilization![36]

It was also asserted that the military expedition had the objective of imposing heavy taxation upon the Ethiopian people as well as forcing the children to learn the Italian language and the Roman Catholic faith.[37] Edouard Trudeau, a French–Canadian Jesuit, wrote of the schools that "in most cases they suffered from a transfer from French or Canadian direction to full Italian control."[38] But Ethiopians who feared that Fascist conquest meant domination by Roman Catholicism were proved wrong. Even in Eritrea, such conversions had been negligible.[39]

Italy's attitude toward the Moslems was entirely different. From the beginning, she showed a benevolence towards Islam that stemmed from a desire to weaken the Christian position and to compensate for the damage Italy had done to her image in the eyes of her North African Moslem subjects. She built a number of mosques and repaired old ones around the country. Mussolini proclaimed in Tripoli in 1937 that Fascist Italy intended "to guarantee to the Muslim peoples of Libya and Ethiopia peace, justice, prosperity, and respect for the laws of the Prophet, and that she wished moreover to manifest her sympathy with Islam and the Muslims of the entire world."[40]

Mussolini's government built schools and even institutions of higher learning for Islamic studies in Harar and Kaffa, but the Ethiopian Moslems continued to teach their children as they had been doing for centuries, while the Orthodox church also, insofar as it was possible, continued its educational activities. Italian movements failed to create either political or religious divisions among the adherents of either religion, but the damage done in other areas of Ethiopia was to call for concentrated efforts of reconstruction by the restored government.

Chapter 4

The Reconstruction Era, 1941–51: Needs and Objectives

When the Fascist invader was expelled from Ethiopia in 1941, a student of Ethiopian history wrote:

> Yet . . . all the elation of victory could not conceal the stark realities . . . : the return to peace and normal ways of a people that for six years or more had lived through war, upheaval, and guerrilla fighting, with all the attendant weakening of normal moral restraints; the . . . arms left behind by the retreating enemy; . . . the disintegration of administration over so far-flung an empire; the dislocation of communications, the lack of transport, and the complete standstill of trade and commerce; the shortage of food and clothing; the elimination of the educated elite whom the Emperor had carefully nursed before the invasion, and the consequent lack of trained personnel; . . . and finally, the British military authorities whose primary aim, and rightly so, was the successful prosecution of the [world] war, then only in its beginning . . . and who could at times be impatient with a self-willed and strange ally. It is against this sombre background that the achievements of the Emperor and the Ethiopian people have to be judged.[1]

The problems of reconstruction were complicated further "by the presence in the country of an Italian civilian population numbering some 40,000, who had to be protected, fed and medically cared for."[2] An Ethiopian government memorandum addressed to the Council of Foreign Ministers meeting in London outlined the chaotic conditions in 1941.

The Government took over a country ravaged by six years of war during which probably three-quarters of its educated citizens were killed in battle or wantonly murdered. . . . Upon the return of the government, the Ethiopians were faced with a mere handful of technicians, an economy which had previously employed 200,000 trained Italians. . . . Although the Italians had some 40,000 registered vehicles to carry the goods of the country, when the [Ethiopian] government took over from the British Military Administration, there were only 6,000 left. It is estimated by unbiased foreigners who were in Ethiopia at the time that 80 percent of the mechanical equipment was removed.[3]

The artificial economy created by Italians for Italians was taken over by the British military administration, which wanted to keep Ethiopia under the British crown and did everything it could to remove or destroy heavy machinery that could have been put to good use.

Rehabilitation was needed in all sectors of society. Law and order had to be established and transport facilities made operational. An efficient communications system and the expansion of trade were urgently needed to provide financial stability for the reconstruction of the educational system, which was viewed as a major task of restoration and which had been largely destroyed or diverted into Fascist ideological channels.[4]

Initial Problems

The real rehabilitation of education was not started until February 1942. There were few people who had any experience in teaching, and the government had to rely on such foreigners as happened to be in the country. Inevitably, courses at all levels tended to imitate those of other countries "because foreign advisors and teachers were instrumental in the formulation of the directives given to the nation's schools."[5] The courses and methods of instruction varied from one school to another, since the English, Swedes, and other nationalities conducted classes in their own way.

Yet the shattered foundations of the public education system had to be rebuilt. Foreign assistance was much reduced because the major countries of the world were still fighting World

War II.[6] The early years were difficult ones for all sectors of the country's battered economy, but especially so in the field of education. The Ministry of Education pointed out:

> The difficulties were perhaps greater than in any other branch of administration. To start with, teachers had to be found; . . . school buildings and furniture had to be retrieved or improvised. . . . Textbooks in Amharic and in English were practically non-existent; other equipment was scarce; . . . at the same time many hundreds of boys, girls and young men, eager to make up for the five years' gap in their education, were besieging the few schools that managed to open their doors.[7]

The demand for schooled and skilled manpower was so pressing that "the actual situation had to be met, and therefore the question of long-range planning was set aside for a later date."[8] The objectives, simply stated, were "to prepare, as quickly as possible, young men and women who could man a modern administration system side by side with those who, educated earlier, had survived the war and years of occupation . . . [and to train] technicians for new industries, for the professions, and for such services as transport and commerce, as well as officers for the armed forces and police."[9]

However, although the urgent need for skilled manpower set the priorities, mass and adult education were not forgotten. The *Ethiopian Herald* was of the opinion that the deepest impact of education would be in this area.[10]

On 24 July 1943, the newly elected president of the Chamber of Deputies told the House, "The fate and destiny of our country depend on what we do for the young."[11] A timely article in the *Ethiopian Herald* went even further: "Our world is a horrible spectacle of undeveloped and misapplied possibilities. . . . How many mute and glorious Miltons have died in silence, how many potential Newtons never learned to read? The supreme task of our awakening minds is the re-education of the world."[12]

It was essential that education should be an instrument for personal and national development and a bridge of peace among the nations. The emperor reiterated these underlying concepts time and again. In 1946 he said: "We call upon all Ethiopians to send their children to the nearest school, for it is suicide and a crime against the responsibility which God places in all parents not to educate one's own children. The catastrophe which was brought about by human hand during the past years can be avoided in the future by religion and the hope in God which be in the hearts of the people. And this can be achieved by education."[13] The stated aim of the Ministry of Education was definitely to educate all the people of the empire.[14]

An Ethiopian scholar added that "the main endeavor of the time was to erase from the minds of the youth, and indeed from the very soil of Ethiopia, the corrupting influence that had been brought from Italy."[15] The short-term need was "to provide a small corps of clerical, technical, administrative and professional personnel to man the government machinery and to get industry going again."[16] As Taddesse Tereffe put it, "Today, the need for more professional people like engineers, medical doctors, educators, agricultural experts and military scientists is the motivating factor in educational ventures."[17]

Postelementary Education

In the first two years after restoration, education was available in the primary grades, but to create the necessary technical and professional personnel a full secondary school was essential. Accordingly, Haile Selassie I Secondary School was formally inaugurated on 23 July 1943 on the site of a former Fascist agricultural station, a few kilometers east of Addis Ababa. Forty-three qualified students from "practically all the provinces of the country" were enrolled, and there were five foreign teachers.[18] The school offered a full four-year secondary program. In the curriculum, two courses of study, one leading to university entrance and the other to technical training, were provided.

The second full secondary school established after the restoration was the General Wingate Secondary School, named for Charles Wingate, a British commander under the Ethiopian emperor in the last stages of the campaign against Fascism.[19] The school began modestly in Gullele district in 1946, in buildings that had been used as a radio station during the Italian occupation. By May 1951, new permanent buildings were erected containing classrooms, laboratories, art, music, geography, and handicraft rooms, a library, an assembly hall for 580 pupils, and administrative offices. There were also four large dormitories, each housing 75 students, and ample space and equipment for physical education. The school was operated jointly by the Ethiopian and British governments to provide "Ethiopian boys of ability with a secondary education on English Public School lines, which will fit them for work in Government departments, in officer ranks of the police, Army and Air Force, and for further professional training as doctors, teachers, lawyers, engineers, etc."[20]

Founded by the late Empress Menen of Ethiopia in September 1931 as an elementary school, the Empress Menen Girls' School was the first and only institution in Ethiopia for female education.[21] It was to play a significant role in the education of Ethiopian women in the coming decades. The Fascist invasion interrupted its work, and eventually the Italians turned it into a hospital for their soldiers. After the liberation it was renovated, expanded, and restored. By 1950–51 the number of students had increased to 615, and by the end of the era it had grown into one of the four general secondary schools of the period.

Tafari Makonnen School was occupied in 1936 by a company of Alpine troops who destroyed most of its equipment.[22] The main building became a barracks, and the dormitory and clinic were used for Italian Army medical stores. In September 1941, the emperor reopened the school. About 700 boys, all day students, filled the available places. By 1945–46, the number of boys had reached 850. Fifteen private houses to accommodate 400 boarders were taken over; an assembly hall, a school clinic, a library, and two laboratories were constructed; and roads were built across the campus and electricity was installed.

In 1946–47 a secondary department with fifty students was opened, and several new buildings were added. In 1949–50, Tafari Makonnen School celebrated its twenty-fifth anniversary. There were fifty–two teachers, twenty–five Ethiopians and twenty–seven foreigners. For the first time in the history of the school thirty pupils sat for the London University Matriculation Examination.

Medhane Alem School in Addis Ababa also had its origin before the Italian occupation, having been inaugurated in 1931.[23] Eighty boarders were paid for by the Ethiopian government. In 1934 the first Boy Scout troop in Ethiopia was started at the school. Closed during the occupation, the school reopened its doors in January 1942 with 25 orphaned pupils who lived nearby, and its name was changed to *Ballabat* (Chiefs) School. In time many students from the provinces were brought there at government expense. Between 1944 and 1949 the school's facilities and enrollment expanded to accommodate 450 boys. In 1951 three years of secondary programs were added, and the following year Medhane Alem became a full-fledged secondary school, well known for its courses in physical training.[24]

The first secondary school to be built outside Addis Ababa was established in September 1948 by the Sudan Interior Mission. Its original name was Medhane Alem Academy, and it was intended as a comprehensive school offering secondary courses in teacher training, commerce, and academic subjects.

Seven academic secondary schools, only four of them complete, were functioning by the end of the era. In addition to the academic postprimary schools listed above, there were technical and vocational schools operated by the Ministry of Education, by other governmental departments, or by private societies.

During the decade a number of technical, vocational, and special schools were established, mostly in Addis Ababa, such as the Air Force Cadet Training Center; the Aba Dina Police Officers Training College and twelve other police schools; Empress Menen Handicraft School; various schools for nurses' aides, sanitation workers, inspectors, pharmacists, and nurses; the Municipal Technical School; the School of Building Technology; the Imperial Body Guard Officers Cadet Training School; the military school at Holeta; the Ambo Agricultural School; the Lycee Gabre Mariam; Berhanih Zare New Adult School; the Theological School; the Technical School; the Commercial School; and the Teacher Training Institute.[25]

When Ras Tafari became regent, he had turned his attention to making at least elementary education available to all the provinces of Ethiopia. When he ascended the throne as Emperor Haile Selassie I, he founded additional schools in the capital and a number in the provinces, but progress was brought to a halt when war broke out.[26] In 1941, the plan for provincial education was reactivated slowly but steadily. As early as 1942 the Ministry of Education appointed provincial education officers to plan for educational needs by standardizing curricula. At the same time the ministry increased budget allotments from the central treasury, built adequate school structures, and increased the number of teachers, textbooks, administrative personnel, and facilities. During the school year 1946–47, modern school buildings were constructed in many centers outside Addis Ababa, and a director of provincial education was appointed.

Expansion in the provinces required additional money, but the ministry reported that education had already been claiming about 20 percent of the national budget. In response to the challenge, the Education Land Tax Act was promulgated in December 1947, earmarking 30 percent of the ordinary land tax for education in the provinces.

Technical and Vocational Education

To meet the growing need for skilled technicians in industry, the Technical School was established in 1943.[27] Housed in an old three-room store in the southwestern part of the capital, the school offered courses of instruction in mechanics, electrical skills, carpentry, and more, while academic subjects included mathematics, French, and Amharic. In 1945 the Technical School was reorganized. The language of instruction was changed from French to English for both academic and vocational subjects. Additional courses such as physics, chemistry, advanced mathematics, and history were introduced. The program aimed to produce technicians and skilled workers at three levels. At the highest level, youngsters were trained for leadership as supervisors and foremen.

The Commercial School, the only government institute of its kind in the country, was started in 1945 in the annex of Menelik II School.[28] The curriculum was drawn up with the help of the school's ten teachers and of businessmen and administrators from the city. Typing was taught to boys and girls in three languages—French, English, and Amharic. Realizing that graduates of the Commercial School would play an important role in the accelerated development of the country, the Ministry of Education, which had founded the school, invested heavily in personnel and equipment. The students were taught modern concepts of business practice, and the first forty-four students to complete the four-year commercial requirements were all immediately employed.

One of the important vocational schools established during

reconstruction was Ambo Agricultural School.[29] The school opened in 1946 as a center for the study of farming in Ethiopia. Although the long-range plan was to raise it to college level, the school remained at secondary level throughout the period from 1946 to 1951. Located in the Guder district in Shoa, the site was chosen deliberately, in fertile and beautiful surroundings, with an agreeable climate, plenty of rainfall, a variety of good soils, and the possibility of irrigation and hydroelectric installations. From the beginning Ambo Agricultural School was well-staffed and well-equipped with agricultural tools and machines. A complete agricultural laboratory was received from the United States. Graduates earned certificates entitling them to work as agricultural technicians in elementary schools, as provincial agricultural officers, as farm managers and advisers, and as assistants of experimental stations. Some were sent abroad for further studies.

The graduates of this and other technical and vocational schools furnished skilled personnel for government and private enterprises, and replaced some of the Italians who had been the only trained technicians in the country. A contemporary report noted that "the Vocational Schools will prove their worth in building up a sufficient number of artisans, craftsmen, and business workers to meet the expanding needs."[30]

Another vocational school of a different nature, operating under the Ministry of Education and Fine Arts, was the Theological Schoool.[31] Opened in 1944 in the compound of the Church of the Holy Trinity in Addis Ababa, the Theological School was to train functionaries for the Ethiopian church. The students had previously been given instruction by priests and deacons of the church at the imperial palace. The Theological School of the Holy Trinity was comprised of three departments, one for junior priests, a deacons' school, and the college itself. Studies included Old and New Testament commentary, the Bible, geography of the Bible, church sacraments, church history, pastoral theology, the Mass, singing (*digwa zemare*), Ge'ez, Amharic, English, geography, mathematics, science, hygiene, and gymnastics. By 1945 some two hundred students were participating.

While undergoing training, the students were busy with practical activities. Senior students practiced preaching and teaching at a number of schools in the capital. Once a week they went

to visit and preach in hospitals or prisons, and on Saturday afternoons they delivered sermons to students and members of the
community in the school's assembly hall. Some students delivered sermons to a larger public on Sundays over Radio Addis
Ababa. A number of promising graduates were sent abroad for
further study.

In 1944, to remedy the severe shortage of teaching staff, the
Ministry of Education and Fine Arts opened the first teacher
training college in one room of Menelik II School.[32] The British
Council provided personnel, an arrangement that was to last until
1948. The school, in addition to primary and secondary sections,
included a professional department, a department of apprenticeship, a department of medicine, and a normal school. At the end
of 1946 twenty-four of the original thirty-two students graduated
and were assigned to responsible teaching posts in several provinces. As the only trained Ethiopian teachers in the country, they
were called upon to perform sundry duties such as administration, accounting, and community leadership, in addition to their
teaching responsibilities. By 1972, five were still with the Ministry of Education.

The two-year program was an effective means of producing
qualified teachers, but it was a slow process. Schools were being
opened constantly, and the supply of teachers was lagging behind.
Accordingly, in 1946–47 the Teacher Training School was asked
to undertake a series of three-month refresher courses for some of
the existing 578 elementary school teachers. The in-service programs continued for three terms; the 83 teachers who attended
spent their afternoons teaching at neighboring schools.[33] In
1947–48, ninety-nine students were enrolled in the Teacher
Training School. Meanwhile, the Ministry of Education had made
it compulsory for all teachers in the provinces to attend summer
courses.[34]

In 1947 the British council withdrew from the project, and a
Canadian, Mr. Steinmann, was appointed director of the training
school. His arrival marked a new phase for teacher education in
Ethiopia. As a professional teacher-educator, he deplored the
tendency to regard the training school as just another kind of
secondary school, but with emphasis on teaching. He therefore
began a gradual shift to professional subjects so that trainee
teachers might impart their knowledge most effectively. Begin-

ning in 1949–50, the ministry raised the level of entry and introduced more advanced courses.

In the years between 1949 and 1951 the school started six-month courses for school inspectors. Each province, it was envisioned, would in time have its own school inspector. As Steinmann explained in his report to the Provincial Educational Officers' Conference, the venture was a forward-looking one. He said then that "inspection should consist not merely in making reports and finding faults, but rather in discovering weaknesses and in showing teachers how they may overcome these weaknesses. Many more inspectors are needed for each province."[35]

The Teacher Training School was training instructors for the elementary schools of Ethiopia, where they were required to teach all subjects.[36] Attention was paid to elementary school needs and students were required to supplement their courses with practice teaching. At first, students accepted this curriculum without question, but in 1948 problems began to develop. Some students expressed dissatisfaction with the professional bias of the curriculum and agitated for greater emphasis on academic secondary subjects. The director stated to the ministry that the proposed curriculum was in accordance with recognized teacher-training practice in advanced societies and asked that the students be directed either to accept it or leave the school. The curriculum was approved, and the school remained a vocational and professional institution. The students who had misconstrued the purpose of the school were ignorant of the real objectives of a teacher-training institute. A recent report says: "A Teacher Training Institute should be a place where men are trained and men are made. None but the best should be entrusted with the education and care of the children of Ethiopia. Remember that you must be a man yourself before you train a man. You yourself must set the pattern he shall follow."[37]

The Teacher Training School expanded rapidly, and in 1952–53 both school and students were transferred to larger premises of their own in Harar. Harar Teacher Training School was thus inaugurated, with eighth grade graduates admitted for a four-year program. The original concepts and the curriculum were based upon the continuation of education and the acquisition of professional skills, plus teaching practice. These were carried over to the reorganized school.

Although Addis Ababa Teacher Training School was the pioneer institution, others were opened to produce elementary school staff. Headmasters of the larger schools were requested to conduct in-service education for their teachers, a plan that left too much to the initiative and imagination of the headmasters, and hence was found inadequate.[38] To augment the supply of trained teachers a committee was set up in 1947, and as a result of its deliberations a series of three-month refresher courses for provincial teachers was initiated.

The refresher courses continued for three terms, with a total of eighty-three teachers undergoing training. They were given a chance to visit schools in the capital and to do practice teaching under expert supervision. By the end of 1948 the training school resumed its regular two-year programs, and the in-service courses continued as a summer program. In 1949–50, sixteen schools throughout the empire were used for the vocation classes, with thirteen hundred students attending. Even with the help of such innovative programs, however, the shortage of trained teachers continued to be a major obstacle throughout the decade.

Higher Education
Postelementary schools were expanding faster than elementary education, which in turn gave rise to a need for further education at the college or university level. This had not been immediately feasible for Ethiopia, but when independence was regained in 1941, the old blueprints for higher education were reactivated and plans for a university college were approved by the Board of Education and the emperor.[39] On 20 March 1950, the emperor invited Dr. Lucien Matte, a distinguished Canadian Jesuit educator who had been serving as head of Tafari Makonnen School, to take the responsibility for the first college in Ethiopia. After Dr. Matte had traveled to Europe to purchase supplies and equipment and to recruit faculty members, classes began on 11 December 1950. Dr. Trudeau pointed out:

It was a humble beginning. There was a staff of nine teachers, the principal included. There were twenty-one students, all men, who had completed high school. The students, all boarders, and some of the staff members were living together on campus, in the building that used to be the Commercial School and was still partly occupied by students of this school. Dormitories, dining-hall, library, classrooms and laboratories were accommodated in this one building. It was simple and poor, but sufficient.[40]

The University College, as it came to be called, included a two-year program leading to an Ethiopian Higher Certificate. Independent of the other schools then in existence in form as well as content, it was to be oriented toward meeting the unique needs of Ethiopia. While Ethiopia was willing to draw upon the experience of foreign universities and personnel, it was felt that her own peculiar heritage and conditions would be the guiding principles in the development of the college.

After the formal inauguration of the college, much heated discussion ensued as to whether the college should be affiliated with a British university. The final decision was to keep the college independent and to work for the recognition of its diplomas and degrees by foreign institutions rather than submit the students to a foreign examination system. Accordingly, in 1953, the University College asked the government of Ethiopia for a civil charter. The charter was granted and published in the official *Negarit Gazeta* on 28 July 1954. The charter granted the college all the usual university powers and privileges. This was the cornerstone of higher education in modern Ethiopia.

The establishment of the University College was a step toward the founding of a university. In 1951 a special committee was appointed and considered "certain propositions for the establishment of the Haile Selassie I University in Addis Ababa."[41] The implementation of its report had to wait until 1961. Meanwhile, it generated widespread interest in the legitimate functions of a university, which in turn led to the establishment of several colleges during the 1950s. In summary, within the decade between 1941 and 1951, a complete structure of Ethiopian education had been built up, covering the whole range from nursery schools to college level—no small achievement considering the late start.

The idea of sending students abroad was resumed with renewed enthusiasm in 1945; some promising young people went even before they had completed secondary education.[42] By 1949 there were 228 students in foreign institutions under government and bilateral scholarship schemes. By the end of the decade there were more than 300 in universities and colleges scattered all over the world. At first they were sent to Alexandria, Beirut, and Greece. Later on they could be found in the United States, England, France, West Germany, Belgium, Finland, Norway, Sweden, Denmark, Switzerland, Austria, Yugoslavia, Cyprus, Turkey, Israel, India, the Sudan, Uganda, Australia, Canada, Japan, Haiti, Portugal, Tanganyika, Pakistan, and Mexico.

Even before 1951, some students had returned to render valuable service to their country. By 1958, 750 Ethiopians had completed their work and returned. The investment made in their education was beginning to pay off in better commitment, higher performance, and more productivity. Despite this, however, it was felt that to continue sending Ethiopians abroad for higher studies was uneconomical. The decision was taken to establish an institution of higher learning in Ethiopia.

Adult Education

Another area of significant need was that of adult education. The postwar scramble for education was ferocious. Children of school age were literally battering at the gates of the relatively few schools that were open. The demand was far in excess of the available personnel and facilities. In addition there were many adults who had had no chance for any kind of formal training, and it was essential that their needs be met. Private individuals and organizations took the lead, but in 1948–49 the Ministry of Education and Fine Arts finally acted. In the majority of the central schools, the headmasters, on their own initiative, conducted evening classes for the people of the neighborhood.

The British Council, through the British Institute, offered evening classes in Addis Ababa and in a couple of provinces. After passing rudimentary tests, young men were admitted at a nominal fee to learn primary English. The institute also offered pamphlets, films, and other cultural and instructional activities, and certificates were awarded annually.

In March 1948, *Berhanih Zare New* (Your Light Is Today), a school and cultural institution, was opened by imperial decree. Endowed by the emperor and located in the heart of the capital, the institute marked a new approach to adult education. Its purpose was ambitious: "The ultimate goal is to branch out into the field of mass education, so that every person in the Empire will become literate in a prescribed period. Plans were being studied this year to adopt a method of simplification of the Amharic alphabet, as a vehicle for achieving this end."[43] However, the prospect of reaching most adult citizens proved elusive for a number of reasons, including lack of equipment, facilities, and teachers.

Education of Women

Girls participated in the traditional system of education far less than boys. It was felt that a woman's place was in the home or working in the fields with her husband. At home a girl was initiated into the practical art of homemaking. Much attention was given to polished manners, politeness, obedience, and reverence for age. Bowing low when greeting elders or strangers and receiving articles in both hands were part of the training of well-mannered girls. Marriages were arranged by parents, and it was considered immodest for a girl to flirt. Once married she became, in many respects, almost equal to her husband: "The Ethiopian woman does not lose her identity in marriage; she retains her family name and continues to be known by it. She is a partner, not a subordinate in matrimony. In case of divorce, the spouses are each entitled to recover what they brought into the marriage partnership, and each has the right to half the property which has been acquired during the marriage."[44]

The women of Ethiopia were not altogether denied freedom, respect, and the enjoyment of culture and higher education that the time afforded. It is recorded that many women were distinguished in secular songs and poetry. The women poets of the city of Gondar were famous and played a significant role in the culture of Gondar at its height. Politically, too, Ethiopian women had played important roles. Empresses were regents by accepted custom during the minority of the heir to the throne, and queens, the mothers and wives of kings, had governed extensive territories and administered justice even during the effective rule of the sovereign. Among such women were the empresses Eleni, Seble Wengel, Mentwab, and Taytu, all of whom had extensive political power in their time. It could be argued that these royal ladies were a law unto themselves and did not represent the common women. However, they did represent the thinking of the ruling class and the church, the two strongest Ethiopian institutions for many centuries.[45]

At the beginning of the present century some girls were sent abroad to study and in Ethiopia itself many girls began to attend the schools established by foreign religious societies. In 1931 Her Imperial Majesty, the late empress of Ethiopia, founded the Empress Menen School for Girls which has been mentioned earlier. Initially fifty female students were registered. The school continued to function until 1936, and reopened in 1941.

The Empress Menen Handicraft School in Addis Ababa was also primarily for girls. This school was established before the war and was disbanded during the occupation. After 1941 it was reactivated, in order to give young women and girls a technical education. Another objective in the reactivation of the school was to preserve and improve "the beautiful handicrafts which had flourished in former times and now were tending under the impact of factory-made goods from abroad to disappear."[46] Gradually this school expanded to include a one-year teacher-training course and a three-year course leading to the award of a diploma.

As table 1 shows, the education of women and girls assumed an accelerated tempo during the early years of the postwar era. It was recognized, however, that there was still a lag in the education of women, and it was decided that henceforth "both boys and girls should be afforded equal opportunities."[47] Nevertheless, any step in the direction of coeducation had to be slow and cautious. The rise in the number of female students had never

TABLE 1.   Female Students as Percentage of
Total Enrollment, 1944–51

Year	Percentage
1944–45	9.9
1945–46	9.2
1946–47	8.7
1947–48	11.4
1948–49	10.5
1949–50	11.7
1950–51	12.4

Sources: Ethiopia, Ministry of Education and Fine Arts, Yearbook 1940–41 E.C., p. 77; Yearbook 1942–43 E.C., pp. 109–17, 143–45, 163–65, 188–81.

been fast or steady; the mean percentage for the seven years to 1951 was only 10.5 percent. This was and still is a problem; young girls seem reluctant to attend or to stay in school.

While emphasis had been placed on reaching as many of the school age and overage population as possible, the Ministry of Education was still unable to provide opportunities for preschool children. However, in sporadic fashion, primarily through the efforts of private organizations and individuals, nursery or kindergarten classes were conducted both in the capital and in some provinces. By the end of the reconstruction era, there were several such schools in existence. This scattered effort did not, however, quench the thirst for kindergartens, especially in the capital.

Curriculum and Methods

The objectives of a curriculum "arise out of the culture of a people, out of their ideals and aspirations, their social and individual values, and their problems that cry for solution."[48] The curriculum in Ethiopia during the reconstruction era, however, was set up to meet immediate manpower needs. It was not well thought out, nor was it tailored to the fundamental wishes of the people or to the characteristics of Ethiopian children. The policy of importing teachers was unsound and inimical to development, but it was adopted because there were almost no other teachers or teaching materials, and no time to try alternatives. An improvised policy had to be followed. Life goes on, and people cannot wait for better times and better things to come.

To bring some kind of balance and uniformity to the structure, content, and methods of instruction, however, the Board of Education formulated a nationwide policy of uniform curricula which covered the first six grades. This made it possible for pupils to transfer from one province to another, from one school to another, or to proceed to higher education by following established procedures.

The new policy sought to make the curriculum not only "uniform" but "adaptable . . . to every community throughout the land."[49] It was intended to fit the Ethiopian scene and at the same time be compatible with standards in other schools and other cultures. This was an honest intention, but in practice the curriculum was foreign both in approach and content.

The first formal curriculum had a 6–6 structure, six years of elementary education followed by six years of secondary. After 1948, the elementary period was extended to cover grades seven and eight, the two years formerly used for preparation. Students were still expected to spend four years in senior high schools or their equivalent.[50]

Beginning in 1948, the Ministry of Education awarded a school certificate to pupils who had successfully completed the prescribed courses of study in the secondary schools. The teacher-training and vocational schools awarded diplomas and certificates of competency. Successful graduates of second-level education were at first sent primarily to Great Britain for higher education, but after 1948 they began to attend American colleges and universities.

The school week covered five full days, Monday through Friday. The average daily attendance was 80 percent of registration and was highest among boarders and in the central schools. Attendance was lowest in rural day-schools, where weather, distance, bad conditions of travel, and the need to help in the home and on the farm caused real hardship.

The shortage of instructional material—unavoidable while a global war still raged—was a serious handicap. In 1942, there was an acute lack of maps, atlases, charts, textbooks, teaching aids, and school supplies, as well as of equipment. Amharic texts, which had been printed before the war, had nearly all been destroyed during the occupation, while the Italian textbooks left behind were useless in terms of both language and content. In 1941–42 the Ministry of Education printed a number of Amharic books to serve as readers in elementary schools, and English readers were also written and published when the language of instruction changed to English in 1944. As far as supplies were concerned, the Italians had left behind blackboards and some inferior chalk, "while the backs of the multitudinous official forms came in useful as writing paper."[51]

The change from Amharic to English placed a heavy burden on learners for whom English was a second or third language. In 1942 the Ethiopian government invited the British Council to set up institutes for teaching English, to provide a library of English books and periodicals, and to procure English textbooks for schools. In 1944 the British Council spent some $200,000 on the purchase of books for use in Addis Ababa.[52]

Meanwhile the Ministry of Education was busy setting up committees to recommend measures for the consolidation of educational policies, curricula, textbooks, and methods of instruction that would be characteristically Ethiopian.[53] In the meantime orders for books were sent abroad and some of the teaching materials—charts, maps, atlases, and textbooks—began to arrive in 1945. From then on, since the war in Europe was over, textbooks, equipment, and supplies could be obtained if the cash was available; most of these teaching materials were foreign-produced, however, for children of different cultural backgrounds.

The government secondary schools suffered just as much, if not more. A student of Ethiopian education writing a decade later observed:

> The secondary schools were almost entirely academic. Everyone directed his attention to the High School Certificate . . . which was the "entrance ticket" to one of the colleges. Commercial, technical and agricultural education was regarded as second–class education, reserved for those who could not make the grade in academic secondary schools, or who had to go to work immediately after finishing their secondary education.[54]

Teaching materials were also criticized for being archaic and conservative. A ministry publication of the early 1950s stated: "Anyone who is acquainted with modern developments in secondary education cannot void being critical of the curriculum and materials of instruction in the academic secondary schools of Ethiopia." The writer added: "It is obvious that a secondary school curriculum which duplicates the curriculum of conservative academic secondary schools in English–speaking countries is not appropriate for us in Ethiopia. . . ."[55]

Problems of this nature could have been minimized or eliminated had it been possible to compensate for them in the methods of instruction, but unfortunately there was no such easy way out. In Ethiopia at this time both materials and teachers were brought from abroad. Furthermore, each teacher brought with him the philosophy of his native land, and he practiced it in Ethiopian schools without much regard for the local situation or for what the other teachers or the school administrators were doing. With appropriate instruction students could have been motivated to develop their critical judgment, independent and creative thinking, and powers of observation and reasoning related to real problems. This was not the case in our schools, however, and many students fell by the wayside before they had completed any meaningful learning. The same ministry publication noted that "the observation of instructional methods in the academic secondary schools would undoubtedly reveal that very little is being done in the area of remedial instruction, the improvement of reading ability, the improvement of study habits, etc. . . . Corrective action should be undertaken as soon as possible."[56]

The curriculum policy issued in 1948 listed subjects for primary grades in detail, as well as instruction on how courses were to be taught. Amharic was the language of instruction for the first two years; there was a gradual transition to English after grade three in the teaching of science, history, art, physical education, music, geography, arithmetic, and handicrafts. English was the language of instruction at the secondary and teacher-training levels.

Textboks used American or British weights and measures, and presupposed a knowledge of the American continent or the British Isles. Perhaps this was the result of two foreign groups trying to do their best for Ethiopian schools, but unable to escape their own backgrounds; yet students would undoubtedly have benefited more from working in an Ethiopian context. Even in teaching Amharic this problem was not solved. For example, because of the Christian heritage of the country and the inability to find suitable textbooks, the Bible was used as a text for the first four grades, but because of the large segment of non-Christian citizens, this had to be discarded. The teaching of English also presented problems. Generally speaking, the curriculum guide was a healthy departure from past practice, but it failed because it was drawn up by people who had too little experience of Ethiopia itself.

The curriculum guide that came out in 1949 provided more specific formulas for grades one through six, but was little more than a rehash of the requirements for grades five and six. It did provide for standardization of instruction for the seventh and eighth grades, which was an improvement. The instructional materials were again based on foreign experience, and were geared no more closely to the needs of Ethiopians than were the texts and materials for lower grades. For example, the prescribed course in science made little mention of personal or community hygiene, nutrition, health or safety measures, agriculture, or the conservation of natural resources. The course outlines were theoretical and dealt with such topics as the solar system, magnetism, expansion of solids and liquids, and the like. Very little of this had any practical relevance for unsophisticated pupils in a rural setting. The curriculum was of course inadequate and was criticized severely. The secondary school curriculum, meanwhile, was oriented toward the requirements of London University's General Certificate of Education Examination, on the assumption that secondary school graduates would further their studies overseas.

From time immemorial the artisans of Ethiopia have been known for their pottery, weaving, jewelry, basketry, straw weaving, metalwork, and woodwork. There had traditionally been a division of labor based on either ethnic, religious, or sexual grounds. Sometimes certain craftsmen were despised by others, and this attitude persists in some parts of the country. Undeniably, the native crafts of Ethiopia have enriched its culture and economy. After the restoration, the government decided to revive these arts in the schools, recognizing that the ability to design and execute patterns and to create useful and artistic objects, is part of the native genius of the Ethiopian people. Modern industrial arts have grown from such roots. It was felt that the schools should encourage the preservation and further development of the native handicrafts by including them in the elementary and secondary curricula.[57]

In rural and provincial schools there were no skilled teachers, so only the indigenous crafts of the community were taught. In larger towns sewing, embroidery, and carpentry were added. Arts and crafts varied from one district to the next, but those taught included rope making, basketry, jewelry, spinning, weaving, knitting, bone carving, simple leather working, simple woodworking, pottery, and gardening. In many schools each pupil had his own garden plot in the compound.

In Addis Ababa and some provincial capitals, sophisticated equipment and relatively well-trained teachers were available. In Empress Menen Girls' School qualified teachers taught the girls spinning, knitting, embroidery, dressmaking, basketry, and other indigenous arts and crafts. In Jimma School of Practical Arts crafts like woodworking and leather tanning were taught as well as simple house construction, mechanics, and bookkeeping. At Kolfe School students were taught to make rope, rugs, and jewelry, and to spin and dye, and to work in silver.[58]

Music is an important part of life in Ethiopia. Traditional music consists of two types, sacred and secular. Unfortunately, the notation and words of sacred music are in Ge'ez, and no attempt has ever been made to popularize its rendition. It is used only in church services by deacons and priests; the majority of laymen do not understand it nor participate in it.

Secular music, on the other hand, has always been the property of the common people, an expression of their feelings about their daily labors, the seasons of the year, and so on. This music has never been written down, nor are there any rules governing note arrangements. When an attempt was made to include music in the school curriculum, therefore, many problems were encountered.[59] The approach was perhaps too negative; because of a lack of teaching material, the authorities tried to teach Ethiopian students Western music, and judged their success or failure on that basis. A 1950 report noted:

> Ethiopian native music is pentatonic as against that of most of the West being diatonic. To delve into study, expand and orchestrate Ethiopian music calls for special skill and, at this stage, great musical research. If the same theme which runs through Ethiopia's modernization, that of preserving as much as possible of the native culture and blending it with the best from the West is to be maintained, then music in Ethiopian education presents some difficulties. . . . It is not as yet established that Ethiopian music as such has been ever reduced to written form, and the instruments used are of purely native fabrication.[60]

The author was speaking of the music of the Western world. Had he tried to find similarities with Eastern music he might not have been so pessimistic.

Despite the difficulties, pupils exposed to music teaching showed "remarkable aptitude" in their sense of rhythm, and tremendous skill in playing musical instruments. "The rule up to the present," said the report, "is to teach the native airs by rote, some of the students and music teachers playing from memory on the piano, and to include Western airs and works as bases for music teaching. The favorite instruments . . . are the piano and the violin."[61] In the larger elementary schools and in secondary schools, music formed part of the regular curriculum. Modern instruments, however, such as pianos and violins, were insufficient, the literature necessary for the teaching of theory was none too lavish, and enough qualified music teachers were still not available.

Health and Physical Education

The importance of physical education was recognized in the 1947 curriculum guide: "Physical education is not merely to improve the physical condition of the children and to secure the full development of their health and physical strength; it is a process through which they are aided in the development of their mental powers and in the formation of their character . . . and therefore rightly forms part of the general curriculum of the Ethiopian schools."[62]

To coordinate physical education and to supervise the distribution of sports materials and equipment, a physical training director was attached to the central office of Addis Ababa. Among the games played were football, basketball, and volleyball, as well as native games. Swimming took place where facilities were available, as did track and field athletics. At the bigger schools, games were organized on a compulsory basis on one or two afternoons a week. The Ethiopian Inter-School Athletic Association was organized during 1949–50 and held annual competitions in football and athletics, the finals of which were always attended by the emperor. The activities of the association were gradually extended to the provinces.[63]

After the liberation, it became apparent that all was not well with the health of Ethiopian children. They had suffered seriously during the occupation. The sickness rate was very high, due to privation, mistreatment, neglect, and malnutrition. Sylvia Pankhurst pointed out:

> Masses of children had existed for years literally without homes. Thousands had been deprived of parents, relatives,

friends and homes. . . . Thousands of young boys, mere children, had been forcibly removed from their villages and
carried off in the Italian army lorries to work on the roads or
to serve the Italians in the towns. These destitute youngsters
were known as "dwellers on the stair," for, possessing no
other shelter, it was their habit to pass the night huddled on
doorsteps.[64]

Children who had gone through such experiences were li-
able to many types of disease, including tropical ulcers, scabies,
impetigo, trachoma, tuberculosis, syphilis, pediculosis, and worm
infestations. Convinced that children could not learn unless they
were healthy, arrangements were made by the Ministry of Public
Health to appoint and supervise nurses' aides to help with minor
ailments and to send the seriously ill to central hospitals. In
addition provision was made for an eye, ear, nose, and throat
specialist to inspect all pupils.

In 1943, as the number of pupils increased, full-time medical officers and school dentists were appointed. Laboratory and
X-ray equipment were installed, and later full-time qualified
nurses were added to the medical staff. The Ministry of Education had by then taken over the administration of school health
services and had begun to purchase bulk medical supplies.

In time most schools were provided with qualified full-time
nurses or, in the provinces, with aides, and qualified physicians
paid frequent visits.[65] During the decade, a Department of School
Health, headed by a full-time physician, was established under the
Ministry of Education. Cases from all Addis Ababa schools and
some from the provinces were taken there for treatment. Each
pupil was provided with a medical record, and each was given
medical examinations and treatment if necessary. The record was
maintained throughout the school years and transferred with the
pupil from school to school. Later on, emphasis was placed on
preventive rather than curative medicine. Diet, clothing, housing,
bedding, lighting, and sanitation were subjected to special study.
Vaccination and inoculation were also introduced.[66]

Examinations and Promotion

The pupils who flocked to the schools were eager to make up for
lost time, and that eagerness was translated into an unprece-

dented demand for schooling. Under pressure of this demand, the government decided to expand the school system.

In the spring of 1941, when prewar schools were reopening one by one in the capital and later in the provinces, most of the applicants were above the normal age for elementary schooling but were keenly aware of the importance of education. A Ministry of Education report pointed out that "standards showed a good deal of variation; and the disparity of ages and of levels of previous education made the composition of classes somewhat peculiar."[67] Some of the students in elementary grades were in their late teens and twenties. To meet the educational needs of youth and the manpower requirements of the country, bright students were promoted from one grade to the next as fast as possible.[68] A fantastically rapid growth in the system ensued. Had the schools followed normal promotion procedures, the first middle school class would have graduated in 1949 and the first secondary class in 1953. In fact, the first secondary school admitted students to its ninth grade in 1943 and graduated its first twelfth grade class in 1947.

This unorthodox procedure has been attacked for contributing to student attrition at the secondary level, and this may be a valid criticism. It must not be overlooked, however, that, if this approach had not been adopted, manpower needs would not have been met. More students—especially average ones—would have been encouraged to drop out and, most important of all, the development of secondary and higher education would have been delayed by at least a decade.

In 1950, the general examination for eighth grade was given to students at the close of grade seven, an unusual procedure that increased the number of students in the upper middle school grades. After this system had started, there was no easy way to stop it, even had there been a desire to do so, and its practice resulted in sending poorly prepared students into secondary schools.

Students desiring to pursue their education to college or university level were required to sit for one of three examinations, the London Matriculation Examination, the General Certificate of Education, or the Ethiopian Secondary School Certificate Examination.[69] The two latter served as the basis for university entrance. In 1948 a group of secondary students sat for the College Entrance Examination of the Board of Regents of the state of New York. Those that succeeded were sent to the United States for further studies.[70] Introduced in 1946, the examinations provided a yardstick for comparing graduates of our secondary schools with those of other lands. Matriculants were either sent to overseas universities or were, from 1950, admitted to the University College of Addis Ababa. Others were sent abroad without passing any examinations or even without completing secondary education. Only more recently have regulations required a first degree from the majority of candidates for scholarships abroad.

Chapter 5

The Reconstruction Era, 1941–51: Patterns of Growth, Management, and Legislation

Patterns of Growth

It is difficult to trace the patterns of growth of government education from the beginning because statistics on the number of schools, teachers, and students, especially for the first three years, are often lacking or contradictory. One fact, however, is clear: in 1941 there were no government schools of any kind. The only formal education in the whole empire was provided by the Ethiopian church. The government schools—indeed the entire educational system that existed in 1951—therefore represented a growth from zero ten years before.[1]

Within the three years after 1941, the infrastructure of the education system was beginning to take a definite form. Table 2 depicts the pattern of educational development during the decade. From 1944 onward, data are available on the total number of schools, but they do not reveal the type of school nor whether it was operated under government auspices.

It can be seen that growth was steady, with an increase of 335 schools betwen 1943 and 1951. At this point, however, the decision of the church to pull out of public education because of the land tax support question had an adverse effect on the continued development of education. The number of schools offering programs of one, two, three, and four years decreased in 1952. As will be explained later, the reason for this fluctuation was the church's withdrawal from primary education.[2]

As we have seen, a start had been made in developing secondary schools and institutions of higher learning, but the number of secondary schools was insignificant compared to elementary schools. By the end of the decade, however, the situation in

TABLE 2.   Growth in the Number of
Government Schools, 1943–52

Year	Number of Schools	Percentage of Increase
1943–44	80	—
1944–45	175	118.8
1945–46	260	48.6
1946–47	380	46.2
1947–48	390	2.6
1948–49	500	28.2
1949–50	540	8.0
1950–51	530	−1.9
1951–52	415	−21.7
Total	3,270	

Source: Ethiopia, Ministry of Education and Fine Arts,
Yearbook 1942–43 E.C., p. 12.

secondary education had been reversed relative to elementary
education and had aroused the alarmed concern of a committee
set up to investigate it. Their report pointed out that the securing
of a sufficient number of competent administrators, technicians,
and professional personnel, essential for the efficient operation
of government, explained in large measure the emphasis placed
on rapid development of secondary and higher institutions.[3]

The same document remarked that it had become difficult to
find a sufficient number of qualified candidates to enter secondary schools. Their rapid development had diverted resources
from the primary schools, while many young people had to wait
even for elementary schooling. It was suggested that attention be
focused on the expansion of primary and middle schools.[4]

Nongovernment Education

During this period some nongovernment organizations had already begun to play significant roles in education. They included,
besides the Ethiopian church, various foreign missionary societies, private organizations, and foreign resident communities
who wanted to educate their children along national lines. Other
institutions were run by Ethiopian Moslems primarily for their
own children. Detailed information on the latter is lacking, but it
is known that Moslem Ethiopians had maintained their own
schools for centuries, and continued to do so. During the occu-

pation the Fascists did not interfere with Moslem schools for reasons of propaganda; indeed, they claimed that they subsidized their expansion. These "Koran schools" sometimes operated with government subsidies, but more often independently. The only estimate regarding enrollment and number of schools is from Ruckmick: "The best figures obtainable put the number at about 6,000 schools with perhaps 40,000 children learning to read Arabic in general and the Koran in particular, but these children do not proceed very far with their general education."

The Ethiopian Jews (Felashas) also operated schools for their own children. Data are also lacking here, but Ruckmick says that "the Felasha population is estimated as having about 300 schools with not more than 1,500 children attending them."[5] Other non-Ministry of Education schools included those for nurses' training, the armed forces, and other quasi-government organizations, as well as those schools run by missionaries.

A modern author has observed that Christian missionaries were not so important in founding secular education in Ethiopia as in other parts of Africa.[6] It is true that they were not so aggressive as in other African or Asian countries, but they had ample reason not to be. Following the unhappy incidents that led to the expulsion of the Portuguese Jesuits in the sixteenth century, Ethiopia, and especially the clergy, had been very wary of foreign missionaries. Once Roman Catholicism had been successfully defied, however, the conduct of the clergy and the people became more relaxed.

In the middle of the nineteenth century both Catholic and Protestant missionaries were allowed to return. Expelled by Tewodros II and by Yohannes IV for a time, they were readmitted by Emperor Menelik II. Since then, most missionaries have remained on friendly terms with the rulers and people of Ethiopia, whose feelings toward them have been ambivalent.[7]

The Shoan king Sahle Selassie expelled missionaries from his territories, saying they would teach his people false religion.[8] Emperor Menelik II also wanted his country to remain independent, saying, "If Europeans come into our house to bring us civilization, we thank them very much, but they must bring it without our losing our sovereignty."[9] Emperor Haile Selassie I similarly stated: "We need European progress because we are surrounded by it. That is at once a benefit and a misfortune. It will expedite our development but we are afraid of being swamped by it."[10]

Nevertheless, the missionaries did make a contribution. By 1935, there were some 180 foreign missionaries in the 119 mission stations scattered over the country, serving 6,717 students.[11] The Italian government made it impossible for Protestant missionaries to stay in Ethiopia, so that by 1940 only eight remained.[12] In 1941 the missionaries were able to return, but some serious questions still remained to be settled before foreigners were to be allowed free rein in such vital fields as religion and education. Misunderstanding between the Ethiopian authorities and mission representatives was inevitable.

In 1944 the government promulgated a decree controlling and defining the activities of missionaries operating in the country. It distinguished between church areas, where the inhabitants were predominantly Ethiopian Orthodox Christian, and open areas, where the inhabitants were predominantly non-Christian. In church areas, missions might establish hospitals and nondenominational schools, but might not proselytize; in open areas they might teach, preach the Christian faith, and found denominational schools.[13] According to Ruckmick, the missionary schools had accounted for the education of 4,500 children by 1950.[14]

Among the oldest postliberation private schools in Addis Ababa was the Princess Zenebe Work School, which opened in 1942. It was situated in a handsome compound donated by Empress Menen and was operated by the American educator Mrs. Ford. Subsidized by the Ministry of Education, the school was coeducational, catering to both boarding and day students. Beginning with a modest enrollment of eight pupils, the school grew to an impressive size and was the pioneer in founding the Girl Guide movement in the capital.

The English School, later known as the Sandford School, was opened in 1942, in response to requests for help from Ethiopian students who had studied abroad during the occupation. It gradually expanded until by 1951 it included students of more than twenty nationalities, some 40 percent of whom were Ethiopian. A non-profit-making institution, it was conducted after the British model as a boarding and day coeducational school, and at this time offered both elementary and secondary programs up to the Cambridge (Overseas) School Certificate. It also had a kindergarten section.

Founded in 1910, the Alliance Française in Addis Ababa was the oldest nongovernment school in Ethiopia. It was established under the direction of the Catholic mission and operated by the Brothers of St. Gabriel. In the period between 1936 and 1941, the Italians diverted the buildings to other uses, and the Catholic brothers were expelled. The school was reopened in 1943 and has remained under the direction of the head of the French diplomatic mission. A coeducational institution, it tried to give its students some knowledge of French language and culture. Graduates either continued their education at the Lycée Gabre Mariam in Addis Ababa or, more commonly, took up jobs in government or in private organizations.[15]

The role of the Ethiopian Orthodox church in the past and today has been described in chapter 1, and much credit should be given it for this initial educational impetus.[16] During the reconstruction era the church continued to operate, but with diminished importance. The church's system of education, and indeed the church itself, had become rigid, defensive, and stagnant, after centuries of attack and of isolation from the rest of the world. Instead of adapting to a changing world, past achievements and outdated methodologies were perpetuated and glorified. If the national church were to hold its ground in the new Ethiopia, reform was urgently needed; and it was initiated by Emperor Haile Selassie I.

As a first step, the Bible was translated into Amharic. Then, beginning in 1942 after long-drawn-out and at times stormy negotiations, the church gained independence from the church of Alexandria, with which she had been associated since the fourth century A.D. The first law after the six years of the occupation to deal with the church was passed on 30 November 1942. It attempted to put the financial situation of the church in order, to create a central treasury, and to provide for the appointment of clergy as well as to influence reforms in clerical education.[17] The Theological College of the Holy Trinity was opened in 1944, as we have seen. The director and three teachers were Copts, the remaining eight teachers Ethiopian, and the courses included secular as well as theological subjects.[18] The reforms, however, were not readily accepted by the church leadership. In 1949, the church claimed exemption from the education tax, which was based exclusively upon rural land ownership.[19] The church refused to pay, claiming that it was providing educational opportunity through its own schools. Its stand was in time sustained by the emperor. As a result the church took most of its schools in eight provinces out of the government system, on the understanding that they would continue to operate them on the lines established by the Ministry of Education. However, wherever there were enough funds, the ministry continued to operate the schools, even though income was reduced by the exemption of church lands from the education tax.[20] Most of the schools transferred to the church between 1949 and 1951 were of lower primary grades, but the loss of 177 schools and nearly half a million dollars of revenue was a heavy blow to the infant educational system then struggling to stand on its own feet in Ethiopia.

It was later discovered that many of the schools so transferred were closed or inoperative. The Long-Term Committee, after reviewing the situation, recommended that the government take the schools over or establish new ones to replace them.[21] This setback in educational development was almost as serious as that of 1936 when the Fascists had closed all the government schools. As Dr. Maaza indicated: "The unfortunate outcome was that an already small and struggling modern school system received its second blow, and an opportunity was lost to combine the educational efforts of an ancient church with that of a government system."[22]

The church continued to maintain schools, mostly of lower grades, some of which tried to follow the ministry's curriculum. During the decade after 1941, a significant number of students attended them.

Teaching Personnel

The demand for qualified teachers throughout the school system had not abated; in fact, the shortage was most acute in 1941. Before the Italian invasion there were some 230 teachers, including some 30 foreigners, teaching in modern schools. During the war and occupation over half the Ethiopian teachers were killed, and many were exiled. Some of the foreigners were driven out of the country. In 1941–42, a major problem was the absence of qualified teachers at even the primary level. To meet this urgent need, some innovations in teacher recruitment were introduced. Anybody with an education, or who had learned the rudiments of reading and writing in church schools, even those who had only completed first, second, or third grade, were hired as teachers.[23]

It should be noted that although the number of government schools and the total student enrollment decreased between 1949 and 1951, the number of teachers employed increased consistently year after year. Overcrowding and excessively large classes were not a problem. In 1951, there were 1,375 teachers and 45,649 students, a ratio of 1 to 30.[24] This happy situation was not to last very long. During the following decade, student enrollment outstripped financial resources and teacher recruitment, and overcrowded classes became the rule.

Foreign personnel had always been a part of the attempt to introduce modern education into Ethiopia. Sixty years ago, when the plan for the first modern school in Addis Ababa was conceived under Menelik II, teachers were recruited from among the Coptic Egyptians, primarily to assuage the suspicions of the Ethiopian church and the conservative elements that modern education would mean conversion to alien religions. In the early 1920s, when Tafari Makonnen School was inaugurated, foreign teachers were brought in to help run the school. By the time the war broke out in 1935, there were about thirty such educators in the country. In 1941 a call went out again for foreign educators to work with Ethiopians to develop the shattered education system. The response was small because of the war, but slowly the positions were filled.

The first groups came from Britain. The headmasters of the leading schools in Addis Ababa were British, and when Haile Selassie I Secondary School opened in 1943, British personnel were in charge. Apprehensions regarding the British appeared, however, and Ethiopia turned away from Britain toward the United States. An American economic mission was invited in 1944, a loan was accepted, and American advisers were appointed in place of the British.

When American aid was not forthcoming in the expected amounts, Ethiopia also turned to Sweden. Sixteen Swedes arrived, most of them teachers. In 1946 the Russians established a hospital. Other countries were also approached for assistance and the response was favorable.[25] British personnel, however, stayed on, and most of the other foreigners were from English-speaking countries, explaining the postwar emphasis on English as the medium of instruction. They included Americans, Canadians, and Indians, as well as Swedes and Lebanese. In 1945 an American named Hambrook became adviser in the Ministry of Education, and another American, C. A. Ruckmick, became superintendent of schools. A few schools were headed and staffed by Americans. The French Canadian Jesuits took over Haile Selassie I Secondary School, Menelik II School, and Itegue Menen School, as well as the technical school in Addis Ababa. The Swedes became the first instructors at the Imperial Body Guard, Air Force, Police Force, and Army Cadet Schools. Beginning in 1948, Indian teachers and administrators were recruited, primarily to staff provincial schools.

The staffing of each school with one nationality created a spirit of competition that was in many respects healthy. In fact, the schools in Addis Ababa were much more "lively, clean, and of a higher standard" in 1949 than they were in the 1950s.[26] By 1949 the Ministry of Education had imported no less than 286 foreigners.[27]

On the other hand, as Margery Perham noted:

> It is . . . regrettable that, in their ever ready fear that a foreigner may gain too much influence or keep out an Ethiopian candidate for a post, they [the officers of the Ministry of Education] have refused to allow a reasonable degree of continuity among the individuals employed or of confidence in them. . . . Without these conditions no valuable influence or tradition can be built into the schools. The Ethiopians may succeed in avoiding culture confusion, but the perpetual changes of plans, persons and nationalities have undoubtedly produced something not far off administrative confusion in education and have discouraged many of those who were honestly trying to do good work for Ethiopia.[28]

In retrospect, Ethiopian educators would probably agree that the foreign teachers and administrators created many problems with which the nation would have to deal in the years ahead. Ethiopia did not always have the means to recruit the people best qualified for the job, even had such people been available. We brought in whomever we could. Yet, looking back, we can see that some outstanding educators were attracted to our cause, and in the circumstances it is difficult to see what other course could have been adopted. In addition, after school personnel had worked here and gained valuable experience, the best people left for America, Canada, or for other African countries which offered more attractive monetary rewards.[29] Some of the most promising young Ethiopians were sent to study abroad (228 of them in 1949), in the hope that on their return they would be attracted to teaching. This, coupled with the opening of the new University College Department of Teacher Education in 1950, was to be the source of future teacher recruitment.[30]

Physical Facilities

The importance of a suitable school plant cannot be overemphasized. Young people need to grow and develop physically, emotionally, and intellectually during their school years. Good buildings, with suitable equipment, furnishings, and facilities, help uninterrupted growth and development. In 1941, as many of the former buildings as possible were restored to their original use; there was neither money nor time to erect new ones for school purposes.

After the liberation, to encourage parents to send their children to school and to rehabilitate homeless and orphan children, provision had to be made not only to educate but to house, clothe, and feed many children. Structures had to serve as dormitories, kitchens, diningrooms, and offices, as well as classrooms. Eventually boarding the children was abandoned, at least at the elementary level, and more classrooms were built. Between 1945 and 1950 more than $3,000,000 was spent on buildings.[31]

The Ministry of Education established an Architects' Department to superintend the building of new schools, especially in the provinces.[32] In Addis Ababa and a few provincial cities, some of the buildings were permanent. Some were originally built as schools, others were taken over and adapted. Some of the buildings had adequate space, lighting, ventilation, and safety standards, while others were deficient. The pressure for space was such that at times partially completed buildings were used. New areas were continually surveyed and reserved as future sites.

Legislation

The first law of the reconstruction era, creating the post of minister of education,[33] was passed only five days after the entry of the emperor into Addis Ababa in 1941. The minister appointed was Mekonnen Desta, a graduate of Howard University in the United States, who had spent the occupation in exile. This legislation was followed by Order Number 1 of 1943 to "define the powers and duties of our ministers." Article 26 stipulated that the minister of education and fine arts was to prepare and submit draft laws necessary for proper administration and to make regulations and issue the orders necessary to carry them out. Article 28 specified that he was, in addition, to develop education and fine arts; to define the curriculum for schools and technical schools; to control private education; to establish an academy for research in languages and fine arts; to inform the people, through publications, of the progress of science and the arts abroad; and to establish public libraries and government museums and issue certificates of higher education.[34]

Decree Number 3 of 1944 regulated mission activities, specifying in which areas such activities were to be permitted. Applications from missionary societies had to be sent to the minister of education, who would designate an area for mission activities. An application would be accepted only if the mission were well established, had a good reputation abroad and adequate funds and staff, and had been established in Ethiopia before 1935 or after June 1941.

Proselytizing for the Ethiopian Orthodox church was forbidden. Missions were permitted to be active only in non-Christian areas, though they might establish hospitals or nondenominational schools in Orthodox areas. Religious instruction was confined to the principles common to all Christian churches. In open areas the societies had the right to teach and preach the Christian faith of their own denomination without restriction, provided that the language used was Amharic. The right to teach foreign languages was assured.[35]

Legal Notice Number 103 of 1947 provided that a 3 percent ad valorem tax would be levied on all imported goods, for the promotion of education and public health in Ethiopia.[36] In 1952, a legal notice increased the tax to 4 percent.[37]

The orderly development of education, culture, and religion

required the involvement of a wide segment of the nation. Order Number 3 of 1947 read: "The direction, administration, supervision and guidance of all functions and controls of Our Imperial Government, relating to education, fine arts, and religious and cultural instruction, within Our Empire shall come under Our exclusive control. . . . A Board of Education and Fine Arts is hereby established. . . ."[38]

Thus the emperor was to assume the education and fine arts portfolio and share responsibility with a board under his orders representing a wide spectrum of opinion, including the church. These arrangements operated for the next fifteen years. Another important piece of legislation established the 1947 land tax for education and provided for its strict enforcement. In provinces where land tenure systems varied, different rates were applied. In Gojam, Tigre, and Begemder, the education tax was 30 percent of the land tax in force in 1947, plus the estimated tithe in cash.[39]

Another law proclaimed at the same time covered expenditure and accounting of local education tax funds. Local boards of education were set up. They were required to meet at least once every six months to keep abreast of local education, make recommendations to the minister of education, examine the balance sheet submitted to them annually by the Ministry of Finance, and satisfy themselves that all education tax was spent on elementary education in the province where the tax had been collected. Except for schools in Addis Ababa, all elementary schools would be supported from the local education tax. All higher education expenses would be borne by the central treasury.[40] General Notice Number 135 of 1950 was the charter of the Boy Scouts Association of Ethiopia.[41]

Management

Until recent years, educational administration in Ethiopia had always been highly centralized. The Ministry of Education and Fine Arts in Addis Ababa was an administrative department of the central government and was entrusted with shaping policies for national education. But the policies were difficult to implement in the face of the shortages of qualified teachers, buildings, and teaching materials. No wonder that improvisation was the order of the day and long-range planning was set aside. Organizational structures did begin to emerge, however, staffing slowly improved, and the whole educational service began to function normally. When the Board of National Education was created in 1947 and the emperor assumed "exclusive control" over culture, religion, and education, the board and the ministry divided the educational administration into policy making and executive arms.[42] The specific tasks of the board were to see that educational standards were maintained in conformity with national objectives and that public morals were not undermined. From kindergarten to university, Ethiopian education was to nurture the spiritual, mental, and physical well-being of the people, so essential to a modern state. The board had to review the budget submitted to it and was also empowered to act with the authority of the minister if the post became vacant for any reason.[43]

In 1941, the newly appointed minister, Mekonnen Desta, faced the formidable task of reorganizing the shattered educational system with inadequate equipment and personnel. "On his shoulders fell the heavy responsibility for reorganizing the whole educational system, under circumstances perhaps more difficult than any other branch of the administrative structure."[44] From 1947 up to the 1960s, however, the post of minister of education and fine arts was assumed by the emperor himself.[45] In 1943 Gashaw Zelleqe was appointed director general. In 1944 Emmanuel Abraham replaced him, and in 1947 he was himself replaced by Akalewerq Habtewold.[46] The incumbent was first named director general and later vice-minister, and he acted under the general guidance of the emperor and the national board of education.[47] Since the chief executive in the ministry for most of this period was the director general, the deputy director was expected to carry a good work load.[48]

The secretary general was responsible to the three executives and reported directly to them. Regulations required that official correspondence must pass through the archives where copies of all documents were to be kept, and the secretary general was charged with organizing and maintaining the archives. The provision of accurate translations of correspondence and documents, instructional material, and other written matter, and the supervision of some categories of personnel were his responsibility.[49]

Until 1960 the Ministry of Education and Fine Arts employed foreign educational advisers. In 1941, although the leading schools were staffed largely by expatriates, the British adviser was the only foreigner in the ministry. He served for more than four years and was later replaced by an American. The advisers were experts who advised the minister or director general on educational policy and on methods of improving the organization of the ministry, and often they rendered invaluable service.[50]

The superintendent of education was entrusted with supervision and inspection of schools, as well as recommendations for the development of elementary, secondary, and higher levels of learning. It was his responsibility to secure information on administration, supervision of teaching staff, instructional standards, curricular conformity, discipline, health and sanitation, and buildings and school grounds. He concentrated on schools in the capital, while the supervision and inspection of provincial schools was delegated to provincial education officers.[51]

During the last half of the period, education had been spreading to the thirteen provinces, although progress was delayed by primitive communication and transportation outside Addis Ababa. A Department of Provincial Education attached to the ministry and headed by a director was created. Responsible to the minister of education, the director made periodic trips to the provinces, where he was responsible for arranging annual conferences, coordinating programs, ensuring fair distribution of materials and supplies, and making general recommendations. There were, in addition, committees for the general examinations, curriculum, textbooks, and others.[52]

Finance

Financial problems were no less pressing. In 1941, money was scarce. The national treasury was empty, trade was at a standstill, and the mechanism of trade with neighboring countries had been destroyed. Until 1943, it proved impossible to draw up a proper budget. The newly appointed officials had no experience in "acting under the right discipline of modern centralized finance." In addition, problems of currency had to be overcome.[53] A rough estimate of revenue and expenditure was, however, drawn up. Except for the years 1943–44 and 1948–49, the budget showed a healthy balance.

In 1941–42, extraordinary revenue constituted the larger part of total revenue. Great Britain, under the terms of the 1942 treaty and despite wartime difficulties, provided a subsidy, but this diminished over the next two years until it reached the vanishing point, leaving the budget with a deficit. When Britain lost most of her privileges under the Anglo-Ethiopian Agreement of 1944, she cut off financial aid to Ethiopia. Fortunately Ethiopia's export market, especially in coffee, was good during most of the decade. In 1944–45, the United States government offered $5,000,000 under lend-lease agreement, and the Swedish government extended credit amounting to 5,000,000 kronor. In 1946 the United States extended credit of $1,000,000, primarily to finance the purchase of war surplus. In 1944 the Export-Import Bank of Washington supplied $3,000,000 (fully paid back in 1946) for the purchase of automobiles, trucks, industrial machinery, gold-mining equipment, educational supplies, and currency notes and coins. In 1947 the National City Bank of the United States advanced a credit of $900,000. In 1948 and 1949 Ethiopia's membership in the International Bank for Reconstruction and Development enabled her to draw a total of $8,000,000. A private United States loan of $324,000 provided aircraft and equipment for Ethiopian Air Lines, the national carrier. Other sources of extraordinary revenue included sales of government promissory notes to the State Bank of Ethiopia, the issuing of coins, and profits on the government's capital investments—government-owned but self-operating enterprises like the state bank, Ethiopian Air Lines, Ethiopian Electric Light and Power Authority, and the Imperial Ethiopian Tobacco Monopoly, or income from the sale of state assets.[54]

The ordinary revenues were derived from business, personal, and land taxes, customs, and import and export taxes. Instead of going deeper into debt, the government enacted a series of taxation laws to raise funds to carry out reconstruction and development projects. The land taxes of 1942 and 1944 brought increased revenue, and in 1944 personal and business taxes were enacted.[55]

Educational developments received additional funding by the 1947 law that diverted 30 percent of the land tax to education. Another proclamation provided for the expenditure and accounting of the education tax by local boards of education.[56] The emperor's goal was that the "Ministry [of Education] should be well organized and developed . . . to raise Ethiopia's standard of education." After 1948, elementary schools in the provinces were financed by the education tax on rural land. All other education was financed by the national treasury.[57]

An official document leveled several valid criticisms at this arrangement. There were additional objections because the education tax was based on the ownership of rural land, and owners of urban property did not contribute to the cost of elementary education. Since the growth of elementary education depended on the growth of revenue, it was obvious that a disparity between the lower and the upper levels of the government school system would develop.

An examination of the finances of all provinces showed that some were less favorably placed than others, so that an inequality of educational opportunity would be obtained and become more and more marked in the future. Secondary and higher-level programs were increasing, while primary education was left to lag behind.[58] An equalization program supported by the central treasury had to be worked out.

Until 1947, most educational establishments were concentrated in the capital; for three years after 1941, very little money was spent on provincial education. In 1944–45, $362,908 was spent outside Addis Ababa, a 7 percent increase over the previous year. Over ten years, expenditure was more than $9,000,000, an increase of about forty-five times. Such an investment represented a nearly sacrificial commitment to education on the part of the Ethiopian government.

Itemized records of expenditure are not available for every year, but the few that are reveal an interesting story. In its eagerness to make education accessible, the government had endeavored to provide free supplies, clothing, board, and dormitory facilities for almost all secondary and higher students and for some elementary pupils. Where board and dormitory facilities were not available, cash was given to the students instead. One observer remarked:

> The period of urgent improvisation existed up to 1947, characterized by a policy of *education at all costs*. Free elementary education was followed by free boarding secondary education and free college education abroad for those who were chosen. It was a costly policy, and the budget for education went up from 4 percent of the total national expenditure in 1944–45 to 12 percent in 1945–46 and 13.6 percent in 1948–49.[59]

Boarding facilities were necessary because many children were orphans, there was a lack of transport, and many homes could not provide a supportive atmosphere for the young people.[60] The purchase of two uniforms a year for those students was an expensive undertaking. One administrator said that ten day students could have been educated for the cost of maintaining one boarding student.[61] A Ministry of Education report suggested: "The advisabilty of this policy in the early years of the development of the school system is not questioned. With the growth in student enrollment, however, the continuation of this policy has involved an increasing drain on the budget of the Ministry of Education."[62] Other methods such as loans were recommended, but the practice of free student support continued well into the 1950s, draining away money that could have gone into education for many more children.

Ethiopia has always been an agrarian nation; about 90 percent of the people make their living from the land. The Education Yearbook of 1949 gives the estimated population of Ethiopia as 15 million and the school age population as 4.5 million.[63] The residents of the capital city numbered three hundred thousand, a small fraction of the total population; but, as in the prewar years, most educational activities tended to concentrate in the capital city. Old buildings were restored, new ones constructed, and schools were equipped and staffed in Addis Ababa. Some $5,000,000 was spent there on schools staffed by highly qualified foreign teachers and provided with costly equipment.

Transport and communication problems restricted the growth of rural education, yet its expansion put a heavy burden on the central treasury. In 1947–48, about $2,056,237 was spent on all provincial education. At the same time, the education tax based on land did not vary by more than $2,000,000 between 1947 and 1973. In 1947–48, $248,264 was spent in Addis Ababa schools for capital equipment, $691,060 for food, and $1,167,688 for new construction. The corresponding amounts for the provincial schools were $68,418, $108,130, and $675,401.[64] The imbalance between urban and rural areas—in the number and quality of schools, teaching personnel, and facilities at every level—created problems whose effects still vibrate in the life of the nation. Well-planned and coordinated development was urgently needed.

Chapter 6

The Territory of Eritrea, 1941–62

Transition

As part of the African campaign, the British commander of the northwestern front took over Eritrea from the Italians in 1941. The British found this large region lying along the Red Sea on the northeastern edge of the country "barren, treeless, waterless, teeming with 45,000 Italians and 100,000 Eritreans."[1] For some time administration remained as it had been under the years of Italian control. There was no long-range planning by the British, who were providing only a caretaker government; many problems were put aside for future solution. Their major problems were to deal with finance, the undeveloped nature of the territory, the absence of trained personnel, the many Italian soldiers and civilians still living in the territory, and the racist laws and practices entrenched there by Fascism. Furthermore, the Italian policy had been to use Eritrea as a market for finished goods made in Italy. Captured documents revealed that "it was contrary to the policy of the Italian government to encourage industries in Eritrea."[2]

The Italian role for the Eritreans was as unquestioning, uncomplaining instruments of the "grandeur of Rome." This policy, and racial segregation, underpinned all their other activities. Regarding education, the Italian government during the occupation ordered that educational activity be kept to a minimum. In 1941, when the British military administration took over, there were only twenty-four four-grade primary schools. "The standard of teaching had been low; its scope designedly narrow."[3] To keep the Eritreans as ill-trained and ill-informed as possible, the Italians systematically developed and strengthened the color bar. "Natives were reminded, specifically and everywhere, of their inferiority in their own country. The municipalities excluded them from all participation. In the central government hierarchy they had no part and were, after fifty years, no nearer to acquiring any; they could at best hope to be low-paid clerks or orderlies. Of advancement or training toward participation in government or of an administrative scheme which could lead to it, there was at no time a trace. There were to be, in perpetuity, rulers and the passive ruled. Meanwhile, native schools were few and poor."[4]

The Italians, of course, had maintained segregated schools—a superior system for Italian children, an inferior one for Eritreans. "In Eritrea," wrote Sylvia and Richard Pankhurst, "there was one school for every 820 Italians as against one for every 50,294 Eritreans. The schools for Eritreans numbered only twenty: they were all primary. In the field of public health there were twenty-five times as many hospital beds for Italians as for Eritreans."[5]

The only schools that had aspired to teach the inherent equality of man or to provide normal standards of instruction were those run by the Swedish Evangelical Mission and a few similar organizations. These had been closed by order of the Italian government in 1932.[6]

When the British took over, they were still fighting Hitler in Europe. Ideological factors were involved, and they therefore felt justified in immediately abolishing the whole body of law designed to uphold white supremacy. At the same time they had to be cautious lest they offend those Italians who were helping them to administer the territory.[7] Gradually, however, they succeeded in creating conditions that permitted the annulment of racist laws.

The Italian neglect of education for over fifty years left the British with a formidable task. There were no trained teachers, no suitable textbooks, and only a few school buildings. The financial resources available for education were severely limited. In time, however, a modest educational edifice was erected. A few schools were opened with a small number of trained teachers recruited from the Sudan and from the few Eritreans with advanced training. After teacher training was introduced in 1943, a steady flow of teachers poured into the schools. Arabic textbooks were brought from Egypt and the Sudan, and Tigrinya textbooks were prepared and printed. Where there were no suitable buildings, funds were raised by voluntary subscription and schools were built;[8] by 1946 there were forty-two schools in Eritrea, with some 3,360 pupils and 100 teachers. There were, however, no secondary or technical schools. The little education available beyond the primary grades was provided by the Ethiopian government.[9] By 1950, two years prior to federation with Ethiopia, one middle-level school and fifty-nine primary schools had been set up.

During the occupation, instruction had been in Italian. Now the British needed English-speaking personnel, and young Eritreans therefore demanded that they be taught English; Italian was abandoned. The choice of a language of instruction in primary school was left to local committees, which invariably favored Tigrinya in Christian areas and Arabic in Moslem ones.

This limited experiment in education found a ready response among a large number of Eritreans, to the surprise of the British. Parents were ready to make substantial sacrifices to send their children to school. In the towns young and middle-aged alike clamored to be given educational opportunities which had been denied them during the Italian regime. To meet the demand for adult education, English institutes were established in the principal towns, and courses in literacy and technical skills were provided. The British Council and administration cooperated in making books and periodicals available. The resource investment was modest, but the enthusiasm aroused in the people of Eritrea for more education, to such an extent that they were ready to make almost any sacrifice, was of great importance.[10]

About 1944, Sylvia Pankhurst, a staunch friend of Ethiopia, made a tour of Eritrea. She was confronted with the stubborn assertion that "Ethiopia could not accomplish in education, or any other field, what Britain could and would achieve for the Ethiopian people." She noted, however, that British officials deplored the shortage of school facilities and materials in the primary schools they themselves had sponsored. In one girls' school, she saw classes conducted in a warehouse which the British director had converted, the girls sitting on the floor for lack of seats. The wool used for knitting was in such short supply that each student had to undo her work as soon as she had completed it so that the wool might be used by other students. "The principal school for boys was housed in what had formerly been a Roman Catholic orphanage. . . . It was grievously deficient in equipment. The text-books were a few sheets . . . stenciled each with a few phrases and stitched together in the centre."[11]

Both the administration and the mission organizations had started the long neglected job of educating Eritreans, but only at primary level. "Secondary education had not been introduced anywhere when the British withdrew from Eritrea in 1952."[12] The development of a complete system of education up to university level was to wait until the territory was reunited with the rest of Ethiopia.

Federation

On 2 December 1950, the United Nations General Assembly voted for the federation of Eritrea with Ethiopia, as an autonomous territory under the Ethiopian flag. An Eritrean constitution was drawn up under the direction of a United Nations commission, in consultation with the people of the territory. The draft constitution was adopted by the United Nations, the Eritrean Assembly, and the emperor of Ethiopia. As Paul and Clapham have noted,

> The steps involved in the federation were complicated and difficult; the preparation and ratification by popular assembly of an internal constitution for Eritrea, the distribution of powers between the "federal" (Ethiopian) Government and the Eritrean Government, the ratification by the Emperor of both the Eritrean Constitution and the "Federal Act" creating the federation, and promulgation by him of federal legislation creating a "Federal Government" in Eritrea . . . to carry out federal responsibilities.[13]

Under the terms of the federation in 1952, education was under the jurisdiction of the Eritrean government, though much assistance was given by the Ethiopian Ministry of Education. Article 31 of the constitution, *Right to education and freedom to teach,* stated that "everyone resident in Eritrea shall have the right to education. The Government shall make every effort to establish schools and to train teachers. . . . The Government shall encourage private persons and private associations and institutions, regardless of race, nationality, religion, sex or language, to open schools, provided that they can give proof of the required standards of morality and competence. . . . Tigrigna [*sic*] and Arabic shall be the official languages of Eritrea."[14]

From the beginning the Ethiopian government tried to coordinate Eritrean and Ethiopian sytems. Amharic teachers were provided by the Ministry of Education, and arrangements were made for students in Eritrea to take the national examinations and to proceed to secondary schools and colleges throughout the empire. A secondary school and a grade school were established,[15] and a naval school opened in Massawa. As time passed, more and more assistance was provided, and Eritrean government schools came to make up the bulk of the system. Nongovernment schools included those run by resident Italians and the mission schools, Protestant and Catholic, which admitted students from all segments of the community. [16] The federal government provided some library books and Amharic textbooks, and in some instances money. The main burden of educational progress from 1941 to 1952 was, however, borne by the Eritreans themselves.

The limited data available during the decade of federation show steady progress. Table 3 shows that between 1955 and 1961, the teaching force, most of whom were nationals, grew by more than 68 percent, a phenomenal rate over so short a period. The number of schools in operation, mostly under the Eritrean government, rose over the same period from 128 to 154. In 1957, the federal government set up the Haile Selassie I Secondary School, and the Eritrean government added a ninth grade to the Prince Makonnen School in Asmara. For the first time two secondary-level schools were operating in Eritrea. As can be seen

TABLE 3.   Government School Teachers in Eritrea, 1955–61

Year	Nationals			Foreigners			Grand Total	Percentage of Nationals
	Male	Female	Total	Male	Female	Total		
1955–56	390	80	470	5	1	6	476	98.73
1956–57	497	101	598	6	2	8	604	99.00
1957–58	525	98	623	1	3	4	627	99.36
1958–59	592	125	717	15	14	29	746	96.11
1959–60	629	118	747	28	6	34	781	95.64
1960–61	676	91	767	18	13	31	798	96.11

Sources: Ethiopia, Ministry of Education and Fine Arts, Government Schools Enrollment, 1959–60, p. 21; idem, School Census, 1960–61 (Addis Ababa, 1961), p. 11.

in table 4, student enrollment at all levels rose from more than eighteen thousand to almost thirty-eight thousand during the same period. It is interesting that the number of female students in primary and special schools was relatively high compared to most of the rest of Ethiopia. The average proportion of female students for the seven-year period is 24 percent. Eritrean youngsters seemed to excel in national and other examinations, showing their need and ability to reassert their identity among the communities of the nation.

The Haile Selassie I Secondary School was the first institution of its type in Eritrea, and was described as the "finest yet erected in all Ethiopia." It was intended to be a boarding school for 450 pupils, but the rapid increase in the demand for secondary education resulted in a change of plan. Three buildings that were intended for dormitories and a dining hall were converted into classrooms, which enabled the school to accommodate 1,000 students. The curriculum consisted of English (the language of instruction), French, science, geography, mathematics, history, and painting. A library period for Amharic books was held weekly by one of the Ethiopian teachers.[17] Library books were supplied by the Ethiopian Ministry of Education and by the United States. Attendance at this school, as in others of its type in Ethiopia, was free. The Prince Makonnen School in Asmara was the only other secondary school in Eritrea and was operated by the Eritrean government Department of Education. In 1958 there were 309 pupils, including 209 boys and 100 girls. In 1949 the school reached full secondary status by adding a twelfth grade.

There were some trade schools of postelementary level such as the Eritrean Vocational Trade School in Asmara. Started in 1954, it was operated by the Ethiopian and Eritrean governments in collaboration with the Point IV general education advisory group established by the Marshall Plan of the United States. The Eritrean government provided the site, including some old buildings from the period of Italian occupation, and electricity. The Ethiopian government and Point IV paid 70 percent and 30 percent of costs, respectively. The program covered three years, and the curriculum included English and Amharic, mechanical drawing, science, physical training, and hygiene. Instruction was given in English except in the purely Amharic subjects. It was a board-

TABLE 4. Student Enrollment in Government Schools in Eritrea, 1955–62

Year	Primary Grades 1–8			Academic Secondary 9–12			Special Secondary I–IV			Grand Total		
	Total	Female	% of Female	Total	Female	% of Female	Total	Female	% of Female	Total	Female	% of Female
1955–56	17,727	3,655	20.61	263	—	—	160	32	20.0	18,150	3,687	20.31
1956–57	22,524	4,368	19.39	334	—	—	226	51	22.56	23,084	4,419	19.14
1957–58	21,918	5,051	23.04	618	29	4.69	214	72	33.64	22,750	5,152	22.64
1958–59	25,283	6,599	26.10	607	23	3.78	300	54	18.00	26,190	6,676	25.49
1959–60	31,382	8,220	26.19	608	29	4.76	297	49	16.49	32,287	8,298	25.70
1960–61	33,059	8,381	25.35	642	24	3.73	304	25	8.22	34,005	8,430	24.79
1961–62	36,606	9,568	26.13	848	53	6.25	524	67	12.78	37,978	9,688	25.50

Source: Ethiopia, Central Statistical Office, Statistical Abstract 1964, p. 145.

ing school: "Tuition, board and lodging, all equipment and tools required for the course, . . . and medical attention when required [were] supplied to the students free of charge." In 1958, 170 students were enrolled; 100 had already completed the course and had received their diplomas. The teaching staff consisted of Americans and Ethiopians, who were rapidly replacing the other expatriates.[18]

Another vocational school was the Empress Menen School of Nursing at Asmara. Jointly established by the Ethiopian Ministry of Public Health and Point IV in 1955 and accredited by the International Council of Nursing when Ethiopia became a member in 1957, the school provided a four-year program leading to an R.N. diploma. In 1958 there were 67 students, and applicants far exceeded the number of places available.[19] There were also a few private schools, and it must also be taken into consideration that many Eritreans had access to secondary and university-level education in Ethiopia or were granted scholarships to study abroad.[20]

Although educational development started late, it grew faster than expected once free of Fascist racist and oppressive policies. This was primarily due to the willingness of the people to undertake the heavy burden of necessary investment and to the enthusiasm of the Eritrean children. The rate of enrollment growth was higher than for any of the twelve Ethiopian provinces or Addis Ababa. The increase in teachers was higher in 1956–57 than that of any other province. All in all, the rate of educational development was faster than in any other part of the empire. This dynamism was maintained beyond the federation period, as we shall see. On 15 November 1962, the emperor declared: "The people of Eritrea . . . desirous of living together with their Ethiopian brothers, have formally requested, by their resolution voluntarily and unanimously adopted on 14 November 1962, that the federation be dissolved. In its place they have asked for the complete administrative integration of Eritrea with the rest of Ethiopia in order to facilitate and speed the economic growth and development of the nation. We have accepted this resolution and have consented to its being placed into effect."[21] With this, Eritrea became the thirteenth province, and its educational development was to be linked henceforth with that of Ethiopia.

Chapter 7

Consolidation and Planned Expansion, 1951–61

Priorities

As we have seen, the reconstruction era was a time of improvisation. When the Ethiopian government was reestablished in 1941, the first priority was quite naturally given to the training of competent administrators, technicians, and professionals essential for the efficient functioning of government and industry, but the rapid development of higher and secondary educational institutions and extended programs of foreign study was emphasized as well. A report covering the 1951–52 period, after listing some of the achievements of the preceding ten years, identified the tasks ahead:

> The Ministry of Education is faced with many very difficult problems. The present status of the Ethiopian school system can be illustrated with the following facts: 20 percent of the entire budget of the Ministry of Education has gone into the employment of foreign teachers. There are 2,013 Ethiopian teachers, most of whom are ill-prepared for teaching. Approximately 60,000 children are enrolled in the schools. Only 35 elementary schools include all eight grades. Only one secondary school exists outside of Addis Ababa [excluding the Agricultural School at Jimma]. Beginning classes often numbering as many as one hundred children are carried on with a third or half of them crowded into a classroom, and the others sitting outside the building in the sun. Learning materials are extremely scarce, and a school library of as many as ten books would be among the best in the smaller provincial schools. Equipment even of the most elementary nature is not available. Although English is the lan-

guage of instruction beginning with the fifth grade, there are no English language newspapers so commonly used in schools of other countries for the study of world affairs and for recreational reading; equipment for crafts activities and science education is found only in some of the larger schools. Viewed from a negative point of view, the situation seems to be extremely discouraging. Viewed positively in terms of the relatively few years during which the Imperial Ethiopian Government has had to build an educational system, *amazing progress has been made.*

The basic need in Ethiopian education is for well-trained Ethiopian teachers. Each year an increasing number of foreign teachers have had to be hired. Teacher training facilities are not being filled to capacity. The number of teachers leaving the profession is greater than the number being trained. Forty percent of the Ethiopian teachers have completed less than four years of elementary education. The training for other teachers has been almost entirely substandard with little attention to teaching methods. Specialists in curriculum development and teacher education are therefore needed to give intelligent direction to programs which can meet this basic need.

Secondary schools have to be established as feeders to teacher education programs and to other programs of higher education in medicine, mining, engineering, public administration, and so forth. Looking ahead two years, the Ministry of Education in 1952 projected plans for the establishment of at least one secondary school in each of the then twelve provinces to make secondary education available outside of Addis Ababa. Hundreds of elementary schools are needed. . . . Learning materials *developed for use in Ethiopia* are essential. . . . Textbooks . . . should be prepared for use in the schools. . . . Audio-visual education equipment would make a decided contribution. Films, slides, and other graphic materials especially for use in Ethiopia should be developed.

As a consequence of European influence in the examination system, the curricula of Ethiopian schools are actually controlled by the nature of the examinations given at the close of elementary schools for admission to secondary school, and at the close of secondary school for admission to college. It would seem very desirable to develop curricula which meet Ethiopia's needs. . . .

In a country where there are a variety of native crafts, the curricula have emphasized woodworking almost exclusively; weaving, basket-making, ceramics and leather crafts, for which native materials are available, are given little attention. An elementary school crafts program, focusing attention on native crafts and potential home industry crafts, is needed.

The whole area of adult education, whether of the literacy type or for homemaking, child care or industrial training, is an area which offers unlimited opportunity.

The greatest need appears to be for technical assistance and qualified specialized personnel to guide, assist and train Ethiopians. . . . Next to the need for personnel is the need for financial assistance for the purchase of equipment. . . . A large portion of Ethiopia's governmental budget is devoted to education. The Imperial Ethiopian Government has built schools at a rapid pace throughout Ethiopia. It has invested heavily in building the superstructure of an educational system. This, however, probably has been done more rapidly than the building of necessary institutions. Ethiopia has a University College that would be a credit to any community in the United States. It has built and equipped the Technical School and the College of Technology. It has planned the Haile Selassie I Imperial Ethiopian University on which construction is under way. It is investing substantial sums for agricultural education and has plans for a Medical College.[1]

By 1952 there were 400 elementary schools, 11 technical and academic high schools, and 3 colleges. An educational structure had been built; yet 50 percent of first-grade pupils dropped out by the end of the second year. By grade five, 90 percent of them had dropped out. The need for adaptation, consolidation, and coordination of the entire educational system was obvious. The task was undertaken in 1953.[2]

The Long-Term Planning Committee
The Point IV educational advisory group arrived in Ethiopia in 1953. The Ministry of Education took this opportunity to launch a

ten-year plan for the controlled expansion of education, and the vice-minister of education accordingly established the Long-Term Planning Committee. The committee's terms of reference were defined at its first meeting in November 1953 as follows: (1) the committee was to be composed of ministry personnel and advisory staff; (2) the terms of reference were to be broad enough to permit the comprehensive survey of the existing school system, schemes of work and academic standards at all levels, and recommendations as to possible reorganization; (3) the committee was to be fully authorized to investigate at first hand and to call for written and personal reports from administrators, school directors, teachers, and others engaged in or concerned with Ethiopian education; (4) the committee was to be encouraged to examine Ethiopian educational problems in the light of experience and developments in other lands; and (5) the committee should not itself be required to work in such detail as to lose sight of the all-important questions of fundamental policy.[3]

The third and final report of the committee was submitted to the Board of Education in June 1955. It recommended the introduction of community schools for basic education; the controlled expansion of the existing primary, middle, academic, secondary, technical, and commercial secondary schools; and the introduction of trade schools, a technical institute, and a college of engineering. Questions of teacher preparation were dealt with, and recommendations made for the financing of all these developments. While the report covered a wide field of educational activity, no claim was made that it was complete:

> In order to supply qualified candidates for higher education, some expansion of the elementary school system is essential. The expansion of this system should be so organized as to bring educational opportunity to a constantly increasing proportion of the Ethiopian people. The content of instruction should be designed to fit the student for better living in his home community and environment, as well as to provide a sound basis for the selection of sufficient able candidates for further training in academic, vocational and technical fields. Care must be taken to maintain appropriate standards of attainment for teaching personnel and in the various branches of instruction.[4]

The committee thus drew up proposals to adapt educational programs to the country's needs, to extend educational opportunity, to train students for positions in government, industry, and commerce, and to improve the qualifications of those engaged in Ethiopian education. A time limit of ten years was set.

The term "controlled expansion" was used in all seven sections of the report, but a better adjective might have been "coordinated," for the committee felt that unplanned expansion had been responsible for uneven development in the government school system and for disproportionate expenditure. The report noted that "although Ethiopia needs an increasing number of academically prepared young men and women . . . there is at present a limit to the number of students who should be selected for such preparation. At least equally important . . . is the development of a system of education designed to promote mass literacy, universalize the official national language, and to help the millions of Ethiopian children . . . to live better, healthier and more productive lives."[5] The committee emphasized that the time had come to think in terms of a shorter period of education and of a different type of education, spread much more widely over the population as a whole. It believed that the quickest possible spread of universal fundamental education, including an effective command of Amharic, was now the basic objective.[6] The community school for basic education was to consist of the equivalent of the first four grades. Specially qualified supervisors were to be appointed by the Ministry of Education, and a one-year training school for community school personnel was to be established by 1956. A tract of fertile farmland on a good road to the capital would be provided for the training school. Housing would be constructed and the site equipped and stocked as a school-farm laboratory by September of that year.

Beginning in 1957, thirty-five such schools for basic education should be opened each year, including twenty-five in communities without government primary schools, and ten in communities where existing schools would be converted into community schools. The estimated total cost of this program over a period of ten years was set at $14,169,000.

By this time the first four grades were designated as primary school. By the end of 1953 there were 412 government primary schools, of which only 168 comprised all four grades. The committee stressed that the basic problem would be to control the development of the various levels of the system so that the entire system would develop in a coordinated manner.[7]

The report acknowledged the church's contribution, past and present. It was estimated that as many as two hundred thousand students were then enrolled in church schools. These schools were extremely limited both in the nature and the length of their programs and naturally were primarily concerned with the teaching of religion, but they did provide an opportunity for children to learn Amharic and Ge'ez. In the period between 1949 and 1951, the government, at the church's insistence, turned over to the church a large number of government-operated schools in eight provinces. The loss of government revenue amounted to $489,000. The committee therefore recommended that church-owned land be subject to the payment of the provincial education tax and that those government schools that were transferred to the church should be reestablished as government schools where this was found to be in accordance with long-term plans for expansion.[8] From 1951 to 1953 the growth rate in primary school enrollment was 15 percent, and in the next year it was nearly 19 percent. Since the annual increase in the number of schools was less than 10 percent, large classes and overcrowding were the inevitable result. During the same two years, although the government was employing additional teachers as rapidly as they became available, the number of teachers in government primary schools increased by only 10 percent, from 1,375 to 1,541. In the following year the increase dropped to less than 2 percent.

A typical primary school had few books or teaching materials. The school was located in a small community in a heavily populated rural area, and many students walked as much as two hours to reach it. With inadequate teaching materials, and up to 150 students in a class, many students lost interest and dropped out, or were frequently absent. Nevertheless, daily attendance in those classes ranged from seventy-five to one hundred. One school director reported that, of a total of 619 students in regular attendance in the primary school, 379 were enrolled in first grade. This kind of a situation was not uncommon. A small four-grade school, surveyed in 1953, had a total enrollment of 129 students, of whom 76 were in the first grade, while grades three and four each had 12 students. Estimates of the number of children in the community aged five to sixteen ranged from 500 to 1,000. Ages in the first grade ranged from five to fourteen.

The planning committee considered various solutions to overcrowding and the consequent high attrition rate, but noted that "the two or three-shift plan with students in attendance on alternate days or every third day cannot be given serious consideration. . . . The remedy for too little educational opportunity for too many students obviously is not less educational opportunity for still more students."[9] Another alternative was to establish a maximum class size, but this would limit educational opportunity to those few students who were fortunate enough to be admitted; certainly such a solution would be extremely difficult to administer. The committee therefore recommended that the supply of qualified teachers be increased, that no new primary schools be established and no schools with less than four grades be authorized to add more grades until there were enough teachers, and that overage students be dropped if their attendance was poor.[10]

In June 1953 the ministry decided not to employ any new teachers with less than an eighth-grade education. The ministry also adopted for the first time a modern salary scale, stipulating that primary school teachers with equivalent qualifications should be paid the same salary as teachers at any other level of the school system. Later, the Long-Term Committee approved these decisions.[11] As late as 1954, however, the quality of teachers remained very low. Fifty-three percent were unclassified—that is, they presumably were not advanced beyond the ability to read and write, and so were probably engaged to teach arts and crafts and some Amharic. The Long-Term Committee pointed out that Ethiopia was deeply indebted to these teachers, working under such difficult conditions. It was therefore recommended that teachers on the job should be given the opportunity, through directed study courses and individual study, to demonstrate within six years that they had achieved the equivalent of the minimum requirement of an eighth grade education. Those who were not able to meet even this minimal standard within the time limit were to be pensioned under a broad program yet to be devised which would provide for retired or incapacitated teachers. It was projected that output would not exceed need

until 1965 and that therefore teacher education should continue
at maximum capacity over the ten-year period.

The term "middle school" was used by the committee to
describe grades five through eight in the government school system. Preparation for high school traditionally constituted their
main function. A basic dilemma existed here, however. The desire to create equal basic education as rapidly as possible con-
flicted with the desire to produce an educated nucleus to meet
the manpower needs of the rapidly advancing society. As the
Long-Term Committee report pointed out, "more money invested in expanding the middle school system means less money
available for use in expanding the basic school system."[12]

In 1953–54, there were twenty-three middle schools in the
eleven provincial capitals, and sixteen in Addis Ababa. The remaining eighty were located in fifty-three of the seventy-five
school districts. Twenty-two school districts had no middle
schools at all.

At that time, 344 Ethiopian and 172 foreign teachers and
directors were employed in the middle schools and there were
four programs for their training: the Teacher Training School at
Harar, regular and special one-year programs at Haile Selassie I
Day School in Addis Ababa, a one-year program for arts and
crafts teachers at Itegue Menen Handicraft School in Addis
Ababa, and a vacation training program for teachers of gymnastics. The Long-Term Planning Committee recommended certification requirements for the training programs and projected that
over four years there would be 190 fewer teachers than the
projected demand. The balance was to be made up by recruiting
foreign teachers.

Finally, the committee summarized its findings as follows:

> If the rate of expansion were limited only by ability to pay
> the financial cost of expansion, there would be little objec-
> tion to permitting any province, district or community to tax
> itself as much as it wished to produce as much income as
> would be needed for any expansion it might desire. Financial
> resources, however, are only one factor limiting the rate of
> expansion of the schools. Teacher supply is a much more
> effective limiting factor. . . . [Also] there is some limit some-
> where to . . . the number of lawyers, doctors, engineers, etc.,

that might be absorbed by the economy. This ability to absorb the highly-educated, smaller proportion of the population is dependent upon the level of education of the masses. Therefore, if this reasoning is sound, the expansion of educational opportunity at the higher levels should in the years immediately ahead be limited and controlled according to plan in the interest of achieving the greatest possible spread of basic education.[13]

The Long-Term Planning Committee also made specific recommendations in respect to the expansion of middle schools and the training of their teachers, and added: "Standard building plans should be prepared by the Architects Department of the Ministry of Education to help school communities to build additional classrooms and buildings with adequate floor space and lighting. The Ministry of Education should bring together all persons whose agreement to these proposals was necessary, to secure their endorsement of the controlled program of expansion, and to set up realistic annual goals."[14]

Controlled expansion was an important element in the academic secondary schools, as well as in the middle schools. Secondary education normally covered grades nine through twelve. Selection of students for the various secondary schools—academic, technical, commercial, agricultural, and professional (teacher preparation)—was made in grade eight. The function of the academic secondary schools was to prepare candidates for colleges and other higher institutions. At the time there were seven academic secondary schools, six in Addis Ababa and one in Harar, but it was felt that they were not producing enough qualified candidates for higher education. Higher institutions existing or projected within the ten-year plan period included the University College of Addis Ababa (1950), the College of Engineering (1952), the Public Health College at Gondar (1954), the Institute of Building Technology and the College of Agriculture (both 1955), the Marine Training Institute (1955), and the Institute of Technology and the Military Training Institute, both projected for 1957. These and other institutions would be able to take care of 4,450 secondary school graduates during the plan period, but it was clear that less than half of the 1,345 students needed for the first four years were likely to qualify.

The committee therefore recommended the expansion of secondary schools, improvement of the curriculum, materials, and methods of teaching, and better selection of students to cut down the attrition rate at that level. Of the curriculum they said that it was "patterned primarily after prewar European practices and comparable to conservative secondary school practices in the United States thirty years ago." They considered the teaching of optional subjects for early specialization, before the student had acquired a general education, unsound and uneconomical.[15] Free maintenance of secondary students was costly ($50,000 in 1954–55 alone), and a system of loans, to be paid back by the students, was recommended. The estimated capital expenditure for expansion of secondary education over the eleven years was $14,000,000.

On the basis of the distribution of students enrolled in academic secondary schools, it was decided that Medhane Alem School in Harar, the Menelik II Secondary, Empress Menen, and Medhane Alem schools in Addis Ababa, the Gondar school, and the Dessie and Ambo secondary schools were to be expanded. The committee noted that in 1954–55 there were seventy-seven foreign teachers and school directors employed by the Ministry of Education. Under the proposed plan, sixty-seven additional teachers would be needed, and with few exceptions they would have to be recruited abroad. They also warned that by 1967–68 the output of the middle schools, even with high selection standards, might exceed the capacity of the secondary schools. This should be recognized by the ministry, and action should be taken to control the academic middle schools and to channel the extra students into suitable higher programs.

The last part of the Long-Term Planning Committee's report dealt with the development of technical-vocational education. The committee estimated that by 1955 there would be need for at least six hundred Ethiopian engineers and high-level technicians, positions previously filled by foreigners. In addition, many more middle-level technicians were urgently needed. The best way to train them was on the job, but since Ethiopia lacked the facilities, the alternative was to provide trade schools. The demand for technical personnel was summarized as follows: 200 to 300 professional engineers, 1,500 to 2,500 subprofessional technicians, and 50,000 to 100,000 skilled workmen.

The College of Engineering had by this time completed its second year of operation and had an adequate physical plant. The Technical School provided training in nine trades and in technical skills. Students were assigned by the Ministry of Education on the basis of an eighth grade general examination, and in 1955 a special aptitude test was initiated. The courses took three or four years but the programs were uneven, and the school was a peculiar combination of technical institute and trade school. The departments of radio, electricity, and auto mechanics demanded high standards of technical achievement, but in the forging and welding, machine shop, and foundry departments the standard was less high. The construction program operated for only one year and was then taken over by the new Ethio-Swedish Institute of Building Technology. Between 1951 and 1954, fifty-three Technical School graduates were sent abroad on apprenticeships in mechanics, carpentry, radio engineering, printing, and so on.

In this field the committee made the following recommendations:

> Until the Engineering College developed full programs, only a few students should be sent abroad, after two years in the College, to train in fields such as chemical, architectural and mining engineering. A program for agricultural and irrigation engineers should be developed and attached to the College of Agriculture. . . . The Technical School's standards should be raised as rapidly as the supply of qualified students permitted. . . . The Technical Institute should accept secondary school graduates for two years' training as radio-electrical technicians, auto mechanics, metallurgists, mechanics, draftsmen and engineering aides. . . . [16]

They added that a trade school was urgently needed. The total estimated cost of technical education for the twelve years between 1954 and 1966 would be $16,292,700, including boarding facilities, or $14,035,700 without boarding facilities. The committee believed it essential that these programs receive active support and cooperation from the Ministry of Education.

The Commercial School in Addis Ababa was established to supply skilled clerical workers for business and government, and it achieved a standard equal to the academic secondary schools and to Harar Teacher Training School by offering a full four-year secondary course for boys and a three-year course for girls. Except for Amharic typing, commercial subjects were taught in English. The staff included Ethiopians, Americans, British, Canadians, Egyptians, Indians, and Persians. Graduating students were prepared for the Royal Society of Arts Examinations in London and for local school examinations. The school's main problem was the lack of an adequate plant. The committee recommended the allocation of $6,536,300 over a ten-year period for dormitories and classrooms. This figure was generous, considering that the total school budget for 1954 was only $215,500. To increase the number of graduates, it was agreed that the annual intake should be increased, and that, until training facilities were locally available, at least two graduates should be sent abroad each year for training as teachers for the Commercial School. Meanwhile, allowances and salaries must be improved to attract competent foreign staff.

In the early postwar period, significant progress had been made in the economic and social fields. In 1944 a ten-year program of industrial development was drawn up by the United States Technical Mission in Ethiopia and was partially carried out. In agriculture and animal husbandry, attempts were made to increase production and to carry out research. A number of important studies were made in mineral and water resources, in agriculture and forestry, in transport and communications, and in the construction of power stations, the establishment of new industries, and the development of fisheries.

On the basis of these studies, separate plans for long-term development were drawn up, including those for road improvement, agriculture, telecommunications, Assab harbor development, water resources in Lake Tana and the Blue Nile, and the ten-year plan for education discussed above.

First Five-Year Plan
The ground having been prepared for a comprehensive national plan, the emperor in 1954 ordered that an assessment of the Ethiopian economy be made. On the basis of the survey and the various studies, the first Five-Year Development Plan was drawn up. It would cover the years from 1957 through 1961, and by the beginning of 1956 a special committee had been constituted to supervise it.[17]

The plan pointed out that in the fifteen years since the restoration, considerable waste in the educational field could have been avoided by better planning. As an example, the committee noted that "the present student capacity of the upper level far exceeds the current flow of students from the lower levels qualified for admission. . . . "[18] The Five-Year Development Plan continued:

There is at present in Ethiopia an acute shortage of skills of all kinds and at all levels. The foreigners who are employed in the public services and who have come in numbers to manage industry and commerce are evidences of the current shortage of skill. It is understandable, therefore, that the government, faced with a scarcity of qualified personnel to run the public services, should aim at the expansion of the higher institutions. This objective, however, cannot be fully and efficiently attained unless the lower levels of the government schools system—the middle schools in particular—are also expanded rapidly.[19]

Although systematic data were not available, the planners tried to assess manpower supply and demand at the degree level for all sectors of the economy. It was estimated that some six to eight hundred people should be added to this group by 1961, and the planners had to assess the likelihood of these requirements being met. Although only 440 students would graduate from home institutions in the five-year period, 640 degree holders would have returned home from overseas institutions, so it seemed likely that manpower needs would be met, at least in respect to engineers and agriculturists. There would not, however, be enough doctors, teachers, or businessmen by 1961. It was hoped that some Ethiopians would acquire enough experience and proficiency to replace foreign personnel. Since the colleges were working below capacity, there was no need for them to expand. They should concentrate on raising standards by the improvement of curricula, teaching materials, and methods.

To meet the need, the technical-vocational schools would have to produce 660 students per year for five years. About two hundred students would return from abroad, after completing studies as technicians. Home institutions and foreign study together would produce only 2,500 technicians, falling short of the minimum requirement by 800. This shortage would be felt in all sectors, particularly in education, manufacturing and electrical industries, construction, and so on; the shortage of technicians would therefore be more acute than that of degreed personnel.[20]

Estimates for the academic secondary, middle, primary, and community schools were similar to those of the Ten-Year Plan for the Controlled Expansion of Education, treated earlier. Again, the shortage of candidates for higher institutions and the need for universal basic education and for equity in financing the school system were repeated.[21]

To what extent were the educational plans and targets set in the Long-Term and first Five-Year Development Plans attained? In considering this, we will examine both the qualitative and quantitative aspects of educational development.

Reference has been made previously to the experiment in community education in the township of Asbe Tafari, in Harar before the Italian invasion. After the invasion, the idea of a community school for basic education was resurrected. In 1943 the inhabitants of Debre Berhan organized the first village school as a community effort. The emperor took an interest in the project and often visited it in the company of cabinet ministers. The Long-Term Planning Committee picked up the idea in 1953 and made a strong recommendation for its acceptance by the Board of Education. The board, accepting the idea in principle, said:

> It is difficult to comprehend the full significance of a national movement aimed at achieving functional literacy in a single language among the sixteen million people of Ethiopia, who now speak more than fifty different languages and dialects, and designed to develop basic abilities which will enable every citizen, both young and old, to meet more effectively his problems in everyday living and to make a greater contribution towards the advancement of his community and the Empire. Yet this is exactly the responsibility of the community school for basic education.[22]

Special teachers for community schools had to be trained. One such training school was established in 1956 at Majete, northeast of Addis Ababa, with the sponsorship of the United

Nations Educational, Scientific, and Cultural Organization (UN-ESCO). The second was set up in Debre Berhan in 1957, with the assistance of the United States Agency for International Development (USAID). The institutions were excellently equipped and staffed by both nationals and expatriates. The one-year course included formal subjects, but most of the teaching time was devoted to practical subjects such as agriculture, health, and manual skills. Each institution was equipped with a brick-making machine for the making of mud and concrete bricks, with which model houses were built by the students. The school at Debre Berhan had a model farm attached, complete with cowshed where cows were milked and a dairy where butter and cheese were made. Vegetables were grown in the school gardens for use at the hostels. There was a large poultry house, and a tree plantation was started.

As time progressed, however, unforeseen problems emerged. Some were attributable to the low academic standing of the students, others to a "reluctance of many students to do practical or manual work while in training." Some students wanted to concentrate only on improving their academic qualifications. In some instances, when the students finally graduated, they were not accepted by the communities because of their youth. In other instances, parents insisted that academic, not practical, subjects be taught at the community schools, saying that "schools were meant to teach the formal skills, and that they, the fathers, were quite competent to teach their sons how to farm, or to look after herds or to plant trees, or to plough, while the mothers were the ones to teach their daughters all about health, child care, cooking and handicrafts."[23]

Furthermore, once graduated, the teachers left their profession in large numbers. After five years 42.2 percent had left the teaching service. The training institution at Majete was phased out in 1960 after only four years, and in 1963 the school at Debre Berhan was converted to a teacher-training institute, admitting students from grade ten. Some of the community schools where these teachers were employed were built by self-help projects, and a few were amalgamated with the other regular primary schools. Some were abandoned after a few years of operation and as early as 1960 had reached the "derelict stage" after parents had transferred their children to other schools which offered an academic education.[24] Thus the community schools were closed down one by one, until in 1964 they were amalgamated with the normal primary schools. The Ministry of Education made these pertinent and candid remarks: "The main lesson to be learned from the Majete and Debre Berhan projects is that good ideas, good equipment, a qualified staff and an ample budget do not guarantee success. In both of the above cases the missing ingredient that was not taken into account, and which led to the projects being abandoned, was that of student, parental and community *attitudes,* which resisted a new approach to education."[25]

Some of the rest of the Long-Term Planning Committee's recommendations were put into practice, but most were not. Perhaps the planning exercise itself had a salutary effect on policy formulation and brought about an awareness of the magnitude and extent of the problems. It is not known why other aspects of the plan were not put into operation. There simply may not have been enough skilled manpower to undertake such major reforms. A Ministry of Education publication said that the plan was too visionary and recommended that too much not be attempted too quickly. It continued:

> To use a modern term, a good job was done in computerizing education in Ethiopia. But there could have been no sociologist on the committee, for it ignored too many variables, chief of which were, firstly, the existing administrative infrastructure, and secondly, vital social and human factors which could have indicated that change can take place only when people have been educated for change. They will be receptive to new ideas only when they understand the reasons for them and where they lead to. They will be fully cooperative only when they themselves have had some say in decision-making concerning the sort of education their children will receive. The parent in the countryside also wants the same educational opportunities as those provided in the cities. Any changes, therefore, in the education system must be nationally rather than geographically or parochially based.[26]

Conflict and Growth

Meanwhile, the system as a whole continued to grow in many other directions. With the establishment of the University College of Addis Ababa, a third tier was added to the government educational system. During the decade between 1941 and 1952, even more than in the previous decade, an increasing number of nongovernment schools appeared. These included church schools, which had of course been in existence long before the government system but which now began to reform their curricular offerings and methodology on a modest scale; schools maintained by foreign Protestant and Catholic missions; and schools operated by private individuals or groups, usually primarily for profit.

The nongovernment schools enrolled about 10 percent of primary school children during the decade.[27] Some of them received some subvention from the government in the form of land, teachers, or at times even of cash. By law, the Ministry of Education was obliged to provide minimal supervision and control over their programs, to see that standards at least equal to those provided by the government were maintained. Higher education, however, was administered under a separate board.

Administration was still highly centralized, in spite of the lip service paid to decentralization. At the end of grade six or eight, a national examination was administered as a prerequisite to promotion. At the completion of the twelfth grade, the Ethiopian School Leaving Certificate Examination (ESLCE) was given. Successful candidates were admitted to the University College of Addis Ababa or sent abroad for further studies.

The basic objective of education was a logical extension of the previous decade. The vice-minister of education stressed that it was still the essential objective of the Ministry of Education to make elementary education available to all children of school age in the country, as finances permitted, and that academic secondary schools should be expanded throughout the provinces and in Addis Ababa.[28]

The objectives of the elementary school program were even more ambitious, although at the same time ambiguous. These were: (1) to foster in children the traditional values of loyalty, unity, and devotion to emperor and country; (2) to spread literacy throughout the nation and provide basic education, in the shortest possible time, in the national language; (3) to help children develop a sense of citizenship in their own country and in the world as a means of acquiring healthy minds, healthy bodies, and proper moral and spiritual values; (4) to enable them to become more happy, useful, and productive citizens; and (5) to give a proper foundation for secondary education.[29]

By the early 1950s, when these objectives were stated, only about two hundred thousand of an estimated school population of one and a half to two million were receiving any type of education at all. Of those, only 70,000 were in government schools. Large areas of the country had no schools. Excluding approximately 900 Amharic teachers, about 200 of the 1,320 Ethiopian teachers had less than a fourth grade education and only 344 had any secondary education. Many existing buildings were inadequate, and there were serious shortages of equipment in many schools. Although Amharic was the native language for many of the children, instruction above the third grade was in English, so that all students at this level were required to learn one new language, and many of them two. The imposition of modern educational methods upon an ancient culture raised many other problems. Long-established patterns of living and traditional social concepts would have to be adjusted to modern modes of thinking without destroying the basic culture of the people.

At the time, the government was spending about one-fifth of its total tax revenues on education and related services, and the limits of the available tax resources were being reached. At the same time it was essential that the ministry should make outlays which were costly in relation to the number of people that education could reach. Foreign teachers, boarding schools (in which all expenses of students were paid by the government), the war orphans, the difficulties of transportation—all these added to the burden.[30] Yet Ethiopia set herself the ambitious aim of spreading education throughout the provinces with universal primary education in mind. To this end, various adjustments in curricula and methods of instruction were tried out.

At the beginning of 1950, grades seven and eight were made a part of elementary schooling. The advantages were many: a more thorough training in English before secondary school, two additional years of school experience for those who never reached secondary school, employment opportunities that would be greater for the more mature student. Furthermore, the decision was felt to be in line with the rest of the postwar world, which was extending the period of elementary education.

The course outlines for grades seven and eight were given in more detail than had been the case earlier. "However, based on foreign tests, they were no more closely geared to the needs of the unsophisticated Ethiopian student than was the earlier volume. For instance, science during those years called for little, if any, mention of personal or community hygiene, human nutrition, health or safety measures. It was highly theoretical in content . . . [and] little of this content had practical application for the pupil in a rural agricultural setting."[31]

The syllabi for the social sciences and other subjects showed a similar lack of relevance. The history books dealt with England and its expansion in Canada and India, and with America and France. Some mention was made of Africa, but only as it related to foreigners like David Livingstone and H. M. Stanley. Dr. Ayalew Gebre Selassie criticized the curriculum for providing unbalanced education and for trying to teach pupils both foreign languages and content at the same time during their elementary years, thus making it difficult for them to master either. He felt that elimination of the language problem would mean that greater emphasis could be given to content.[32]

It was accordingly decided to teach English as a subject beginning in the first two primary grades, and above grade three all instruction, except the course in Amharic, was to be given in English. The reasons advanced were that available qualified teachers were conversant with English and much of the teaching material was available only in that language. Amharic, however, was not lacking in advocates. Among the reasons listed in favor of Amharic as a language of instruction was that it had been the court language of Ethiopia since 1270, thereby gaining prestige and acceptance among a significant number of Ethiopians. As things stood in the 1950s and earlier, anyone who wished to be employed in the government services or to wield national influence had to have a good command of the Amharic language. Additionally, Amharic was the only language spoken in Ethiopia with a script of its own. The other languages spoken in the country employed the Amharic script, if indeed they had any written form. Amharic, furthermore, was the only language with a rich literature and prestige of its own; it had formerly been the language of diplomacy and the means of communication not only within the country but with the outside world as well. It was the only language spoken by a large number of Ethiopians (whether as a first or second language). Finally, the language had the inherent flexibility to grow with the advance of culture, science, and technology.

The opponents of Amharic as a language of instruction in the schools argued that Amharic could not replace English because of its limited vocabulary. Years of isolation had prevented the language from developing, as it had similarly affected other aspects of national life. As a result of the absence of contact with the European world, Amharic had been unable to borrow and adapt scientific and technical terms from other languages. Second, it was argued that Amharic was spoken by a minority of people within the country, and by none outside it, and that the educated Ethiopian, at least, should speak and understand well one international language. Third, it was argued that printed matter, especially textbooks, was not available, to say nothing of qualified teachers.[33]

The linguists, many of whom had been scholars of Semitic languages for decades, had already pointed out that Amharic had the inherent strength and flexibility to accomodate itself to the linguistic needs of a modern society. Professor Marcel Cohen stated that, "Amharic was no more prepared for the development of the modern sciences and techniques than were the European languages before the evolution of European culture. It is well known that these languages employed Greek elements in constructing the words required for modern sciences, using a few ancient Greek words and many newly-formed combinations of Greek elements which have now been assimilated into the modern languages. Amharic, in its turn, is obliged to borrow for the same purposes. . . . The future promises well for Amharic as a national language. . . . "[34] After weighing the pros and cons of the issue, the Ministry of Education in the mid-1950s adopted Amharic as the language of instruction, first through the primary grades and later on for all grades, without minimizing the costly commitment that this policy might entail initially in research and production of teaching material.

In the meantime, the problem of language was discovered to be at the root of much of student attrition and class repetition. It was also discovered that, because of the difficulty of comprehending material presented in English, students increasingly and consistently resorted to memorization of bits and pieces of facts to pass examinations. This in turn contributed to the deterioration of the quality of education.[35] All these points were taken into consideration when the decision was made to use Amharic as the language of instruction. The intention did not, of course, solve the larger problem of implementing the decision.

Along with the decision discussed in the preceding paragraphs, deliberate efforts were made to Ethiopianize the entire curriculum. Toward this end, the director of the Department of Research and Curricula, Million Neqniq, presented a report at the General Education Conference convened in Addis Ababa in 1957. He pointed out that the school program and imported textbooks were not adapted to national needs. He also believed that the use of English in the early grades was absolutely unsound.

Following the report, the director general of the Ministry of Education, Kebede Mikael, formed another committee to explore the best means of training primary school teachers. The committee recommended that the grade structure be reduced from eight years of primary school and four years of secondary to six years of primary, with Amharic as the medium of instruction. The two years of junior and three years of senior secondary school would be taught in English. The committee also favored a greater emphasis on culture as expressed through morals and music, on handicrafts, and on those courses that would develop the aesthetic values. For female students, courses in home economics should be provided, and physical training courses should be offered to all children.

A drafting committee was established to prepare curriculum guides, and in September 1958, it presented new guidelines to the Board of Education. The guidelines were approved, but were first to be tried out at five schools selected for the experiment, three of which were the Addis Ababa schools of Amha Desta, Medhane Alem, and Asfa Wossen. In the meantime, work on research and production of teaching materials appropriate for various grades was being carried out in the Department of Research and Curriculum Development of the Ministry of Education, which had been established in 1956.[36]

This new experimental curriculum guide differed from the one drawn up in 1947.[37] It reflected the thinking of Point IV personnel, along with the research results and recommendations of the Long-Term Planning Committee, especially in respect to community schools and to language instruction. The introduction stated that the first six years were to be taught completely in Amharic, with English taught as a subject as early as possible. They laid special stress on making elementary education a wider, more meaningful, and more useful experience.

The first four years, organized especially for older boys and girls, were meant to fulfill the "Community Education Program." Most of the time was devoted to practical training for those who might, at the end of the four-year period, return to work in their respective communities as more useful and productive citizens. As alternatives, these young people could attend vocational schools for a year and then become semiskilled workers, or could complete their primary education in two more years as a foundation for later education.[38]

Since all teaching was to be in Amharic and English was to be taught as a language, children from homes where Amharic was the spoken language were expected to begin learning English early, provided there was a teacher qualified to teach it.[39] It was specified that all subject matter should be integrated into a whole. When more than one teacher was responsible for a class, frequent staff meetings and discussions could facilitate understanding and cooperation among teachers.[40]

At the beginning of each year the school director was expected to administer screening tests to new applicants so that they might be grouped according to ability. At the end of the fourth year a general examination was to be given to determine the achievement level of those who would be leaving school, and a diagnostic test was to be given to younger pupils who would continue. The final examination, given by the Ministry of Education at the end of the sixth grade, would decide which students might be directed to a one-year vocational school.[41]

In the area of community resources there was a new departure. The curriculum guide stipulated that a well-organized school should work in harmony with the community. For example, men and women of the community might be willing to teach their special skills to children. Further, the school was to provide activities in line with the principal occupation of its community and thus make the program "a living and effective part of the community."[42]

Meanwhile the new curriculum was being tried out in the five selected schools. Almost all reports were favorable, and so the change was effected in most of the government primary schools. As far as the secondary level was concerned, existing practices would continue for the time being.[43]

Construction of school buildings continued at a slower pace than during the reconstruction decade. Still, some new structures of varying size and quality went up and some old houses were converted. In general, improvisation was the order of the day in school plant expansion as well.

The type of building also varied, and schools in the capital differed from those in the provinces. The former were more modern in structure and design. Except in the provincial capitals, those in the provinces were less impressive, in most cases built of local materials by local workmen. A 1954 report of the ministry indicated that the erection of new structures was retarded by the enormous cost of getting materials and men.[44] The establishment of a Department of Architecture in the ministry helped in the selection of school sites, the drawing of plans, and the approving and supervising of construction.

During the decade, at least one senior school was established in each of the provincial capitals, whereas formerly there had only been one, in Harar. These extensive building ventures placed a heavy burden on the limited resources of the ministry, yet school construction had to go on. Investment continued, and some of the buildings erected during this period are still in good condition. At the time, there was considerable opposition to building schools that "looked like palaces."

Equipment and library facilities were expanded. The director of research and curriculum noted that the production of teaching and learning materials in 1956 and 1957 increased more than 50 percent over all educational materials ever produced at any one time in the history of Ethiopian education, but that still more updated materials were needed to serve not only government schools, but church and private schools as well.[45]

Teaching Personnel
Since the restoration, the finding of qualified teachers in sufficient numbers for all schools had been a formidable problem. In fact there were only the national teachers (untrained, inexperi-

enced, or both) and foreigners (in most cases neither well-trained nor aware of Ethiopian realities). The former were chosen on the dubious criteria of ability to read (some of them were able to write as well) and willingness to teach. As a result many unqualified people had been brought into the system, and although it was a necessary expedient at the time, it was difficult later either to retain them or to lay them off when better qualified people became available. This dilemma was to continue to plague the school system well into the 1970s.

In the early 1950s, for example, many of the elementary teachers were unqualified. Out of 1,541 government elementary teachers in 1953–54, 814, or 53 percent, were classified as Amharic, arts and crafts, or physical education teachers. What this meant was that the Amharic teachers had a rudimentary knowledge of reading and writing, but that for the rest of the group the ability to read and write was not mandatory. Hence it might well be assumed that over half the teaching force was made up of illiterates and semiliterates. Of the rest, 12 percent were classified as having attained an education equivalent to grade one to four. Only 3 percent had an eighth-grade education, and only 2 percent had the required preparation of grade eight plus one year of teacher training. This was indeed a dismal situation which prompted the ministry to take action—action which, although overdue, would nevertheless rectify the situation.

When the first systematic salary schedule was developed in 1953, the Ministry of Education adopted a policy of employing only those new teachers who had an eighth-grade education. In 1954, the Long-Term Planning Committee approved the requirement that primary school teachers should have completed the eighth grade plus one year of teacher education. Requirements for physical education and arts and crafts teachers had not yet been decided upon, but the direction of general policy indicated that this should be the minimum requirement for all teacher certification. It was less than might be desired, but as the committee said, "It is all that may reasonably be expected in the years immediately ahead."[46]

As late as 1954, the quality of teachers remained very low. Fifty-three percent were presumably not advanced beyond the ability to read and write and to teach arts and crafts, with some Amharic. As we have seen, the Long-Term Committee recommended that teachers were to be given at least six years, up to September 1961, in which to meet the minimum standards, after which date they might be retired with a pension at the discretion of the ministry.[47]

At the same time, more teachers for primary and secondary schools were to be prepared to replace teachers who did not meet the minimum requirement for certification by September 1961, who had left, or who had been selected for preparation to teach in the new schools for basic education. New teachers were needed for incomplete primary schools and for the 1955–65 planned expansion. Upgrading the teaching force was not easy given the pressure for admission to schools by an increasing number of children, and by the end of the decade a vast proportion of the teachers were still underqualified. A survey conducted in 1962 by the Bureau of Educational Research and Statistics of the ministry revealed that some 62.4 percent had only elementary education or lower, without any type of teacher training; about 13 percent had three to four years and 16 percent one year of teacher training; and 9 percent had some community teacher training at various entry levels.[48]

The elementary teacher program was started with the help of the British Council, and later of Canada. Fortunately both groups were devoted professionals. In 1952 the first teacher-training school was transferred from Addis Ababa to Harar. In the following year, training programs were started at the Haile Selassie I Day School in Addis Ababa. In 1956 the Majete Community Teacher Training School was opened under the sponsorship of UNESCO, and the following year the Debre Berhan Community Teacher Training School under the auspices of USAID became operational. Their development has been traced above. In 1958 a number of one-year programs were initiated by several of the senior secondary schools.

The Ethiopian government was not the only institution that carried out the heavy responsibility of educational development in the country. Foreign mission societies, the Ethiopian Orthodox church, and other private organizations were also conducting viable programs in the country. The various institutes and colleges produced over three thousand teachers in nine years. This commendable addition to the teaching force was still far from meeting requirements, but if the ministry were to produce teachers at this rate and retain them on the job, the future augured well.

Indeed, had this trend continued, the severe shortage of teachers would have been minimized over the years. Unfortunately, however, qualified teachers began to turn to other, better-paying positions in the country. A 1960 survey made by the Ministry of Education revealed that, of those teachers who had graduated within the first decade from one-year teacher-training programs, 23 percent had left the profession; of the four-year program graduates, 28 percent; and of the Community Teacher Training graduates, 42 percent;—an average rate of about 30 percent. The largest attrition occurred among those from the Community Teacher Training program, an interesting phenomenon in view of the fact that this group was trained specifically to work in the rural setting. Dr. Aklilu Habte, who made a study of the teacher wastage problem, observed that "several school directors in the fourteen provinces visited by the writer characterize the teachers who leave their schools as active, responsible teachers, teachers who generally come forth with suggestions for the improvement of their schools. If those who leave teaching have the qualities ascribed to them by their directors, then the school system is being deprived of the members who are most likely to give useful service to the nation."[49] The most usual reasons given for leaving were economic hardship, unfavorable administration or working conditions, lack of further educational opportunities, the difficulties of living and working in rural areas, the feeling of being forgotten by educational authorities, indiscriminate recruitment to the teaching service, and the low social prestige accorded teachers by government officials and local community members.

It is not surprising that economic factors headed the list. The quasi-governmental and private organizations that these young people entered paid them much higher salaries than the Ministry of Education. As for administrative inefficiency, Dr. Aklilu reported: "Teachers seem to have lost all faith in the Ministry of Education and its officials. . . . The Ministry is sometimes pictured as a remote island peopled with incompetent and corrupt clerks and administrators, whose sole preoccupation . . . besides coffee-drinking and gossip . . . is the devising of ways and means to oppress teachers."[50] The perceived oppression and suppression of teachers by central and local ministry officials increased with the distance of their schools from Addis Ababa. They felt they were looked upon as menials to be moved about at the whim of officials, that favoritism prevailed, and that the ministry had no way of distinguishing competent individuals from incompetent ones. They feared they had no one to protect them from "exploitation, unfair treatment, unjustifiable mishandling by officials, or unfair accusations by students and parents."[51] Teachers felt insecure and apprehensive—materially as well as psychologically—and it is not surprising that they preferred to work where they were more likely to be given fair treatment.

Another reason given for leaving the teaching service was unfavorable conditions, by which teachers meant the absence of teaching aids, chalk, blackboards, or desks, and, of course, optimal classroom size. School directors assigned teaching duties regardless of the teacher's qualifications and regardless of the applicability of what they might be teaching to children of different localities. It was pointed out that "school directors . . . are selected on the basis of every criterion except ability and professional qualification." This alone caused teachers to resign in disgust.[52]

The secondary school teachers who taught in the 1950s were mostly foreigners. In 1955 the Long-Term Planning Committee wrote that "with very few exceptions all secondary school teachers, other than the teachers of the Amharic language, are foreigners. Dependence upon foreign teachers, of course, should be corrected as rapidly as equally qualified Ethiopian teachers become available. . . . In the meantime, increasing the number of foreign teachers presents no new problems except as it involves a heavier drain on the budget of the Ministry of Education. . . ."[53]

Equal in importance to the quantity of teacher output was the quality of teachers produced. The constant objective, of course, was continuously to improve quality by maintaining a reasonably high academic standard of entry to a teacher-training institute, liberalizing the curriculum along practical lines, developing a greater sense of responsibility and maturity of outlook among the trainees, and introducing more professional training including community involvement. These were the aims of those responsible for teacher training. A Ministry of Education publication pointed out:

Most African countries have departed from the old traditional colonial viewpoint that students with primary education are good enough to teach in the lowest of the primary
grades. . . . Modern educational thought confirms that the
youngest children should have the best teachers and not the
worst, for it is in the lower classes that the academic foundation is laid, behaviour patterns are established, and disci-
plined study habits are taught. . . . If it is considered necessary to train children in independent thought, in habits of
industry and intellectual integrity, then our teachers must
possess these qualities in ample measure. . . . None but the
best should be entrusted with the education and care of the
children of Ethiopia.[54]

Training administrative staff was essential. In a meeting of the
provincial education officers held in 1950, it was resolved to begin
the training of Ethiopian school inspectors, or supervisors. The
training lasted for six months, and by 1952 thirty-seven young
educators had been graduated and training discontinued for four
years until more inspectors should be needed. When training was
resumed, school directors were brought into the program. By
1960, 124 school directors and inspectors had graduated.[55]

These educational leaders were, in the first instance, drawn
from among the primary school teachers. With their inadequate
academic backgrounds, they lacked sufficient academic preparation and command of the English language to be able to profit
from their training. Meanwhile, classroom teachers were undergoing academic and professional training during the long rainy
months, and in a matter of a few years this group of teachers felt
that they had achieved a higher standard than the school directors and inspectors. A solution to the problem was found in the
1960s, when the administrative staff participated in a summer
and one-year training session at university level.[56] For the time
being, this improvisation in the training of school directors and
supervisors served the immediate needs of the government
school system.

Qualitative Characteristics

In the meanwhile, the number of schools and students had continued to increase. During this decade more than at any previous

time nongovernment organizations accelerated their involvement in the development of Ethiopian education. As far as numbers were concerned, by 1961 there were 1,100 schools of various levels in the empire—663 government, 178 mission, 128 private, 55 church, and 75 community schools. The teaching force was 7,155 of whom 5,091 were in government, 942 in mission, 648 in private, 242 in church, and 232 in community schools. Of the total number 15.5 percent were female.

The total number of students was 244,368, of whom 239,831 were in primary grades, 3,598 in special schools, and 939 in higher institutions. Twenty-three percent of them were female, although the higher grades had a much lower percentage than the lower.[57] There were now 45 academic secondary schools with 6,782 students, of whom 730 were females, and 32 special schools (vocational-technical and teacher-training), with 3,598 students. The enrollment in institutions of higher learning was 939. Of the primary school pupils, about 13 percent were enrolled in the capital, 20 percent in Eritrea, and 66 percent in the thirteen provinces (including Bale which had been carved out of the Harar province).

Table 5 sets out the government school enrollment by grade level and sex for a period of ten years. For the year 1952–53, there were over sixty thousand students enrolled in all government schools at all levels. Out of this number, 87 percent were in the four lower primary grades, 10 percent in the middle schools (grades five through eight), 3 percent in the academic and special secondary schools, and only 0.2 percent in institutions of higher education. This shows that the middle and secondary schools were not well attended, confirming the complaint made at the beginning of the decade that not enough candidates were being prepared to enter the higher educational institutions. At all levels the number of female students was proportionately low, reaching almost zero at college level.

As can be seen in the same table, 1960–61 shows, with minor modifications, a similar pattern. While the lower primary school enrolled 87 percent of the total student body in 1952–53, in 1960–61 the percentage had been reduced to 76 percent. The enrollment in the middle grades had increased from 10 percent to 18 percent in 1960–61, in the academic secondary and special schools from 3 to 5 percent, and in institutions of higher educa-

TABLE 5. Enrollment in the Four Divisions of Government and Community Schools 1952–62

Year	Primary Schools Enrollment (Grades 1–4)		Percentage of Total			Middle Schools Enrollment (Grades 5–8)		Percentage of Total			Academic Secondary and Special Schools Enrollment		Percentage of Total			Enrollment in Institutes of Higher Education		Percentage of Total		
	Male	Female	Male	Female	Total	Male	Female	Male	Female	Total	Male	Female	Male	Female	Total	Male	Female	Male	Female	Total
1952–53	45,397	6,969	75.49	11.59	87.08	5,416	637	9.00	1.06	10.06	1,471	141	2.45	0.23	2.68	100	0	0.16	0	0.16
1953–54	52,744	8,505	74.33	11.99	86.32	6,610	829	9.31	1.16	10.47	1,923	202	2.71	0.28	2.99	142	0	2.20	0	2.20
1954–55	58,846	10,587	73.02	13.13	86.15	7,556	842	9.37	1.04	10.41	2,353	240	2.91	0.29	3.21	199	2	0.40	0	0.24
1955–56	66,089	14,397	69.43	15.12	84.55	9,886	1,269	10.38	1.33	11.71	2,820	381	2.96	0.40	3.36	335	10	0.35	0.01	0.36
1956–57	80,261	18,446	68.03	15.63	83.66	12,758	1,760	10.81	1.49	12.30	3,802	483	3.20	0.40	3.63	450	16	0.38	0.01	0.39
1957–58	88,584	21,524	65.65	15.95	81.60	16,414	2,452	12.16	1.81	13.98	4,892	472	3.62	0.34	3.95	578	27	0.42	0.02	0.44
1958–59	88,307	22,953	61.76	16.05	77.81	20,274	3,453	14.18	2.41	16.59	6,036	1,201	4.22	0.84	5.06	716	44	0.50	0.03	0.56
1959–60	89,896	26,301	58.91	17.24	76.15	23,307	4,669	15.27	3.60	18.34	6,771	871	4.40	0.57	4.98	778	49	0.51	0.03	0.54
1960–61	96,271	28,757	58.51	17.48	75.99	24,855	5,426	15.11	3.30	18.41	7,136	1,142	4.34	0.69	5.03	883	56	0.54	0.03	0.57
1961–62	95,644	30,092	56.57	17.80	74.37	26,133	6,809	15.46	4.03	19.49	8,037	1,385	4.75	0.82	5.57	919	49	0.54	0.03	0.57

Source: Ethiopia, Ministry of Education and Fine Arts, School Census for Ethiopia, 1961–62, p. 20.

tion from 0.2 to 0.6 percent. Small though the change was, these increases presumably reflect the recommendations of the Long-Term Planning Committee, and at any rate they indicate progress in the desired direction. Enrollment of female students during the decade showed a slight improvement, but it was insignificant at the higher grade levels.

In 1951–52 the number of schools was 520. There were 1,375 teachers, and total student enrollment was fifty thousand.[58] During the following year, as depicted in table 6, the number of schools decreased by 13.5 percent, but the number of teachers increased by 12.3 percent and enrollment by 20 percent. The decrease in the number of schools may have resulted from the ministry's continuing to transfer schools to the church as in the previous decade, but the phenomenon cannot be fully explained; the reports are incomplete. The increase in the number of teachers reached 64 percent in 1954–55. The largest steady growth recorded, however, was in the number of students. This unevenness in the growth rate of schools, teachers, and enrollment resulted in overcrowded conditions for students.

In 1951, the Long-Term Planning Committee had bemoaned the shortage of qualified secondary school students for entry into the various colleges. The first Five-Year Development Plan had specifically pinpointed the need for middle-level

TABLE 6.   Number of Government Schools, Teachers, and Students, and Percentage of Increase, 1951–61

	Schools		Teachers		Students	
Year	Number	% Increase	Number	% Increase	Number	% Increase
1951–52	520	—	1,375	—	50,000	—
1952–53	450	−13.46	1,544	12.29	60,131	20.26
1953–54	455	1.11	1,541	−0.19	70,958	18.00
1954–55	435	−4.39	2,523	63.72	80,625	13.62
1955–56	453	4.13	2,752	9.07	95,026	17.86
1956–57	469	3.53	3,117	13.26	111,832	17.68
1957–58	501	6.82	3,541	13.60	134,715	20.46
1958–59	484	−3.39	3,927	10.90	140,719	4.45
1959–60	483	−0.20	4,053	3.20	147,876	5.08
1960–61	492	1.86	4,293	5.92	152,884	3.38

Source: "Education Report," Ethiopia Observer 5, no. 1 (1961), pp. 61–73; Ministry of Education and Fine Arts, School Census for Ethiopia, 1960–1961, pp. 10, 11, 16.

technicians to man the growing economy of the country. As might be recalled also, at this time there were only about seven academic secondary schools, one commercial school and one technical school in the whole empire. Accordingly, between 1953 and 1960, several academic and technical-vocational-professional schools were built.

By 1960–61 there were twenty-six schools that included some secondary education, fourteen of them located in the provinces and twelve in the capital. Eleven of them went through grade twelve. Furthermore, two secondary schools were built in Eritrea, and there were ten mission and seven private secondary schools over which the ministry had no effective control. Therefore, their rate of emergence (and disappearance) probably had little to do with the national development scheme.

With the increase of secondary schools, however, academic standards were lowered, and this in turn resulted in an increased dropout rate. "It is . . . regrettable," notes Dr. Trudeau, "that the Ministry of Education went on building and opening new secondary schools, but did not follow up with good staffing or good teaching facilities." It would have been "much more economical and much more fruitful, academically speaking, if the Government had centered its efforts on the existing seven schools."[59]

One of the major problems confronting second-level education was staffing. In 1953–54, only 10 percent of the secondary school teachers and administrators, primarily Amharic and Ge'ez teachers, were Ethiopians, as the Long-Term Committee knew when it advocated Ethiopianization. But until the complete replacement of these foreigners had been effected, the ministry had to maintain its policy. Dr. Trudeau laments:

Year after year, a last-minute trip by officials to foreign countries brought the urgently needed personnel, but it was a last-minute selection. These teachers arrived in schools late in October or November. . . . They were handicapped from the start! Ethiopia saw good foreign teachers leave for other countries, often in Africa, where they were more respected and better rewarded. Beautiful plans for controlled expansion of secondary education became useless, because practice did not follow policies.[60]

The steady deterioration of the quality of secondary education was measured by the high rates of student dropout and of failure in the Ethiopian School Leaving Examination.

A special category of second-level education consisted of the technical-vocational and teacher-training institutes. In 1953 there was one technical school for the whole empire, with 225 students. Because of the serious shortage of skilled technicians, many private and quasi-governmental organizations trained their own employees in schools poorly equipped and staffed.[61] The main responsibility for training technicians for the growing economy rested with the Ministry of Education. The number of schools and students was very low in comparison with the academic secondary schools and in relation to the demands of the economy. This fact can be explained primarily in terms of the cultural background of the society and the government's inability or unwillingness, or both, to provide appropriate incentives. Thus Dr. Trudeau aptly summed it up: "In 1961–62, technical education was still a poor, undeveloped sector in the educational system, with less than a thousand students and about 105 of the overall secondary school enrollment. This situation was not encouraging, especially on the eve of an economic expansion drive."[62] The number of graduates was therefore relatively small, considering the great need of the country.

The Ten-Year Education Plan recommended almost no specific measures regarding women's education. Nevertheless the lack of it was a serious weakness of the educational system, and still is.[63] On the whole there were more girls in the nongovernment than in the government schools. The private schools had the largest number of female students, followed by the mission, church, and community schools, in that order. This is not surprising, since the private and mission schools were operated by foreign, mostly Western, groups, who brought with them the custom of coeducation.

To free the educational system from traditional antifemale attitudes, two approaches were used. First there was the trend started when the first girls' school (Itegue Menen School) was opened in 1931. The *1947–49 Year Book* stated, "Their Imperial Majesties have . . . advised that henceforth, both boys and girls should be afforded equal educational opportunities."[64] The second step was to place girls and boys in the same classrooms. In

1950 a ministry report noted: "Coeducation, practically a new phase of Ethiopian education, is geared to the urgent needs of the hour." Three years later, out of a sample of thirty-six primary schools surveyed, thirty-one were coeducational. This fact represented "a definite major shift," following policy directives sent by the ministry to all elementary schools.[65]

We have indicated that in the 1950s the nongovernment organizations had resumed their educational activities after an interruption of nearly fifteen years. During this period the church, the foreign missionary societies, and other private organizations had established at least a few primary schools and had attracted a significant number of students. The missionary societies had the largest number of schools, teachers, and students, followed by the private schools, the church schools, and the community school system. These schools, mostly of the first level, together constituted about 10 percent of the total number in operation during the first half of the decade, and about 23 percent toward the end.

The government and nongovernment schools together achieved an impressive rate of growth during this period. Enrollment for grades one through twelve increased in all from 50,350 to 267,252 pupils. The growth rate of the nongovernment schools was higher, a trend which was to continue throughout the following decade.

In the 1940s, students who desired to continue on to college had to pass the London Matriculation Examination or its equivalent. In the 1950s, the Ethiopian School Leaving Certificate Examination (ESLCE) was instituted, and it became the main avenue that led to university admission. At first, as can be seen in table 7, more than half the twelfth-grade students registered for the examination; of those some 62 to 75 percent passed in the years 1951 through 1958. Thereafter, however, there was a continued drop until by 1962 only 23 percent were passing. The phenomenon can be understood better if one recalls that during these years the various colleges (including, from 1961 on, Haile Selassie I University) were starving for qualified candidates. What was actually happening was that almost half the twelfth-grade students chose not to sit for the examination, and of those who did, many failed.

Indicators of the efficiency of an educational system include

TABLE 7.   Students Passing the ESLCE, 1951–62

Year	Number of Students Enrolled in Grade 12	Registered for ESLCE	Percentage of Total Enrollment Registered	Number Passed ESLCE	Percentage Passed Students Registered for ESLCE	Of Total Enrollment in Grade 12
1951–52	138	83	60.1	63	75.9	45.6
1952–53	176	86	51.7	64	75.8	36.3
1953–54	313	105	33.5	73	70.0	23.3
1954–55	278	159	57.1	88	55.5	31.6
1955–56	310	163	52.5	103	63.2	33.2
1956–57	468	153	32.7	111	72.5	25.7
1957–58	606	317	52.6	197	62.2	32.5
1958–59	673	441	65.5	180	40.8	26.7
1959–60	917	412	44.9	168	40.7	18.3
1960–61	851	532	62.5	192	36.0	22.5
1961–62	1,163	718	61.7	167	23.2	14.3

Sources: Bjerkan, "Plans, Targets and Trends in Ethiopian Education," p. 222; Trudeau, "Higher Education in Ethiopia," pp. 16–19.

the number of learners who successfully pass general national examinations, the number who successfully complete and are promoted from one grade or level to the next, and their performance in life careers once they graduate from the educational system. While it is not always possible to evaluate the last factor, it can be ascertained that in terms of success in examinations and of holding students within the system until graduation, our system of education did very poorly. Although this problem was recognized by the Long-Term Planning Committee as early as 1952 or 1953, little was done to lower student wastage.

Thus, in 1952–53 only 44 percent of first-grade students were promoted to the second grade. Two years later only 30 percent of the same group were promoted, and so on until eight years later only 18 percent were still in the system. The picture was even worse for the period between 1953 and 1955, for which we have complete information. Beginning in 1955–56, some improvements were noticeable, but student wastage still remained intolerably high.

At the second level of education, the picture was somewhat better. In 1955–56, about 81 percent of those in grade nine were promoted to grade ten. Two years later 50 percent were promoted to grade eleven, and eventually 34 percent entered grade twelve. Throughout the period from 1952 to 1960, tenth-grade promotions averaged about 80 percent and eleventh-grade promotions about 53 percent. Only a relatively small percentage reached grade twelve. The wastage rate in all cases was far too much, even after making allowances for recruitment to other fields of training.

Reasons were adduced to account for wastage at all levels. At the elementary level, these included the distances that small children had to travel to school, parents' conservatism regarding schooling, language problems, teaching inefficiency, overage and underage learners, conflicting objectives of traditional and modern education, and family socioeconomic problems.[66] Another major reason may have been the growing decrease in educational expenditure in comparison with that of the reconstruction era. During the decade between 1951 and 1962, budget allocations did not match the fast expansion of the educational system.

Legislation and Finance
There was less new legislation affecting education during the consolidation and expansion period than in the previous decade. One of the two laws that did appear, however, was unprecedented in the annals of our history. This was the revised Constitution of 1955.

In 1931, the emperor had declared that the Ethiopian people, completely isolated as they were from the rest of the world and from modern civilization, were in a backward state and that their sovereigns were therefore justified in ruling over them "as a good father guides his children."[67] He added, however, that sufficient progress had been made to warrant the granting of the first constitution in 1931. Since this occurred just four years before war was declared on Ethiopia, the new instrument of modernization was not given enough time to make an appreciable impact on the national scene.

The restored government in 1941 upheld the 1931 Constitution, which provided the legal framework of the era of reconstruction and improvisation. It was already apparent by the 1950s, however, and especially so after Eritrea was federated with Ethiopia in 1952, that a new constitution was necessary to encompass the needs of changed times. Thus a revised constitution was effected in 1955.

Here we have time only to touch upon those constitutional articles or clauses that have specific implications for education. Article 38 specifies that there shall be no discrimination with respect to the enjoyment of all civil rights. Article 40 stipulates that there shall be no interference with the exercise of the rites of any religion or creed. Freedom of speech and of the press is guaranteed in Article 41. Articles 45 and 47 guarantee the rights to assemble peaceably and to travel within the empire and change domicile therein. Article 47 states that the Ethiopian subject has the right to engage in any occupation and to that end to form or join associations. Article 48 states that "the Ethiopian family, as the source of the maintenance and development of the Empire and the primary basis of education and social harmony, is under the special protection of the law." In Articles 61 and 64 Ethiopians are guaranteed exemption from unlawful search and seizure and given the right to vote. A gain for education under the constitution was that the minister of education became a member of the cabinet on equal terms with other cabinet members.[68]

Throughout this century, the desire for universal education in Ethiopia has been paramount. As may be recalled, Empress Zewditu promulgated a law requiring all citizens under a certain age limit to acquire the ability to read and write. Emperor Haile Selassie ordered the formulation of a policy that would lead progressively toward universal education. The Long-Term Planning Committee recommended universal education and the community schools of the 1940s and 1950s pointed toward this cherished goal.

In 1955 there appeared, in Amharic newspapers only, an official notice stating that everyone between the ages of seven and eighteen should receive at least elementary education, which would be available free at government schools. Illiterate persons over eighteen were instructed to learn, with the assistance of the clergy, Amharic reading and writing. All employers were to provide learning facilities for their employees. Finally, the minister of education was to draw up the necessary program and ensure its implementation.[69] This scheme fell short of becoming a national law. Still, it generated healthy discussion among Ethiopians for a long time.

This same wish was to be expressed in the 1961 Conference of African States, where Ethiopia, along with other African countries, pledged to make primary education available to every

Ethiopian child by 1980. Although this was later dropped, the 1972 Education Sector Review organized by the ministry of education would declare that primary education should be available to all within thirty years or less.

When attempts were made to put plans into effect, it was found that additional technical and financial assistance would be increasingly required, and the Ethiopian government sought it from bilateral and international sources. Since 1941 Ethiopia had been receiving some help from external sources in the form of cash, equipment, facilities, and personnel. We have seen that aid and credits were extended first by the United Kingdom and later by the United States and Sweden. The main international participation in the development of Ethiopia, however, came in the 1950s, when three loans totaling $8,500,000 from the International Bank for Reconstruction and Development (IBRD) were used to rehabilitate the road network, to establish a bank to make small loans to agriculture and industry, and to improve and extend the telecommunication system. Since Ethiopia had a good record in meeting interest and principal repayments on its foreign debts, it was relatively easy to secure additional foreign credit in the years to follow.[70]

The Technical Cooperation Program, or Point IV, was enacted by the Congress of the United States in 1950. The Act for International Development was based on the premise that technical and economic cooperation represented the best method to enable countries to use their own resources, to overcome major obstacles to their progress, and to energize their development processes. The program also envisioned that "in addition to technical cooperation, which basically is the transferring of knowledge and skills from one country to another, funds [were] needed for direct utilization in economic development projects permitting capital improvements."[71] This cooperative venture covered a wide range of projects, but here we shall deal only with education. Late in 1950, after various diplomatic exchanges, the emperor appointed a Point IV Inter-Ministerial Committee, whose proposals were discussed with representatives of the United States in 1951. In June an official request for assistance in the development of primary and secondary schools was made. The proposal was that an Ethio-American Education Service be established in Addis Ababa to cooperate with the Ministry of

Education on specific problems and that a qualified administrator be sent to help plan specific projects and to report on their execution, as well as on equipment and personnel. No action was taken, however, until after the arrival of the United States director of technical cooperation on 1 May 1953.

In June 1952, the two governments agreed to cooperate on "Technical and Science Education in schools of Secondary and Elementary level, and the Technical College in Addis Ababa." Joint funds were set up, and control of the venture was invested in a special representative of the two countries, who would, however, have no control over the ordinary operation and management of Ethiopian schools. In March 1953, Dr. William Wrinkle arrived in Addis Ababa as Chief Technical Cooperative Administration (TCA) education adviser to the ministry. Other advisers followed, and fruitful cooperative efforts were put into motion.[72]

Point IV undertook to upgrade the quality of existing teachers and to train new ones for all levels, and helped to develop new teaching materials for use in elementary and secondary schools. In addition, it sought to improve the teaching of languages and established guidance, testing, and measurement services in the ministry.

The Ministry of Education and Point IV advisers, we will recall, initiated the program at Debre Berhan to prepare teachers for the villages which, although short-lived, promised a response to community needs. The two units also established a communications media center to produce teaching materials. In short, the Point IV-ministry venture was the most influential single program after restoration.

The United Nations, through UNESCO and the United Nations Children's Emergency Fund (UNICEF), had already begun to contribute to the development of education. (More will be said of United Nations activities later.) The bilateral and international agreements entered into by the Ethiopian government contributed significantly to the qualitative and quantitative development of all levels of education.

As far as the central administration was concerned, the structure and organization remained basically as it was in the reconstruction decade. The emperor continued to retain the ministerial portfolio, and the vice-minister continued to carry out the day-to-day administrative transactions, while the National Board of Education provided guidelines regarding policy formation and implementation.

At this time the ministry commissioned an independent organization to make a thorough study of the whole administrative setup. The study appraised the status quo and first commended the achievements of the past ten years: "The Ministry of Education . . . has been faced with a situation in which acute recognition of problems, careful and patient planning, and effective and well-timed steps have been required and have been much in evidence." It went on to say, however, that the ministry needed to be organized to administer as effectively as possible the day-to-day activities for which it was responsible and to prepare itself to take over with trained local personnel the task of developing, on a continuous basis, a truly Ethiopian educational system.[73] In several respects the ministry was not organized to accomplish in the most effective manner either of these objectives. As more facilities and trained personnel became available, the ministry sought to achieve the following objectives:

1. Unity: specialized educational programs, such as agricultural and other technical education, should be integrated into the Ministry of Education;
2. Appropriate staff services;
3. The most effective use of foreign personnel in an advisory capacity. Ethiopian personnel should be assigned to positions within the regular organization of the ministry as counterparts to technical advisers; and
4. Clear channels of authority and accountability.

The report went on: "The present organization . . . does not provide the desirable characteristics set forth above." Some of the defects listed were that the Vice-Minister and Director General were too overburdened with details to give the necessary time and attention to policy and planning; there was no single point of contact for provincial education officers or school directors with the central office; certain services, such as budgeting, planning and research, and supervision of school maintenance, had not been established; and the records system was inadequate. Additionally, organizational arrangements within the ministry lacked attention—such matters as the training of Ethiopian personnel for supervisors and curriculum specialists and the providing of facilities for review and evaluation of programs. Administrative processes were encumbered by an overuse of committees without sufficient coordination of their work, and the selection and placement of teachers and students were marked by inadequacy and confusion.[74] To what extent the document was accepted at that time is not clear, but some of the recommendations were put into effect after 1961.

Government education was financed from four main sources—the central treasury, the education tax on rural lands, public contributions, and economic and technical assistance from abroad. During the decade between 1951 and 1961, the operation and administration of provincial elementary schools were financed as before by the 1947 tax on rural land, and all other educational facilities and programs were financed by national treasury allocations derived from general tax revenue.

During the period from 1948 to 1954, total educational expenditures increased by 28 percent. The sharpest increase, 56 percent, occurred in national fund expenditures for schools above the elementary level. During these years the provincial and national divisions of financial support remained close to a forty to sixty ratio, while the proportion of funds devoted to elementary education, both in Addis Ababa and in the provinces, declined, with a corresponding increase in the proportion of funds devoted to education above the elementary level. Since the establishment of the education tax, the national share of education finance had decreased.[75]

Table 8 reveals the financial disparity among the various provinces and the consequent need to extend equal opportunity to all children of the nation. An expert appointed by the Long-Term Committee reported:

An examination of the financial position of all provinces shows that some provinces are less favourably placed than others. Hence the system of financing has created an inequality of educational opportunity . . . which will be more and more marked in future years. Urban property owners do not contribute to the cost of elementary education in spite of the fact that their children are the main beneficiaries since schools tend to be established in urban areas.[76]

TABLE 8.   Educational Expenditure by the Ministry of Education, in Ethiopian Dollars, 1951–62

Year	Head Office and Addis Ababa Schools	Provinces	Total	Percentage of Increase
1951–52	5,201,735	4,070,222	9,271,957	—
1952–53	6,098,859	4,206,725	10,305,584	11.14
1953–54	5,549,368	4,910,760	10,460,128	1.49
1954–55	7,724,415	4,803,167	12,527,582	19.76
1955–56	9,295,109	5,595,449	14,890,558	18.86
1956–57	10,205,757	6,191,596	16,397,353	10.11
1957–58	8,393,444	7,199,433	15,592,877	−4.9
1958–59	11,573,785	6,451,752	18,025,537	15.60
1959–60	12,546,002	9,564,933	22,110,935	22.66
1960–61	8,395,779	6,448,006	14,843,785	−32.86
1961–62	10,204,727	9,153,090	19,357,817	30.41

Source: Data from Ministry of Education, Physical Planning Section, (April 1972).

Yet the disparity continued to exist. The nation's general commitment to education was indicated by the total amount of money devoted to it. Table 9 shows that when a comparison is made between total government expenditure and expenditure on education, the mean percentage for the ten-year period was only about 10 percent.

TABLE 9.   Expenditure on Education as Percentage of National Expenditure, in Ethiopian Dollars, 1951–61

Year	Actual National Budgetary Expenditure	Expenditure on Education	Percentage
1951–52	84,413,000	9,592,000	11.42
1952–53	103,119,000	10,055,000	9.75
1953–54	112,300,000	10,600,000	9.44
1954–55	122,700,000	10,700,000	8.72
1955–56	124,800,000	13,900,000	11.14
1956–57	144,900,000	15,500,000	10.70
1957–58	175,500,000	17,100,000	9.74
1958–59	197,800,000	19,400,000	9.81
1959–60	216,340,000	20,917,000	9.67
1960–61	224,593,000	23,794,000	10.59

Sources: "Education Report," Ethiopia Observer 5, no. 1 (1961), p. 71; Girma Amare, "Education and the Conflict of Values in Ethiopia," (Ph.D. dissertation, Southern Illinois University, 1964), p. 101.

Taking all factors together, it seems that public education, which was and is the largest system in Ethiopia, was beset by shortages of resources, the major one being financial resources. In the distribution between urban and rural communities, the latter were always shortchanged. Although responsible officials took cognizance of these inequalities, little was done to rectify the imbalances.

Accomplishments and Challenges

After World War II, then, the period of reconstruction and urgent improvisation gave way to one of consolidation and planned expansion. This was indeed a period of bold innovation as far as planning went. Most of the plans, however, unfortunately remained on paper, even the parts that were endorsed by the National Board of Education. The few that were implemented, such as the community schools, were unable to be maintained, primarily for lack of commitment and perseverance on the part of those entrusted with carrying them out.

The decade between 1951 and 1961, however, was not without dramatic progress in the area of educational outlay and enrollment. Writing toward the end of the period, the director of the ministry's Department of Research and Curriculum Development noted that, "In spite of some planning defects, the advance hitherto made in the sphere of educational development must be regarded as one of the solid achievements of the postliberation period. This remarkable pace of educational expenditure, one presumes, must have been the result of a recognition, not that a poor country cannot afford education, but that a poor country cannot afford to do without it."[77]

Now, what of the future? The author just cited listed the most urgent needs of education, and it is a list with which we are already too familiar—planning, administration, teacher training, learning materials, financing, and the expansion of coeducation. He added that, even though the nation might require more highly skilled people to man the economy, elementary education needed to be advanced on a countrywide basis; and that "with only 3 percent of the school-going . . . population in the classrooms, we have to adopt a drastic and determined new look into the future."[78]

Maaza Bekele, in charge of the ministry's Department of Curriculum Development, saw the problems of the future from the qualitative point of view. Noting that the curriculum structure consisted of eight years of primary education, four of secondary, and three to four of higher education, each period followed by one of the three formidable national examinations, she felt that this structure had caused teachers and students alike to see education as a matter of securing certificates. She furthermore questioned the validity of the bits and pieces of imported learning that had been superimposed on an "ancient and revered culture," and questioned whether our schools were producing young people who appreciated the valuable aspects of their own society and their own communities. She added:

> It seems that we need to try to shift the emphasis in our education system from examinations and put it upon some specific aims, such as helping children to meet the challenges presented by a developing nation in a changing world; to help children . . . find solutions . . . which are practical, intellectual and emotional; to help them become aware of the relationship between them and their environment, . . . to stimulate in them the desire, within the range of individual ability, always to continue the process of education, and to share acquired knowledge and skill with others.[79]

While educators were probing for solutions to existing problems, there was also the problem of the cultural milieu. Already, alarmed voices were being raised regarding the traditional culture. A Ministry of Education publication warned: "For the moment the modern developments may seem to be of primary importance; but they must not be allowed to get out of hand, to the extent that they swamp the traditional culture. Ethiopia's contribution to the world's cultural prosperity will be superficial and banal unless it is permeated with her own special sense of the past and its continuance as present reality."[80] These were some of the challenges that had to be met as we ventured into the 1960s and beyond.

Chapter 8

The Decade of Africa, 1962–72

Conference of African States

For Ethiopia the educational momentum that had started soon after liberation was to continue. There was faith in and enthusiasm for the powerful role education could play in nation building, and a considerable proportion of the national resources was going to be invested in it. But the emphasis had shifted from education for its own sake to education that would produce those skills that would be needed for the development of the country. Deliberate national planning was continued; yet this decade was different because, for the first time in our history, we began to interact directly with other sovereign African states and to compare educational notes with them. The comparison was to bring traumatic shocks and salutary new motivations.

The beginning of the decade was also the end of the first Five-Year Development Plan (1957–61), later extended to include the fiscal year of 1962. This decade was to see two more nationwide efforts, the second and third Five-Year Plans (1961–66 and 1966–73). The most dramatic plan, however, was the one that emerged in May 1961 at Addis Ababa.

The year 1960 has been called the "Year of Africa,"[1] and rightly so. Within a single year, seventeen states gained their independence. As illustrated in table 10, there were forty independent African states by 1963. These events effectively launched what we have called the Decade of Africa.

Realizing the unprecedented speed with which Africans were throwing off the chains of colonialism that had held them for so many years, the international community wanted to play an active role in the social and economic development of Africa. In February 1960, therefore, a preliminary meeting was convened by UNESCO in Addis Ababa, where it was decided that a larger conference should be held in the near future.

147

TABLE 10. African States Listed with Date of Independence

Country	Day	Month	Year	Country	Day	Month	Year
Angola	11	November	1975	Mali	20	June	1960
Algeria	1	July	1962	Mauritania	28	November	1960
Benin	1	August	1960	Mauritius	12	March	1968
Botswana	30	September	1966	Morocco	2	March	1956
Burundi	1	July	1962	Mozambique	25	June	1975
Cameroon	1	January	1960	Namibia (South-West Africa power being			
Central African Republic	17	August	1960	transferred to the Nambians)			1978
Chad	11	August	1960	Niger	3	August	1960
Comoro Islands	6	July	1975	Nigeria	1	October	1960
Congo	15	August	1960	Rwanda	1	July	1962
Djibouti	8	May	1977	Senegal	20	June	1960
Egypt[a]	23	July	1952	Seychelles	28	June	1974
Ethiopia[b]		—		Sierra Leone	27	April	1961
Equatorial Guinea	12	October	1968	Somalia	1	July	1960
Gabon	17	August	1960	South Africa[c]	31	May	1910
Gambia	18	February	1965	Sudan	1	January	1956
Ghana	6	March	1957	Swaziland	6	September	1968
Guinea	2	October	1958	Tanzania	9	December	1961
Guinea-Bissau	24	September	1974	Togo	27	April	1960
Ivory Coast	7	August	1960	Tunisia	25	March	1956
Kenya	12	December	1963	Uganda	9	October	1962
Leshotho	4	October	1966	Upper Volta	5	August	1960
Liberia	26	July	1847	Zaire	30	June	1960
Libya	24	December	1951	Zambia	24	October	1964
Madagascar	25	June	1960	Zimbabwe (Rhodesia, power in process of being			
Malawi	6	July	1964	transferred to the [black] majority)			1978

Sources: Respective embassies (Addis Ababa, October 1973); *Economist* intelligence unit; *Africa*, London, 1973, pp. 1–212; *CBS News Almanac*, 1977; *Information Please Almanac*, 1978.

[a]*The date indicated is National Day of Egypt.*

[b]*The oldest independent state in the continent, except for the brief usurpation by Italy, 1936–41.*

[c]*Power remains in the hands of white minority government.*

The 1961 UNESCO Conference of African States for the Development of Education was held in Addis Ababa from 15 to 25 May, bringing together thirty-nine governments as participants and twenty-four more as observers, ten United Nations agencies, and twenty-four international nongovernmental organizations. The purpose was "to provide a forum for African States to decide on their priority educational needs to promote economic and social development in Africa and, in the light of these, to establish first tentative short-term and long-term plans. . . . "[2] The report of the conference later noted that "the voice of Africa was clear and impressive—the needs for education in Africa were made known."[3]

The thirty-five states representing Middle Africa submitted their national plans for education and for the means of achieving them, and these were debated and studied by four commissions and in plenary sessions. The conference's stated plans for education in Africa were as follows:

1. Short-term plan targets (1961–66)
    a) An annual 5 percent increase of enrollment at the primary level, which would mean an increase in enrollment from the then existing mean of 40 percent to 51 percent by the end of the plan.
    b) An increase in enrollment in second level education from 3 percent to 9 percent. During the short-term period, this was to receive highest attention.
2. Long-term plan targets (1961–81)
    a) Universal, free, and compulsory primary education.
    b) Education at the second level for 30 percent of those who completed primary school.
    c) Higher education, mostly in Africa, for 20 percent of those who completed secondary school.
    d) Constant improvement of the quality of African schools and universities.

Both plans called for the training of teachers in sufficient quantity and quality at all levels and the expansion of adult education.

Enrollment targets expressed as a percentage of the appropriate age-group were:

	1960–61	1965–66	1970–71	1980–81
Primary level	40%	51%	71%	100%
Secondary level	3	9	15	23
Tertiary level	0.2	0.2	0.4	2

3. Overall development of education
   a) Primary education
      (1) Reduction of student dropout during the six years of primary education from 60 percent to 20 percent or less.
      (2) Class size in the primary schools to be reduced from 45 to 35.
      (3) Regarding primary school teachers, 10 percent were to have secondary school education plus three years of teacher training; 45 percent elementary schooling followed by four years of professional training; and the remaining 45 percent to have elementary education followed by two years of teacher training.
   b) Second-level education
      (1) Thirty percent of pupils who completed elementary studies were to be admitted to the second level. Of these, one-third were to have six years of academic secondary education and two-thirds were to enter vocational, technical, or teacher–training institutions.
      (2) Student wastage during the six years of secondary education was not to exceed 15 percent of initial enrollment.

Twenty percent of the students completing secondary education were to go on to higher education. Sixty percent of these would be enrolled in scientific, vocational, and technical courses, while the rest would pursue literary, social, or behavioral science studies. The educational pyramid aimed at by 1980 was 100 (primary), 23 (secondary), and 2 (tertiary). Further, it was decided to allot 5 percent of the total expenditure to adult and other types of education not covered by specific provisions.[4]

At the second level of education, the conference recommended that more places should be provided for an increased number of qualified students, so that the critical shortage of second-level manpower would be met to a greater extent. To this end urgent attention was to be given to curricula reform, including emphasis on technical and agricultural education.

To finance this expansion, all African member states and associated members were to raise the percentage of national income earmarked for education from 3 to 4 percent by 1965 and to 6 percent by 1980. At the same time, appropriate measures were to be taken to reduce costs by improving organization and administration, by avoiding wastage and duplication, and by speeding up the Africanization of personnel.[5]

Other important conferences followed. The 1962 Tananarive Conference on the Development of Higher Education in Africa sponsored by UNESCO encouraged the development of African colleges and universities which would be required to contribute to the unification and building of African nations. These institutions of higher learning were made responsible for the rediscovery and teaching of the history, culture, and social structures of Africa. A conference of African ministers of education held in Paris in 1962 took the findings and recommendations of the two previous conferences a step further by making allowances to those countries which had very low school enrollment. In like manner, the March 1964 conference in Abidjan recognized that regional plans for education were to be interpreted in the light of the national development plans of each country. In July and August 1964, a conference in Lagos concentrated on the utilization of natural resources as well as of human resources. It also made recommendations regarding scientific research and the training of scientists.

All these conferences played significant roles in the development of education in Africa. Perhaps the single most important conference since 1961, however, was that held in Nairobi, Kenya, in July 1968. Known as the Conference on Education, Scientific, and Technical Training in Relation to the Development of Africa, it undertook a review of what had been taking place in education during the Five-Year Short-Term Plan of 1961 to 1966. The findings were that, while overall enrollments in the states that had signed the Addis Ababa accord had increased substantially during the period, they had all fallen short of the target, with the exception of higher education enrollment. The shortfall in elementary education (a million less than the total anticipated) was critical in light of the high dropout and repetition rates reported at that level. The mean percentage rate of yearly increase in enrollment, instead of being 5 percent of the school entering group, was only 1.77 percent.

It was only in higher education that the plan was more than attained, and this was reflected not only in higher enrollment. More people were studying in home universities rather than in overseas institutions. Only in scientific and technological fields was the goal not achieved.

On the other hand, population growth as projected at the Addis Ababa conference for the African states was far lower than expected. The targets set in 1961 were for the most part unfulfilled, but the Nairobi conference retained them as objectives to be aimed at through 1980.[6]

For Ethiopia, these events were her first opportunity to evaluate her social conditions as compared with those of other African countries, former colonies now emerging as full-fledged sovereign nations. If freedom and independence were to be measured in terms of secular educational achievement, Ethiopia did not like what she learned:[7] she was at the bottom of the hierarchy. Dr. Trudeau, a longtime educator, commented:

> UNESCO official statistics and reports were now revealing . . . that all this educational progress in Ethiopia was comparatively small. Educational achievements in other African countries had been . . . much more impressive and had left Ethiopia lagging behind, especially at elementary and secondary levels. Ethiopia, a symbol of African freedom on the political scene, a country of great prestige led by a much respected leader in Africa, was shocked by the facts brought to light at the Conference. . . . Ethiopia had to . . . back its political leadership in Africa with educational and economical leadership.[8]

While still fresh from the traumatic awareness that Ethiopia had fallen behind other African states in the development of education, the then minister of state for education and fine arts, Haddis Alemayehu, set up a committee of top officials of the ministry to evaluate the educational programs of the country and to make recommendations. The chairman was Million Neqniq, a professional educator. In August 1962, barely a year after the Addis Ababa conference, the committee submitted a report that reiterated the great significance for Ethiopia of the plan for educational development in Africa, and concluded: "The basic documents prepared for that Conference . . . showed that in terms of the numbers of students currently enrolled in her schools and of the national investment in education, Ethiopia has fallen seriously behind most other African countries. This means that a correspondingly greater effort must now be made."[9]

Dr. Trudeau remarked that the committee had not set educational targets so high as those proposed by UNESCO, but that they seemed more realistic; yet they were rejected by the government as too expensive.[10] Furthermore, in terms of percentage of government expenditure, gross national product, and per capita income, Ethiopia was not exerting as much effort as most of the other African states—facts well known to government authorities.[11] As if admitting defeat in the race, Ethiopia began to look inward and concentrate on her own five-year national development plans.

Second Five-year Plan

As we have noted above, the end of the first Ethiopian Five-Year Plan coincided with the Addis Ababa conference. During the plan period (1957–61), the number of students enrolled at all levels, including the special schools, had increased 65 percent, or about 11 percent each year. The total number of graduates from special secondary schools increased by 72 percent. The number of special secondary schools increased 4.4 times, while the number of academic secondary schools trebled. In higher education, 403 young people graduated from the various programs offered by the six colleges, and 883 were still enrolled at the end of 1960–61. During the same period, 1,101 graduates returned from abroad, while 979 were still pursuing their studies overseas. Significant strides had therefore been made in this area. Nongovernment schools had enrolled about a third of the students, a fact appreciated by the government.[12]

The plan document noted, however, that in spite of improvements secondary and higher education at the end of the first Five-Year Plan were not fully developed, and these schools were attended by only 4.3 percent of the total number of students. Even the primary schools comprised barely 10 percent of school age children. Other problems were high student attrition, low female enrollment, and the lag in the production of teachers.[13] In launching the second Five-Year Plan, these hard facts had to be taken into consideration. Dr. Trudeau points out:

> A new approach to education, a new philosophy of education had replaced the drive of the post-war years. The philosophy of 'education at all cost' had been replaced by the calculated approach of the economist: invest for what you can get in return. Educate only as many as can be absorbed by the developing economy and administration, educate only the type you need.[14]

This philosophy prevailed throughout the second and third Five-Year Development Plans, which in essence constitute the decade under consideration. Accordingly, these plans stressed the priority of those forms of technical education best suited to efficient, fast training of skilled personnel; a balance in general academic education so that it did not develop excessively at the expense of technical education; adjustments in length of studies, hours of work, and educational programs to ensure the fastest production of qualified personnel; and the financing of these comprehensive programs by encouraging communities and local populations to contribute money, materials, and voluntary labor.

Primary education was to be expanded, since it provided not only the necessary background for further education, but also for recruitment of the needed manpower. "Nevertheless, a certain limit must be set, . . . having regard to the scarce resources and the need of developing technical education in particular."[15] Emphasis was also placed on more equal distribution of educational opportunities between urban centers and rural areas.

The grade structure was changed so that six years of elementary were followed by two years of junior secondary and four years of senior secondary schooling, or a 6–2–4 system.[16] Under the new structure, recruitment was from grade eight for the specialized schools (Addis Ababa and Asmara trade schools; Ambo and Jimma agricultural schools; the Addis Ababa Commercial School; the training institutes for elementary teachers at Addis Ababa, Debre Berhan, Harar, and Asmara; and two schools of handicrafts and fine arts at Addis Ababa). Recruitment for entry to the Bahr Dar Polytechnic Institute followed completion of tenth grade. There was also some recruitment from grades nine and eleven by governmental and nongovernmental agencies. Both degree and diploma candidates were to be recruited for higher education after having completed the twelfth grade and having passed the ESLCE.[17]

The new curriculum of the Ministry of Education, fully operational in 1963–64, incorporated several new features. It included both academic subjects (Amharic, arithmetic, social studies, science, and English) and nonacademic subjects (health and safety, morals, agriculture, arts and crafts, homemaking, physical training and games, and music). Special attention was to be paid to languages. Amharic was now the language of instruction in the first six years, but in cases where Amharic was a child's second language, special adaptations were to be made to meet the specific needs of the pupils.[18]

Committee on Secondary Education

In 1965, the Council of Ministers appointed a committee of high-level education officials, including representatives from USAID and UNESCO, to study problems connected with the twelfth grade examination. The committee reviewed the programs of the elementary schools as well, as an important part of the total process. While agreeing in principle with the curriculum changes, the committee expressed dissatisfaction over the lack of implementation. For example, in respect to Amharic, it pointed out: "To develop the language as an effective teaching medium, great attention must be paid to the development of new vocabulary and the expression of scientific concepts in Amharic. There has been little control over these processes, and even the books published by the Ministry of Education are uncontrolled in terms of vocabulary, [and] graded difficulty in language construction."[19]

The committee found few qualified Amharic teachers in the school system at any level, and felt that in general they had been appointed "on the principle that anybody can teach Amharic." There had been no control over the teaching of Amharic, so that there was a "growing state of confusion in which terminology and concepts are not consistent or adequately expressed. . . . " Thus, since Amharic was the language of elementary instruction and was the national language as well, it was recommended that the Ministry of Education in cooperation with the university should prepare suitable Amharic learning material and should encourage the recruitment of teachers for training in the language as a special subject.[20] The committee made these final remarks: "Principles of psychological and physiological development, applicable perhaps to certain age-groups in Western Europe and America, have been applied to the Ethiopian education system without question, and, in the absence of suitable Amharic local data, are being taught in teacher training institutes. The committee feels that this points to an urgent need for a great deal of basic educational research. . . ."[21]

A revised curriculum for secondary schools was published in 1963. It was an attempt "to bring Ethiopian secondary education into line with the needs of the Ethiopian student, his country and his continent."[22] The objectives were redefined as follows:

1. *a)* To produce people who can think objectively and dispassionately.
   b) To . . . open the heart to the interests and concerns of others and the world at large.
   c) To develop inner resources of spirit.
   d) To prepare one to participate efficiently in the productive work of the world so that one may contribute something of value to society. This includes both love of work and appreciation of the dignity of all labor, and insistence on high standards of efficiency and workmanship. These aims are practical as well as moral assets.
2. General secondary school thus defined should be such as to arouse in the young Ethiopian a spirit of inquiry in all fields of knowledge, to allow him to appreciate fully his duties as a citizen, to give him a genuine understanding of his national and regional environment, to strengthen his appreciation of his traditional and cultural values; and by making him conscious of the wealth of the world's culture and the continuing progress of science, to give the feeling of being one with the whole of mankind.[23]

The junior secondary school was to provide the Ethiopian adolescent with a "common core of knowledge, skills, under-

standing attitudes and habits essential for effective citizenship."
He was to develop the "ability to communicate thought, to think
effectively, to discriminate among values, and to use sound judgment in problematic situations"; to master the English language;
and to select a course in line with the needs of the senior secondary or specialized schools, or to become a semiskilled worker.[24]
The senior secondary school was designed to enable young
people to enter a university, an institution of higher technical,
agricultural, or industrial education, or to find employment in
the intermediate levels of public administration or private enter-
prise, "personnel at this level being those most urgently needed
in Ethiopia at present."[25]

A new revised curriculum guide (1967–68) was intended for
the newly emerging comprehensive secondary schools that emphasized technical and vocational skills rather than academically
weighted courses. It also made provision for a wider experience
and a broader training, covering agriculture, industrial arts,
everyday commercial needs, and intensive concentration on English language skills. From grade eight, some 60 percent or more
would be selected to continue either in the general secondary
schools or in specialized schools. The latter were terminal and
prepared students for specific crafts, trades, or professions. The
senior general secondary schools were not terminal in this sense;
their central objective was to develop "a foundation of trainabil-
ity."[26] Students leaving from grade ten, a recognized tap-off
point, or from grade twelve would often undertake some specialized course or receive on-the-job training in the public or private
sectors. Some might sit for the ESLCE examinations; if successful, they could be admitted to one of the faculties or colleges of
the national university.

The committee appointed by the Council of Ministers also
commented upon the practical areas of industrial arts, home economics, commercial training, and agriculture. They felt that in
some subjects the curriculum had not been fully developed,
while in others it was nonexistent. The agricultural syllabus was
simply a list of headings, and industrial arts had not been carried
beyond grade eight. No books or materials had been produced
to cover these courses, although in some schools foreign materials were available. On the whole, there seemed to be some confusion of thought as to whether these courses were meant to

widen cultural horizons or whether they were simply to be looked upon as job training. The committee then recommended that the schools should begin to take the form of multilateral institutions providing either education in an academic stream leading to university attendance or general education and specific training of a terminal nature in nonacademic areas such as industrial arts, commerce, agriculture, and home economics.[27]

The report of the committee expressed concern over the lack of teaching materials. They identified the factors that hampered the provision of equipment, textbooks, and supplies to schools as lack of a proper scale of equipment and supplies; problems of relations with the auditor general's office; inefficiency in distribution; out-of-date regulations; lack of organization in recent years; and the absence of adequate financial resources. The committee had noted that there was no consistent method of distributing textbooks. Students purchased their own or had textbooks rented to them or issued on signature, and some students were denied textbooks altogether. The committee concluded: "There will be little possibility of any large change for the better in the effectiveness of Ethiopian education until this situation has been reviewed with the objective of creating realistic regulations."[28]

A 1971 conference of secondary school directors in Addis Ababa also raised the textbook problem. "No textbook at all, not even one reference book for the teacher, is available for certain subjects. There is a dearth of basic reference books, e.g., a small low-cost dictionary. . . . But even when the books are available, they rarely arrive at the schools in time for the school's opening, because of the complex channelling and intricate bureaucracy involved. . . . "[29] After 1970 the policy was that all students should be required to purchase their own books at cost, but field surveys indicated that only a small fraction were able or willing to do this, while the rest went without.

The lack of teaching materials and qualified teachers, as well as the language problem, contributed to handicapping the students at both the primary and secondary levels. This effect could have been minimized, if not entirely overcome, had they not been additionally handicapped by a traditional approach to teaching. Most teaching was routine lecturing, most learning rote learning, and most teachers taught for the examination and not for the inherent values of the subject. The committee recommended to the ministry that it should develop teaching aids and a variety of in-service programs for teachers.[30]

Structural Revisions

The administration and supervision of education had meanwhile evolved into a complex governmental structure. After April 1966, the portfolio of minister of education and fine arts was transferred to a cabinet minister, and the National Board of Education became nonfunctional, although it was never officially dissolved. According to a UN Report of 1969, the Ministry of Education then had a staff of about 15,000, the largest of all the development ministries. More than 10 percent of the staff were expatriates, of whom 1,450 were secondary school teachers and 81 were nonteaching personnel.

There was in general a great excess of personnel, especially in the administrative services. This was accompanied by a "low level of efficiency"—the consequence of the poor quality of recruitment, so that the best people were attracted by other government agencies or the private sector—and poor management, with responsibility not intelligently allocated. At the same time, there was a shortage of qualified, professional staff in some departments.[31]

In 1963–64, teacher training was standardized and entry level fixed at grade ten, with a two-year program provided. The committee appointed by the ministry in 1965 set up an official national curriculum, stipulating that 50 percent of learning time be devoted to teacher training. Between 1967 and 1969 this conventional approach was supplemented by two curriculum workshops conducted by the ministry with participation by subject specialists, UNESCO representatives, and others. The results of the workshops were forwarded to the teacher-training institutes (TTIs) as official curriculum guides, but with the passage of time disparity arose again between one institute and another.

For each of the fifteen major administrative divisions (fourteen provinces and Addis Ababa, Bale having been created after the union with Eritrea), a Provincial Education Office was established, headed by a provincial education officer (PEO). The PEOs and their staffs were regarded as local representatives of the ministry, having responsibility for the whole range of educational activities within their provinces.

Soon after the establishment of the land tax for provincial elementary education in 1947, provincial education boards were instituted to supervise the expenditure of these revenues. It had been intended that the boards would assist the PEOs in this regard, but apparently they failed to carry out this function and were of little support.

The provinces are divided into 102 *awrajas* (districts). At the head of most of the *awrajas* was an officer responsible for education activities within his district. Lacking experience and training and uncertain of their authority, they were termed a "stumbling block in the development of Ethiopian education."[32] By 1965 most of the *awrajas* had officers with no qualifications at all, who could not be expected to render any useful service to the cause of education. Each government elementary school was headed by a director directly responsible to his *awraja* officer, but in 1965 it was found that, of 992 elementary schools, only some 180 were headed by a director trained for the job. Assignment was supposed to be made on merit and capability, but more often than not "elementary school directors were appointed otherwise than on the basis of professional ability."[33]

Qualified secondary school professionals were also in short supply. By 1966 there were only three foreign school directors in government secondary schools, and young, inexperienced Ethiopians were put in as directors. There continued to be a large turnover of directors, and the secondary schools suffered from a lack not only of experienced direction but also of continuity in administration. Hence, there was a serious dislocation— one is tempted to say crisis—in all five of the component units of education: students, teachers, facilities, curriculum, and administration. It would have been all too easy for the committee, as they said, "not to be so blunt and critical, but this would have been self-deception and contrary to the real interests of Ethiopia and her people."[34]

Teacher Training

The Ministry of Education and the university jointly decided to launch in-service programs for education officers, and about a hundred candidates were selected for a one-year course at the university. The ministry paid full salary during training. Certification programs included professional courses such as school administration and curriculum, as well as academic courses. Between 1963 and 1970, 740 people graduated. Later, the in-service activity was conducted during the long summer vacations.[35] Graduates replaced some of the unqualified personnel, but more remained to be done to upgrade the qualifications of school leaders.

Around 1962, the three-tier system (6–2–4) became operational. In line with this development, teacher training at all levels was reorganized and improved. In 1964 the government entered into an agreement with UNESCO and UNICEF for the further improvement and expansion of teacher education. The objectives included strengthening primary teacher training and the organization of in-service programs. A separate Teacher Education Department was established with the ministry. An adviser and two teachers were provided by UNESCO, and a salary subsidy for up to twenty-four Ethiopian teacher instructors was offered.

Under this agreement, all existing teacher-training institutes were equipped with teaching aids and instructional materials at a cost of $12,500 for each institute. Although four, and later five, TTIs were functioning under pressure, the number of graduates was not able to match the demand. As a result, it became necessary to resort to various shortcuts. This could be done so long as quality was not sacrificed for quantity, but with limited teaching personnel and facilities the goal was very hard to achieve.[36]

Between 1963 and 1969 a number of attempts were made to standardize the curriculum of the TTIs, but with the passage of time and the frequent turnover of instructional staff, disparities continued to occur between one institute and another. This created serious problems for students, as they were required to sit for national examinations after being taught from syllabi that had never been coordinated.

As far as content was concerned, the curriculum of the TTIs included rural science, arts, crafts, wood carving, leather work, nutrition, child care, dressmaking, and cooking. These subjects were designed to make elementary education oriented to everyday life, but teachers were often required to teach subject matter without much relevance. This was reflected in the barrenness of elementary school premises—no gardens, vegetable plots, or tree plantations, no handicrafts or music.[37]

"One of the main problems associated with the curriculum is the apparent lack of correlation between what is taught at the institutes and what students are required to teach in the schools," the ministry reported. The problem rested primarily with the elementary school system. Teachers were taught to handle subjects such as rural science, physical education, and home economics in a very practical way, and thus were taught to be generalists, yet when they reported to their posts they were required "to teach as specialists in a narrow academic range, and the practical and functional subjects were frequently neglected."

The qualifications of teachers generally had been low throughout the previous twenty years. During this decade marked improvements took place. In 1962–63, 62 percent of the teachers were of eighth grade level or lower, with no teacher training. By 1967–68 that percentage was reduced to 12 percent, and by 1970–71 the number of teachers of elementary education level without teacher training was reduced to 5 percent.[38] Wastage of elementary teachers leveled off at about 10 percent during the decade. The effect of this high rate of turnover was felt the more because most of the people who left the profession were the better qualified ones.[39] The ministerial committee attributed the high turnover to unfavorable salaries (as compared with alternative employment) and the lack of a satisfactory salary increment policy; the widespread feeling among teachers that they occupied a low status in society; poor administration and unprofessional treatment by officials in the provincial education offices and headquarters; and the prospect of service in hardship areas without due reward.[40] The committee felt and rightly added that it would be possible for the Ministry of Education to take more interest in the teacher as a professional trying to do a difficult job. "Teachers must not be allowed to feel neglected, ignored or trodden upon by the various levels of officialdom. They must be given assistance and encouragement. . . . "[41]

After the new grade structure (6–2–4) came into full operation in 1963–64, the need to prepare special teachers for the different cycles was apparent. For the junior secondary school curriculum, designed to provide general education as well as vocational, trained teachers were needed. Haile Selassie I University assumed the responsibility of producing these teachers, who were recruited from those who had completed grade twelve and had passed two or three subjects of the ESLCE. They were given two years of training in the university and a third year out in the country as part of their service requirement. This scheme worked well for some years, but as time went on the objectives of training for these teachers became confused. When it was realized that the Faculty of Education was not producing the kind and number of teachers required by the ministry, a Junior Secondary Teacher Training College was established in 1969 in Addis Ababa by the ministry.

However, for lack of a well-qualified staff of its own, the new college had to rely on part-time teachers drawn from the various faculties of the university and elsewhere. As the Teacher Education Division of the ministry noted: "What had eventuated was not so much a Junior Secondary Teacher Training College as a junior University, teaching an academically oriented curriculum . . . unrelated to the needs of the junior secondary schools."[42]

In the meantime the qualifications of junior secondary teachers remained very low. The teaching force in 1971 was 1,582 nationals and 115 expatriates. Out of these, 7.6 percent had the necessary diploma, 1.4 percent had a university degree, and 51 percent were TTI graduates. In other words, only 9 percent of the teachers were really qualified to teach at the junior secondary level.[43]

Teachers for the senior secondary schools were either graduates of the Faculty of Education of the university, expatriates recruited under contract, or Ethiopian graduates of overseas universities. In 1965 the estimated number of senior secondary school teachers was 424 Ethiopians, 349 foreigners, and 297 volunteers, mainly from the United States Peace Corps and from France. The 646 foreign teachers thus constituted the majority in secondary schools. The committee established by the Council of Ministers felt that the senior secondary teaching force fell far short of the required standards. For instance, only forty-nine of the Ethiopian teachers employed had degrees, many of the United States Peace Corps volunteers had no experience in teaching, and the 194 Ethiopian University Service students had not yet completed their training. Only 40 percent of the senior secondary teachers were Ethiopian (and only 10 percent of these were qualified), and many of them taught sports, home economics, handicrafts, and so forth. Many who were unqualified were teaching Amharic. Of the expatriate staff, nearly half were volunteers, and these served for only two years. Perhaps only a fifth of the senior secondary school teachers had adequate qualifications and teaching experience.[44]

The committee observed that the salaries of Ethiopian graduate teachers were not competitive with those in other professions, a fact largely responsible for the small number of Ethiopians serving in the field. The committee added rather sadly: "It has become clear to the Committee that young Ethiopian graduates do not regard secondary school teaching as a satisfactory career. . . . a number of students have actually repaid sums as large as $500 to the University to free themselves of any obligation to teach. . . . Serious steps must be taken by the Ministry of Education to stop this wastage of specially trained personnel."[45]

The committee found that the average salary of an expatriate teacher was only $10 per month above the starting salary of an Ethiopian graduate, and the average increment received was $30. This was ridiculous in view of the fact that the average length of service was about six years. Then followed the bitter comment: "Not only has the Ministry of Education taken no reasonable steps to retain its valuable core of expatriate teaching staff but, in a highly competitive market, . . . it has offered conditions which have become increasingly unlikely to attract good teachers to the country. Initial salaries . . . have remained unchanged for at least the past 20 years."[46]

Finally, the 1966 report of the ministerial committee concluded:

> The present personnel are woefully inadequate in numbers, training and experience in all categories. . . . To a certain extent, it is true to say that the Ministry of Education has not been adequately financed for this purpose, but, at the same time, a great deal of the responsibility lies with the Ministry of Education itself since the personnel policy and administration can only be described as careless, haphazard, illogical and chaotic. The impact of this situation on the quality of education which is made available to the nation's children cannot be overestimated.[47]

Over the decade in question the percentage of female students in teacher-training schools had increased from 2 percent to almost 18 percent. In 1970, more girls applied than could be accommodated, but the representation of women teachers in the school system was still much lower than in any other country, including others in Africa. For instance, by 1970 26 percent of the teachers in Africa as a whole were female. The comparable figure for Latin America was 46 percent and for Canada, Australia, and New Zealand, 66 percent.[48] By comparison, Ethiopia's 10 percent was small indeed. Clearly, much more effort was needed to attract women teachers into the school system.

On the whole, however, the quality of teachers at all levels of the grade school system had greatly improved during the decade between 1962 and 1972. In the elementary schools, the objectives of Ethiopianization had been virtually realized, but at the level of the general secondary, TTI, and vocational-technical schools, the majority of the teaching staff were still expatriates, with all the instability and higher expenses that this circumstance entailed.

Furthermore, in 1970, only 18.4 percent of Ethiopian senior secondary school teachers met the minimum standard, 48.6 percent had not had any kind of teacher training, and 16 percent were graduates of elementary school training institutes.[49] Thus the general situation for secondary school teachers was not much brighter than in 1965.

School Plant
It will be worthwhile to give some consideration to the school plant in which these developments took place during these years. The ministerial committee of 1966 found that, in general, elementary education was housed in minimal physical surroundings, very often in a bad state of repair, with no allowance made for specialized accommodations like libraries, workshops, or laboratories. Most elementary school students had little introduction to practical work and had no experience in using a school library.[50]

In June 1965, it had been agreed by the Ministry of Education and the International Development Agency of the Swedish government that the latter would provide a group of Swedish volunteers to help construct elementary school classrooms under the supervision of the Building College and the Ministry of Education. Over the next three years, 109 elementary schools were built,[51] and in 1968 the agreement was extended to coincide with the third Five-Year National Development Plan. A special unit known as the Elementary School Building Unit (ESBU) was es-

tablished within the Ministry of Education. It was stipulated that
ESBU would build and furnish elementary schools in rural areas
and that the two governments would each contribute 50 percent
of the cost. The Ethiopian government undertook to provide
appropriate accessible sites in Addis Ababa and to pay the salaries of the Ethiopian personnel. The Swedish government paid
the cost of Swedish experts and consultants and provided for the
training of Ethiopians outside the country. As long as the contract was in effect, maintenance was to be undertaken by ESBU
and to be paid for jointly.

The plan called for an expenditure of 64 million Ethiopian
dollars during the five-year period. The plan targets were not
fulfilled: only $29 million was forthcoming from Ethiopia. As of
March 1973, however, some 3,644 classroom units had been
completed and furnished.

Although the Ethiopian government assumed final responsibility, it was actually the communities where these schools were
built that raised the matching funds. They learned to cooperate
for the common good, and the program gave them a sense of
achievement and the feeling that the schools did indeed belong
to them. The building activities were spread over the fourteen
provinces. Happily, the rural areas, which had previously been
neglected, received 85 percent of the schools. Sixty-two percent
replaced government primary schools, and 38 percent were located where no primary school had previously existed.[52]

The need for additional elementary schools was partially met
by this new and rather imaginative arrangement, and more buildings were constructed by local community efforts. The agreement with Sweden was extended until the end of 1974.

Secondary school buildings varied from good to very bad.
Some of the original ones, mainly in Addis Ababa, were constructed with the requirements of the secondary program in mind
and did provide for library, workshop, and laboratory needs. As
the system expanded to new locations, however, less and less
provision was made for the special requirements of secondary
education. As the 1965 committee pointed out, the second-level
schools were created to a large extent out of existing elementary
school classrooms, at the expense of elementary enrollment. On
the whole, the secondary schools in Addis Ababa and Asmara
were better equipped than in any other part of the country.[53]

After lengthy negotiations that began soon after the 1961 Conference of African States, the Ministry of Education in December 1974 concluded an agreement with the International Development Association (IDA), an affiliate of the International Bank for Reconstruction and Development (IBRD), for a loan to be used for the expansion of secondary education over a four-year period. The credit enabled the ministry to increase enrollment and to reorganize the structure and curriculum. New schools were erected nearer the homes of rural people, thus effecting a more equitable and rational geographical distribution of secondary schools throughout Ethiopia.

The project was designed to produce eighty-three general secondary schools. Of these, forty-two were senior secondary schools, twenty-one were existing schools that needed extension, ten were existing schools that required rebuilding on new sites, and ten were completely new. All but one of these were also to have junior secondary sections, of which almost all were new constructions. The project also included the construction of forty-two separate and new junior secondary facilities.

The plan additionally made provision for the extension of technical, vocational, and elementary teacher-training institutes. The Addis Ababa Technical School and the Asmara Trade Institute were to be enlarged and the equipment upgraded. At Dire Dawa and Jimma, two vocational training units were to be constructed, equipped, and furnished through the loan. The Addis Ababa Teacher Training Institute was to be expanded to an enrollment of 500 and an output of 250 per year. A new teacher-training school was to be established at Jimma, with a capacity of 300 and a yearly output of 150 trained teachers. The project included the construction of student hostels and teachers' housing at certain locations where these facilities were needed, and the provision of six "master teachers," who would travel to supervise the general secondary system. For all these items a total of 23.15 million Ethiopian dollars was requested and granted.[54] In 1965, the ministerial committee noted: "The details of this project [the IDA loan] give some indication of the inadequacy of the present secondary school system. Of the total capital sum . . . all but $471,000 . . . is to be spent on the rebuilding and extension of existing secondary schools."[55]

The program was held up by delays in payments to contractors. In 1968 it was estimated that, if there were no further delays, an additional 27 schools might be ready for use in September 1969.[56] This was, of course, far short of the 84 schools envisaged, and even if payments could have been made on time at that late hour, it was not anticipated that the first IDA agreement could be carried out by the end of the 1969–70 school year as planned.

In April 1971 another loan agreement was concluded between the Ethiopian government and IDA. The $23,750,000 interest-free loan was largely to be devoted to teacher training, and the largest sum of all was set aside for the establishment of the Academy of Pedagogy at Bahr Dar, with its own training facilities.[57]

Dynamics of Growth

As the school plant expanded, the growth pattern of the government educational system as a whole was steady though uneven through the decade. During the school year 1970–71, there were about 800,000 students taught by 19,000 teachers in 2,500 schools. This meant that enrollment was growing faster than the recruitment of teachers or the expansion rate of school facilities and, further, that heavy teaching loads and overcrowded classrooms were the inevitable consequences.

The growth rate of the nongovernment system was higher. This was another indication of parents' desire for more education for their children. Since the government system was not responding as fast as the need, people were resorting to nongovernment schools, most of which were concentrated at the primary level. Within the nongovernment school system, the mission schools enrolled the largest number, with an average growth rate of about 9 percent. The growth rate in the private schools averaged 10 percent and in the church schools 3 percent. The rate of growth in the private schools was significant, a direct reversal of what had prevailed some thirty years before, when people had to be cajoled into sending their children to school at all. It is also worth noting that the average enrollment of girls in government primary schools remained at 28.4 percent during this period, but a steady gain, beginning at 23 percent in 1960–61 and reaching 29 percent in 1971–72, was encouraging.

Among nongovernment schools, mission and private schools

had initially the highest percentage of female students, the church schools the lowest. In 1970–71, the private schools had gone far ahead (35 percent), followed by the mission and church schools in that order. Female enrollment in the church system had grown faster than in the rest, however, from 16 percent in 1960 to almost 30 percent ten years later. More girls were turning to the private schools, indicating a change in attitude on the part of female students and their parents toward education. Growth patterns were uneven from one year to the next; sometimes even negative growth was recorded. Enrollment of female students grew faster than male enrollment throughout the entire period but remained relatively low in specialized schools.

During this period, the aims of education also changed, and there was some emphasis on technical and practical education. The system originally designed to produce administrative personnel for government services had now broadened into a comprehensive structure supplying diverse sorts of people for a variety of levels of government and private employment. Most important, however, was the fact that educational objectives now included the long-range aim of universal education. Although qualitative progress was made and the system developed structurally, there were still very many problems needing urgent resolution.

Even though the system expanded more than fourfold during this decade, the students enrolled in 1973 for full-time education at the various levels still represented only a small fraction of the young people in the country.

Table 11 presents a comparative study of government elementary school enrollment (ages seven to twelve years) as a percentage of the total age-group. In 1956, the 129,379 pupils enrolled in all government elementary schools represented only 4 percent of the total age-group. By 1961 the figure had grown to 5 percent, by 1965 to 8 percent, and by 1972–73 it had reached 14 percent. It can be argued, of course, that the figures did not include those children enrolled in nongovernment schools, but certainly elementary enrollment figures were far below those envisaged at the Addis Ababa conference in 1961, which had anticipated that there would be some 75 to 80 percent elementary enrollment by 1973.

As the Ministry of Education's annual report of 1968–69 indicates, the city of Addis Ababa and the provinces of Shoa and

TABLE 11.   Enrollment in Government Elementary Schools as
             Percentage of Primary School Age-Group, 1956–73

Year	Total Enrollment	Percentage of Age-Group Enrolled
1956–57	129,379	4.2
1957–58	142,471	4.6
1958–59	149,410	4.7
1959–60	162,700	5.0
1960–61	147,805	5.3
1961–62	100,533	5.3
1962–63	204,410	5.9
1963–64	234,440	6.6
1964–65	257,436	7.2
1965–66	283,275	7.7
1966–67	312,207	8.2
1967–68	338,737	8.8
1968–69	382,360	9.7
1969–70	430,758	10.7
1970–71	470,983	11.5
1971–72	525,695	12.4
1972–73	588,868	13.5

Sources: Ministry of Education and Fine Arts, Current Operation of the Education System in Ethiopia, p. 89; Central Statistical Office, Statistical Abstract 1971, p. 195; Ministry of Education Planning Unit and CSO for data, years 1966 through 1973, to reach estimated primary school age groups.

Eritrea shared 25 percent of the primary school age population. These three areas had 41 percent of the total primary school enrollment and 50 percent of that in grade six. Increase in enrollment continued to favor those privileged locations,[58] although approximately 90 percent of the Ethiopian people lived in rural areas. The report said: "If many of these [rural] areas are to be provided with primary schools and an effective system of education, this activity must be matched by parallel efforts, particularly with regard to the development of communication and the regrouping of rural or nomadic peoples."[59]

In 1968–69 there were still thirteen awrajas in which even primary school enrollment was not likely to reach 5 percent of the school age population. These included Lasta, Ambasel, Wadla, Delanta, Were Himeno, Genale, Delo, El Kere, Garamuleta, and the five awrajas of the Ogaden. In the third Five-Year Development Plan, it was proposed to reach into the backward areas with at least primary education. The ministry had tried to bring about an equitable distribution, but as late as 1973 the solution to the problem continued to be elusive, and the school system in the favored regions continued to expand faster than in the disadvantaged rural areas. As late as 1972–73, out of the 418 *weredas* (subdistricts) in the country, 28 were without an elementary school. The situation was even worse at the second level of education.

Second-level education included not only junior and senior academic or general secondary schools, but also the vocational-technical schools and the teacher-training institutes. Since 1963, grades seven and eight had been called junior secondary schools, and grades nine through twelve senior secondary schools. The technical-vocational and teacher-training schools were approximately the equivalent of grades ten through twelve. Within the senior secondary school system there were the academic and "comprehensive" schools. The former concentrated on traditional academic subjects, while the latter included commercial, technical, industrial, and home economic fields, as well as the academic subjects. In the comprehensive secondary schools, students were encouraged to choose their area of concentration according to their capacity, aptitude, and interest. The technical-vocational streams were usually regarded as terminal, while the academic streams led to the possibility of university admission. In practice, however, either group might sit for the Ethiopian School Leaving Certificate Examination. In 1971–72, there were 76,338 students in the 368 junior secondary schools and 61,353 in the 105 senior secondary schools. By contrast, enrollment in the 6 vocational-technical schools was only 5,737, and there were 2,875 students in the 10 teacher-training institutes. The government system enrolled about 85 percent of the junior secondary school students, 90 percent of the senior secondary school students, and 96 percent of the TTI students. At the vocational-technical school level enrollment in the government schools was only about 60 percent. At the primary, general secondary, and tertiary levels, enrollment had exceeded the set targets, but in the special areas such as technical-vocational and teacher-training, plan targets fell short by as much as 50 percent in some instances.

At second level there were 368 junior secondary schools, of which 242 were government-controlled. The senior secondary schools totaled 105, of which 59 were government-operated in

1972–73. There were 60 vocational-technical schools, of which 26 belonged to the government. Of the 10 TTIs, 5 belonged to the government.

The main technical-vocational schools of the ministry were the Technical School (Addis Ababa), the Vocational Trade School (Asmara), and the Polytechnic Institute (Bahr Dar). In addition there were other trade, nursing, and vocational schools operated by other ministries and nongovernment organizations. In 1968–69 the enrollment in technical-vocational schools was about 15 percent of that in senior secondary schools. Approximately one-third of the students were in four schools under the Ministry of Education, one-fourth in thirty other government schools, and the rest in forty private or mission schools. The increase noted in enrollment was almost entirely concentrated in nongovernment schools.[60]

On the whole, at all levels of education in the different types of schools, teacher-student and classroom-student ratios remained higher than expected. The comforting aspect was that at the elementary level, although the teacher–student ratio fell short of expectations, the quality of teachers improved greatly over the years. The pupil retention rate grew from 37 to 45 percent between 1968 and 1970.[61] At the junior secondary level, the quality of teachers was very much below expectation. As late as 1972–73, more than 60 percent remained unqualified.

In the senior secondary schools, reliance was placed on recruitment of Peace Corps and other volunteer teachers from America and Europe, as well as on foreign teachers on contract, most of them from India. Many of the Haile Selassie I University students were engaged to teach during their one year of national service. The rest of the teaching force was made up of Ethiopian teachers, the majority of whom were unqualified. Thus the number of unqualified teachers was high, and the quality of senior secondary school education was adversely affected by its rapid, uncontrolled growth and consequent overcrowding. Workshops, laboratories, and libraries were in short supply.

The committee that examined the quality of Ethiopian education during the last half of the decade noted: "The Committee has reached the clear conclusion that, in encouraging a quantitative growth in the education system in recent years, insufficient attention has been paid to the quality and type of education given. Resources have been limited but, at the same time, resources have been wasted. Many students have emerged from various levels in the school system ill-equipped for employment or further training."[62]

As we have seen, student attrition had always been a problem. One way to assess an educational system is to determine how many learners progress from one grade to the next with the minimum of student wastage. In 1960–61, 57 percent were promoted from grade one and the yearly progression was 77, 78, 71, 81, 82, and 101 percent respectively through the eighth grade. Thus the higher the grade, the higher the retention rate. The same held true for the rest of the period. At the same time, there was improvement for all grades as the years progressed. Two other facts stand out: the attrition rate was too high between first and second grades, but it declined slowly throughout the period.

At the secondary level, however, wastage was not entirely due to attrition. Many students were "tapped off" at grades nine, ten, or eleven for further training in the teacher-training institutes, the Air Force, and some twenty other government and nongovernment agencies. In 1964–65, 2,129 students were tapped off by no less than fourteen different agencies.[63]

The ministerial committee, after carefully examining the problem of student attrition in 1966, concluded that "money and effort spent on a child who enters grade 1 but does not complete grade 6 are money and effort thrown away and scarce resources wasted. At the moment, only one child in six of those who enter grade 1 completes the elementary course."[64] What was said in 1966 would, with slight modifications, apply just as well in 1973.

Educational Technology

Given Ethiopia's varied physical characteristics, comprising for the most part a complex of plateaus and deep gorges, mountains and steep escarpments, communication—especially during the long rainy seasons—is difficult. Nevertheless, if education, including adult education, was to make headway, various forms of mass media would have to be utilized.

Schools located away from the few major urban centers had little access to resources that would assist the teacher in the classroom. Newspapers, magazines, and supplementary books were rare, and even materials from which teachers could make their own illustrative teaching aids were either in short supply or nonexistent in many of the rural schools. At the same time, the shortage of trained personnel meant that experience and proven ability were often thinly spread, and it was not always possible for support services to reach the inexperienced teacher in remote locations. Finally, we know that the vast majority of school age children were not able to find a place in the formal school system and might reach adulthood without having had any basic education or training. A solution other than the traditional classroom approach had to be found.

In response to these needs, the establishment and use of new educational technologies, especially those of radio and television, were imperative. Hence in 1968 the Ministry of Education established an educational media center in Addis Ababa, which would produce, transmit, and store on tapes educational radio and television programs; provide ancillary services for photographic works and graphics, as well as library services for visual and sound materials (films, slides, tapes, wall charts, and the like) for schools; and furnish maintenance services for mass media equipment.[65]

The mass media offered an important new tool for literacy and basic education, as well as for regular classroom instruction. Experiments in the teaching of reading and writing by radio, initially conducted by experts in radio education supplied by a local business firm, had been going on since the early 1960s in the Ministry of Education. The experiments had been encouraging,[66] and it was decided to expand them.

After the establishment of the new Mass Media Center, an educational radio project was started in earnest in 1969. During the first semester, lessons were beamed to fifty-six elementary schools in Menagesha *awraja* (around Addis Ababa). In November, 262 radio sets were distributed to senior secondary schools, and senior secondary transmissions were added to the broadcast schedule. Radio lessons were prepared to supplement the teaching of Amharic, English, history, geography, and science. A total of 151 hours of original broadcasts was transmitted to the schools. The following year there were 180 hours of original broadcasts, with emphasis on lessons geared for primary rather than secondary schools. A total number of 126 primary schools, 59 secondary schools, and 10 adult education centers were involved in the radio project by the end of 1971.[67]

A full trial year of educational television was carried for the first time in Addis Ababa in 1965. Programs in English, biology, chemistry, physics, geography, and health were transmitted to fifteen secondary schools in the city. Wtih the assistance of the United Kingdom, staff were trained and the nucleus of an educational television center established. All secondary schools in the area were supplied with television sets, and about 3,000 students received television instruction as part of their regular school attendance. By 1969–70, 49 schools with 68 television sets were participating, and the following year saw an increase to 103 schools and 143 sets.

Later the emphasis shifted to the junior secondary schools and to adult education broadcasts. More attention was paid to upgrading the quality of lessons transmitted, and telecasts were extended to a few outlying areas. In the Mass Media Center a new videotape machine with a fifty-hour supply of tapes was installed, and the center received 175 television sets for distribution to schools from the United Kingdom and Japan.

Modern technology needs to be put to even wider uses. In the solution of innumerable problems—lack of teachers, shortage of equipment, inexperience of instructors for practical work, shortage of visual material, large class size—the wise use of modern electronic devices would be a boon.[68]

The "Your Light Is Today" night school had been established in 1948 in response to a need for adult education, and in the early 1960s there had been a program for adults known as "fundamental education" under the supervision of the ministry. In 1967 the Adult Education and Literacy Department, headed by a director general within the Ministry of Education and Fine Arts, was created.

In 1968 the National Advisory Council was formed to be responsible for guiding the nationwide literacy drive. In the same year the United Nations Special Fund (UNSF) Work-Oriented Literacy Project was initiated and it soon undertook to coordinate its work with that of the Mass Media Center. A research project in mass media communication for literacy purposes was started, and a monthly newspaper launched for new literates.

Although the beginning was promising, the project encountered problems of insufficient staff and shortage of funds. Only ten of the thirteen experts to be appointed by UNESCO/

UNSF actually came, and several of them were late in arriving. Out of thirty-one professional positions, only ten were filled, and of the nonprofessional establishment only seven out of twenty-seven were actually on the job. This state of affairs not only hampered the work of the project but also reflected on the degree of commitment to the project on the part of the Ethiopian government. In spite of the difficulties, the 1971–72 annual report of the ministry struck an optimistic note: "In the last few years, 1,213,088 adults were taught to read and write and 180,168 attended primary, secondary and college level schools. This year, 1,122,920 have attended. . . . "[69]

A number of experimental materials were produced, intended for wider application later, and ways in which educational activities of this kind might fit into a pattern for rural regeneration and development were explored.[70] A major question was whether the newly literate would remain so or lapse back into illiteracy after a few months, if nothing were done to maintain learning activities and interest.

Legislation and Finance

During the decade there was a limited amount of legislation relevant to education. After 1947, the only tax for the support of education was the rural land tax for the elementary schools, which we have discussed above. Secondary and tertiary education were financed from the central treasury. As time progressed, it became clear that the richer provinces were better off than the poorer ones in terms of elementary educational development. Further, while the rural landowners and the poor peasants shouldered the burden for education, the salary earners and urban property owners who were benefiting the most were not directly contributing their fair share of tax. Although it did not achieve what was first hoped, the Additional Educational Taxes Proclamation was supposed to reduce these imbalances. This law provided that, beginning in 1970, an education tax would be payable annually by all those subject to urban land tax, at a rate equal to 30 percent of the amount payable. Further, it included a 2 percent tax on personal income.[71]

In 1970–71, the total amount of tax collected rose to over $12 million, and in the following year to $14 million, doubling previous collections. This seemed to be the answer for primary education but the Ministry of Finance insisted that the added tax money was part of the general revenue and not necessarily earmarked for education. In fact, much more than the earmarked money was required; hence it was essential that more money be invested by the central treasury.

During 1970–71, total funds available to the Ministry of Education and Fine Arts came to $77 million, out of which $67 million was raised by the Ministry of Finance through taxes and other fees. Community contributions for the building of primary schools came to approximately $1 million, and foreign grants and loans provided $9 million.

The Local Self-Administration Law was passed in 1966 to provide for *awraja* self-administration in such matters as public health, education, transportation, water supply, agriculture and community development, trade, and commerce.[72] The law was never actually applied, although newly trained *awraja* administrators were appointed in some nineteen districts.

In 1968 a charter was granted to the University of Asmara, a private institution supported by the religious congregation Piae Matres Nigritiae of Italy. The emperor allocated $200,000 in government funds towards the operation of the university, and the ministry was represented on the Board of Governors.[73] In addition, the National Commission for UNESCO was established under the Ministry of Education to coordinate educational, cultural, and scientific activities in close cooperation with UNESCO, and to facilitate cultural exchange between the people of Ethiopia and the people of the world.[74]

In 1966, the emperor transferred the portfolio of minister of education which he had assumed in the early 1940s, and a National Commission for Education was established in 1969. The commission was charged with studying and proposing ways to implement general educational objectives such as uniform educational opportunities for children and adults.[75] It was also empowered to engage experts for specific projects as the need arose and was given an annual budget.[76]

The responsibilities of the commission were broad and comprehensive. It heard testimony from people engaged in Ethiopian education, staff as well as students, and participated in the Education Sector Review concluded in 1972. Aside from these activities, however, it remained relatively inactive, and it can now be considered to have been superseded by new organizations created since February 1974.

From 1960 to 1974 capital expenditure for education was relatively small, and this adversely affected its quality. Expenditure by the ministry in 1970 was only 30 percent greater than in 1960. Teacher salaries were the largest element in recurrent expenditure, claiming over 90 percent of the total at the primary level. The same ratio obtained at the general secondary level, but teachers' salaries in technical and vocational institutes represented only approximately 75 percent, and in teacher-training institutes about 60 percent, of recurrent expense. Overall, salaries represented about 87 percent of costs, leaving little money for such important items as school supplies, school plant maintenance, and travel for supervision.

External assistance for education had played an important role in Ethiopia in the past. The ratio of external assistance to domestic resources had been increasing over the decade and was relied upon heavily by the Ministry of Education.[77] Still, foreign aid, offered in many forms—fellowships, technical assistance, capital investment, and loans—often had strings attached that were costly and disadvantageous. As the ministerial committee pointed out: "Frequently aid is offered on terms which do not represent any real advantage to Ethiopia, and such aid must be refused. For example, countries sometimes stipulate . . . that equipment and constructional materials must come from the aid-giving country. The high cost of such arrangements gives little benefit to Ethiopia. . . ."[78]

The financial efforts of the Ministry of Education were augmented by other agencies of government, semigovernmental organizations, foreign missions, private persons, and the Ethiopian Orthodox church. Government agencies other than the Ministry of Education and the university together spent $22 million on education. Of the rest, the private organizations raised most of their money from tuition and fees, the mission societies from external sources. The total expenditure on education during 1970–71 by all agencies and organizations came to $141.1 million.[79] At this time the Ministry of Education controlled $77.3 million, or approximately one-half of all expenditure on education in Ethiopia. Haile Selassie I University controlled $25.4 million, almost one-fifth of the country's expenditure, and the two together accounted for $102.7 million or 73 percent of all education expenditure.[80]

The problems confronting the Ministry of Education were more than those of obtaining and spending budgetary allocations, however. The ministerial committee identified a number of crucial problems faced by the ministry in arranging adequate financing of the school system. For example, budget estimates prepared by the Ministry of Education had never been approved in full, and the ministry had never received the total budget as published in the official *Negarit Gazeta*. Due to delay in approval processes for purchasing or for increments of staff salaries and due to the delay in the receipt of funds from the central treasury, it was often difficult for the ministry to make use of specific funds that had been approved in the budget. As a result, the provincial tax earmarked for education remained static. There was always a big gap between approved budget and actual expenditure; large funds were returned annually to the Ministry of Finance, and this was used as an argument against increases in the Ministry of Education's next budget.

In a 1967 publication, Mulugeta Wodajo wrote:

> The consequence of this acute shortage of funds was that the unit expenditure (excluding foreign aid) has been on the decline during the past ten years—from about Eth. $145 per child to about Eth. $86 in 1957 (Eth.C.). This is quite a sharp drop, especially in view of the fact that the Government now spends very little for elementary school construction, as most of this is now done by the communities themselves, with matching funds from the Swedish Government. Whatever the future of Ethiopian education may be, the nation should not be led to believe that at present everything is fine with the schools, for in the final analysis it is how much the Government is devoting from its own resources that is the real measure of the national effort and commitment to education.[81]

One way of evaluating Ethiopia's commitment to education is to compare her investment efforts with those of other African countries. In terms of the ratio of tax revenue spent on education, Ethiopia lagged behind. A group of economists who assessed the amount spent by Ethiopia concluded:

Ethiopia suffers from a lower GNP *per capita* than most countries in Africa. This creates a low tax base. But taxes collected are also a smaller proportion of the low GNP than in most other countries. And finally, out of the low tax revenue, a smaller proportion than in most other African countries is set aside to be spent on education; thus expenditure on education as a percentage of GNP (or GDP) was only 1.4 percent in 1968 against 2.5 (to) 6 percent in other African countries. . . . It is of course this fact that also explains that the Ethiopian enrollment ratio is lower than other African countries.[82]

It should also be noted that the unit costs of education for secondary schools were very low by international standards, and this permitted higher enrollment than would elsewhere have been possible.

TABLE 12. Ratio of Public Education Expenditure (PEE) to GNP and to Public Budget Expenditure and Ratio of Tax Revenue to GDP of Selected African Countries (in percentage)

Country	Ratio of PEE to GDP or GNP		Ratio of PEE to Total Public Expenditure		Ratio of Tax Revenue to National Income or GDP		GDP	
	1957–59	1965–68	1962–63	1966–68	1951–60	1961–67	1968	1969
C.A.E.[a]	2.1	3.3	10.6	17.0	—	15.6	19.6	−67
Ethiopia	—	1.4	7.9	10.0	—	8.1	8.7	8.9
Ghana	2.5	3.9	19.5	18.7	—	13.3	12.7	—
Kenya	3.0	4.5	22.9	18.4	13.4	12.1	13.8	—
Morocco	3.2	4.0	15.2	17.1	—	13.5	14.4	—
Nigeria	—	2.5	14.0	—	8.8	9.8	—	—
Sierra Leone	—	3.3	18.7	18.8	—	15.2	18.9	—
Sudan	—	5.4	29.1	20.3	9.0	10.9	—	—
Tanzania	2.7	2.8	—	—	—	11.6	14.8	−67
Uganda	4.0	2.8	19.5	12.5	—	12.1	13.9	13.8
Zambia	1.6	6.2	20.1	12.9	24.9	31.2	49.9	—
Average Africa	2–2.5	4	16.3	16.9	—	—	—	—

Source: Education Sector Review Conference, "Final Report:—Financing of Education," p. 52.
[a]Central African Empire

TABLE 13. Public and Private Expenditures of Selected Countries as a Percentage of Their GNP

Country	1960	1963	1964	1965	1966	1967
Ethiopia						
Public	—	1.4	1.1	1.2	1.4	1.4
Private	—	0.4	0.4	0.4	0.4	—
Kenya						
Public	4.6	4.8	4.8	5.6	—	—
Private	0.1	0.1	0.2	0.2	—	—
Malawi						
Public	3.6	—	4.6	4.9	5.4	5.0
Private	0.0	—	0.7	0.1	—	0.2
Sudan						
Public	2.5	1.9	2.2	2.8	4.5	5.4
Private	—	0.4	0.4	0.2	—	0.0
Zambia						
Public	1.8	3.6	4.3	6.0	6.2	—
Private	0.1	0.3	0.5	0.4	—	—
Canada						
Public	—	5.5	5.5	6.3	7.2	8.1
Private	—	0.1	0.2	0.2	0.1	0.1
Argentina						
Public	2.0	2.9	2.6	3.3	3.6	—
Private	0.3	0.3	0.6	0.4	0.5	—
Korea, Rep. of						
Public	—	—	2.5	1.8	2.0	2.4
Private	—	—	0.8	1.1	1.2	0.9
Australia						
Public	1.4	3.2	3.3	3.6	4.1	4.0
Private	—	0.7	0.7	0.6	0.6	1.1

Source: Education Sector Review Conference, "Final Report:—Financing of Education," p. 53.

More recently, further attempts were made to establish Ethiopia's relative position vis-à-vis other African countries. To establish the basis for such comparisons, determinants such as the relationship between public expenditure on education (PEE), gross domestic product (GDP), and gross national product (GNP), as well as the relationship between PEE per capita and GNP per capita have been used, as shown in tables 12 and 13. Other important determinants of the per capita expenditure on education were the school enrollment ratio, the tax effort, and the degree of urbanization. These determinants were used to measure the education efforts of African countries and are considered to be valuable indicators of effort.

The education profile of Ethiopia as seen against the diffuse and statistically unclear background of African developing countries was summed up by a group of experts commissioned to make a study of the problem in 1972.

> Ethiopia has one of the lowest enrollment ratios in Africa, which, coupled with high pupil-teacher ratios and comparatively low teacher salaries, gives Ethiopia the position of one of the countries falling far short of its potential as compared with other African countries. . . . The means available are spent on a comparatively lower proportion [in] primary education than in many other countries. There has been progress in Ethiopian education as measured by expenditure on education; percentage-wise, it might be even faster than in many other countries. But due to the low base, the gap seems to have widened during the 1960's. . . . However, the fact that other countries which have had as low a GNP per capita as Ethiopia only 10 or 20 years ago now manage to spend a much higher amount and larger proportion on education than in the past, spells out hope for Ethiopia.[83]

During the Decade of Africa, the education gap between Ethiopia and other African countries had grown wider and wider.

Chapter 9

Toward the Year 2000

Over the last twenty years the development of the Ethiopian educational system has been viewed with dissatisfaction, principally because it has failed to satisfy the aspirations of the majority of the people and to prepare in any adequate way those passing through its ranks. The most glaring of its shortcomings arose from the fact that both its objectives and the experiences it offered to children and youth were unrelated to Ethiopian realities, and thus its product was a younger generation unaware of and unappreciative of its own cultural heritage and roots. The school system was too elitist, rigid, and unresponsive to the various local needs. It sought to prepare students primarily for the next scholastic level and emphasized the passing of rigidly set examinations, whereas in fact most students dropped out before they attained employable skills. Educational opportunity was not equitably distributed among the regions of the country, favoring instead only a few provinces and urban centers, and administration was therefore highly centralized. In sum, flexibility and local community participation and initiative were inhibited in curriculum planning, personnel, and budgetary allocation and control.

For obvious reasons pressures were building up for change, from teachers, parents, and students. In response to these demands, the National Commission on Education was created in 1969 and charged with the responsibility of formulating an overall prospectus for Ethiopian education and of devising a workable method for the equitable distribution of educational opportunity. The commission spent its first year conducting hearings with students, parents, government officials, teachers, school directors, and private individuals, but little else was done and no tangible results were achieved.

In 1970 a team of university instructors, under the auspices of Haile Selassie I University with the author as chairman, developed proposals for a thorough review of the senior secondary school system. If the proposals were to be effectively carried out, they would require the cooperation of the Ministry of Education. After lengthy negotiations lasting over ten months, the ministry refused its obligations. The underlying reason for this refusal, as we learned, was the ministry's fear that the weaknesses in the operation of the schools would be exposed, embarrassing the ministry officials and the government in the eyes of the public. Nevertheless, public pressure continued to mount.

The Sector Review

At last the Ministry of Education felt compelled to respond to the need for a review of the entire educational sector. In 1971 an agreement was signed between the government and the International Development Association (IDA), an affiliate of the World Bank, by which IDA agreed to finance thirty-seven man-months for the carrying out of the project. Fourteen task forces, four of them appointed by the National Commission on Education (itself a relatively recent creation), and five small working groups constituted the core of the participants. There were eighty-one members, of whom fifty-one were Ethiopians drawn primarily from Haile Selassie I University as well as from the Ministries of Education, Agriculture, and Community Development, the Planning Commission, and a few other agencies of the government. Foreign members included government employees and representatives of UNESCO, International Labor Organization (ILO), the Ford Foundation, and Harvard University Development Advisory Service. The Education Sector Review was then launched to analyze the whole educational and training procedure, together with its capability for promoting economic, social, and cultural development; to suggest, wherever necessary, those means of improvement and expansion that would best promote social development and national integration; and to specify priority studies and investments to this end.

Various Ethiopian government agencies were consulted in the drawing up of the terms of reference. A symposium was held early in 1972 to consider the papers prepared by task force members and other invited individuals. This was followed by a conference held the following July to assess progress and to evaluate and finalize the draft report, which frankly stated: "The debates over fundamental concerns have shaped the nature of the ultimate recommendations and proposals of the Sector Review. At the same time they have evidenced a renewed faith in the future that portends well for the Ethiopian people."[1]

The report found that urban population was increasing generally at the rate of 6.6 percent annually, while rural population was growing by only 2.1 percent. If these trends continued, by the year 2000 the total population would be more than fifty-two million, with approximately two-thirds of the people in rural areas and one-third in towns and cities. Table 14 presents the total population figures as well as the numbers of children in various groups for selected years. These figures, based on Central Statistical Office estimates, were used to project educational requirements and costs for the country. The report made the difficulties clear:

TABLE 14. Population Estimates and Projection for 1 January of Selected Years, 1963–2000 (in millions)

Year[a]	All Ages			School Ages	
	Total	Urban	Rural	7–12	13–18
1963	20.7	1.5	19.2	3.3	2.7
1967	22.8	1.9	20.9	3.6	3.0
1969	24.0	2.2	21.8	3.8	3.2
1970	24.6	2.3	22.2	3.9	3.2
1971	25.2	2.5	22.7	4.0	3.3
1972	25.8	2.7	23.1	4.1	3.4
1973	26.4	2.8	23.6	4.3	3.4
1974	27.1	3.0	24.1	4.4	3.5
1975	27.8	3.2	24.6	4.5	3.6
1976	28.6	3.4	25.1	4.6	3.7
1977	29.3	3.7	25.6	4.7	3.8
1978	30.1	3.9	26.2	4.8	3.9
1979	30.9	4.2	26.7	5.0	4.0
1980	31.7	4.4	27.2	5.1	4.1
1985	36.1	6.2	29.9	5.8	4.8
1990	41.1	8.7	32.4	6.7	5.5
1995	46.6	12.2	34.4	7.5	6.2
2000	52.7	17.0	35.6	8.4	7.1

Source: Ethiopia, Ministry of Education and Fine Arts, Draft Report: Report of the Education Sector Review (Addis Ababa, 1972), p. II–A–1.

Note: Totals may not add up because of rounding.

[a]Years are G.C.

> There are great diversities. . . . The population includes
> farmers in the central highlands using oxen-drawn ploughs
> and living in scattered dwellings and isolated villages, in-
> cludes more densely concentrated groups in the Ensete
> [local crop] area of the south, pastoralists, desert nomads,
> and of course the urban dwellers. These groups differ
> widely, not as regards their way of life, region and language,
> but as regards the extent to which they are in touch with the
> more modern sectors of society and are subject to various
> forms of administrative control.[2]

It was rightly emphasized that Ethiopia's economy and educational system should be vitally and intimately interrelated, because
educational growth is dependent on finance, and economic growth
is dependent on the skilled personnel produced by the educational system. The Education Sector Review concluded that the
output from subsistence agriculture could increase very slowly, so
that by 1977 the dollar volume of the nonagricultural sector
would exceed that of the agricultural sector. By the end of the
century, however, two-thirds of the population would still be living in agricultural areas and earning their living from the land.

For the years 1969 to 1990, it was assumed that the average
per capita income would increase from $91 to $198. Total urban
income would increase more than fourfold, as would urban
population, but the average per capita income of this group
would rise only marginally, from $680 to $713. Rural incomes
would climb somewhat faster—from the low base of $109 in
1969 to $135 in 1990. Therefore, since the economy would be
growing more rapidly than the school age population, an increase
should be feasible in per capita expenditure for education. However, "the low level of rural incomes would provide a formidable
challenge for those concerned with education and development
generally."[3]

The review then turned to objectives, but it was felt that the
lack of a clear statement of national ideology (a major source of
complaint during the study) would make the task difficult, if not
impossible. It was generally agreed that Ethiopia, "a nation richly
endowed with national resources and cultural heritage," had the
following aspirations: to strengthen national unity by economic
growth and development and thereby ensure adequate living

conditions for all; to develop a democratic society founded in freedom, equality, and justice; to foster in all citizens a firm sense of right and responsibility; to shape a society appreciative of its heritage but imbued with a spirit of dynamism and innovation; and to build a self-reliant nation that would participate constructively in the African community of nations and the world. These were the comprehensive goals that education would have to reflect.[4]

The broad range of proposals and recommendations with respect to educational objectives was consolidated into three major alternative strategies on which future development could be based. In each, a major emphasis was placed on making basic education available to the maximum number of people as fast as possible, while second- and third-level education was to be made available as required by population and economic growth. Since the review has been internationally hailed as a model for educational development for the Third World, a brief outline of each strategy is given below.

Alternative Strategy I provided for a continuation of the existing 6–2–4 grade structure, but with significant changes. To achieve the goal of universal education, primary education would be expanded as rapidly as possible. Curricula would be made more practical and relevant by the inclusion of work-oriented and environmental studies. Economies in recurrent and capital costs would be achieved by operating the schools in two shifts of three and one-half hours each daily and by raising the annual number of days of school attendance from 180 to 220.

Alternative Strategy II suggested that the formal school system be restructured on a 4–4–4 basis, accompanied by major changes in curriculum and instructional methods in first- and second-level schools. As in all proposals, instruction would be oriented toward student participation rather than rote learning. Course material would be integrated into cohesive areas of study, instead of being taught as a number of discrete subjects. The language of instruction throughout would be Amharic, with other Ethiopian languages used as necessary in the early grades to teach Amharic. This second plan put strong emphasis on nonformal education, which would be institutionalized and programmed under "community practicums." Community practicums would serve those graduates of minimum formation education (MFE) who did not go to middle school. The concept would combine continuing education with some elements of apprenticeship. A higher level of practicums would be provided for those who left the second-level schools without going into third-level education.

To meet local and individual needs, different types of community practicums would be offered. Some would offer training in specific skills associated with such productive activities as potteries, tanneries, blacksmith shops, cement factories, sugar refineries, drafting, and surveying. Here participants would spend most of their time in practical on-the-job training and the rest in related classroom instruction. Participants would include those already employed in a particular field, as well as those being prepared for employment. The director of a practicum was envisioned as a skilled technician, craftsman, or extension agent who would provide on-the-job training. Classroom teachers would be recruited and trained for the purpose, and might include regular teachers in government schools who would be paid to teach in practicums after school hours.

Community practicums would not be part of the formal education system, but would be closely associated with it. School facilities would be made available after regular school hours for classwork. The craftsmen offering on-the-job training might also serve as community assistants, directing practical training in the spill-out MFE program. Each school associated with a community practicum would offer guidance to the director in curriculum and programming and would assist in determining textbook and workbook needs.

Strategy II thus would place a much greater emphasis than Strategy I on nonformal education. In the final year more than two million people would participate in organized nonformal programs, representing about 11 percent of the eleven-to-thirteen-year age-group and 8 percent of the nineteen-to-thirty-four-year group. Taking into account the number who would have participated in intervening years, the cumulative exposure to nonformal education would be appreciable over the course of time. In the ten-year period before the year 2000, nonformal educational programs would have been made available to more than three-quarters of the eleven-to-eighteen-year age-group and to more than half the nineteen-to-thirty-four-year age-group.

Alternative Strategy III, on the other hand, suggested two parallel channels of formal education: a 4–2–4 system that would include four years of MFE, followed by two years of junior secondary school for selected students and an additional four years of senior secondary education for certain students from the latter group; and a 2–3 program comprising two years of "basic formation." The two channels would be so coordinated that students could transfer from one program to the other. Strategy III would permit attainment of the goal of universal mass education within a relatively short time. By 1979–80, 39 percent of the nine-to-twelve-year age-group would be enrolled in school, and the rest would be attending basic formation programs a few years later. By the year 1983–84, nearly 90 percent of the children would have entered either a nongovernment program or a minimum formation.

This high proportion would be made possible by the use of the lower-cost minimum formation program. Participation rates would continue to climb. By 1989–90 about 57 percent of the nine-to-twelve-year age-group would be enrolled in minimum formation and nongovernment schools, with most of the other 43 percent headed for basic formation a few years later.

After 1989–90, basic formation would be gradually phased out, permitting the channeling of all funds and enrollment into four-year minimum formation programs. By the year 2000, basic formation would have served its purpose—that of rapidly expanding educational opportunity—and it would be discontinued. Virtually all relevant age-groups would then be enrolled in government MFE or in nongovernment schools, as follows:

Age Groups	1979–80	1984–85	1989–90	1994–95	1999–2000
Seven to ten (MFE and non-government)	44%	45%	50%	64%	80%
Thirteen to fourteen (Basic formation)	31%	31%	40%	40%	26%

Table 15 summarizes the three alternative strategies in terms of enrollment and expenditure for the years 1979 through 2000. Under all three, expenditure would be the same for higher education, mass media, administration, and subsidies for nonrecurrent expenditures.

TABLE 15.   Summary of the Recommended Strategy—Expenditure and Enrollment

	1979–80	1984–85	1989–90	1994–95	1999–2000
Expenditure, Total	190	263	387	564	835
Minimum					
Formation	52	74	98	166	305
Basic Formation	19	25	42	53	51
Second Level	38	49	68	86	109
Third Level	33	47	67	97	139
Nonformal	20	28	47	68	97
Other	28	40	63	92	133
Enrollment, Total	3,056	3,649	4,906	6,215	7,940
First Level	1,988	2,336	3,071	4,197	5,273
Second Level	220	257	301	353	416
Third Level	10	13	17	22	28
Nonformal	838	1,043	1,517	1,643	2,223

Source: Ethiopia, Ministry of Education and Fine Arts, *Draft Report: Report of the Education Sector Review* (Addis Ababa, 1972), Exhibit V–F–1.

Finally, after extended evaluation and debate, the Education Sector Review adopted a modification of Alternative II that would incorporate some aspects of Alternative III. The strategy finally recommended, which is depicted in figure 1, was as follows: four years of minimum formation education (grades one to four), to be available to all children as rapidly as finances permitted; two years of basic formation for youths who had been unable to attend elementary programs; four years of middle school and four years of senior secondary school for a limited number of graduates of MFE and basic formation; and extensive nonformal educational programs for youth and adults. It was projected that the net school participation rate would continue to increase until some 90 percent of the children born in 1982 would have access to education, and Ethiopia would in effect have achieved universal educational opportunity.

The expansion rate at the second and third levels of education was seen as dependent on the nation's needs for skilled manpower, and enrollment would therefore be adjusted accordingly. The final result would include an extensive nonformal educational program in community practicums and community center operations to serve youths and adults, related to the formal system and to overall programs of community development.

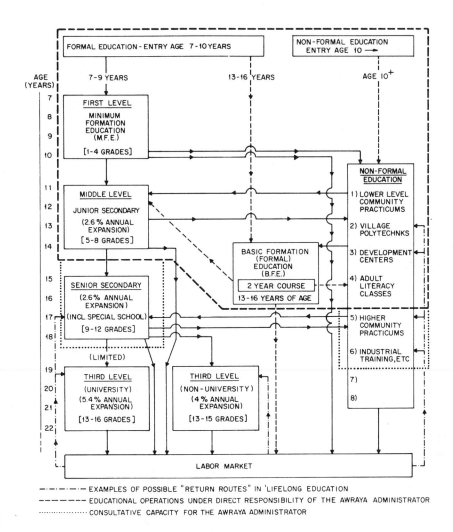

Fig. 1. Flow of students in the adopted strategy. (*Source:* Ministry of Education and Fine Arts, Planning Unit, "Summary of the Decisions of the Council of Ministers in the Education Sector Review Proposals" [Addis Ababa, 1973].)

Community centers would be established and expanded, particularly in rural areas, where farmers might be trained in improved agricultural methods. Farm cooperatives and model farms would be established to serve as distribution points for fertilizer, seed, and other supplies. The centers would also train housewives in home economics, child care, sanitation, nutrition, sewing, and the like, provide adult literacy courses, and conduct training in practical crafts.[5] The structure of the program would depend on local initiative, geographical location, and the extent to which they were related to *awraja* self-government plans. Community development centers would be closely related to the formal school system. They would serve also as operation bases for public works, which in turn would provide productive employment for youths and young adults, who could develop roads, dams, and forestation projects. Funding would be shared among the Ministry of Education, other interdepartmental governmental agencies, and the communities.

Effective implementation of the recommended program would of course require significant changes in teaching methods, curricula, and teacher attitudes. The TTI programs would be completely revised, with emphasis being placed on practical professional, rather than on academic, courses. English would not be taught as a subject at this level, and the language of instruction would be Amharic, since graduates would be teaching in Amharic in first-level schools. Candidates would be limited to those sixteen years or older. A one-year TTI program would be followed by a year of practice teaching and a summer seminar. In addition, a large-scale in-service training program would need to be launched. A separate department within the Ministry of Education and a National Advisory Council on Teacher Training (named in January 1974) would be established.

The Education Sector Review regarded the existing educational management as too highly centralized to achieve the necessary speed and efficiency. It asked that first-level educational matters be primarily the responsibility of the *awraja* Boards for Human Resources and of the local people. At the secondary level, the *awraja* and the provincial educational officers would take over the program.

The sentiment of participants in the review was best expressed by a concluding statement of the chairman: "Today we have before us a national model which is based on the impressive achievements of the past and turns the educational system around, making it stand on its head as it were, in order that it may . . . meet Ethiopian development needs for the coming three decades."[6] In making their final recommendations, the members were not unmindful of the problems of implementation. The Education Sector Review Conference had made it clear that, while the new plan could not be expected to solve all educational problems, the review should be regarded as a broad evaluative study focused on the most fundamental concerns. It attempted to point to horizons and to give direction to those responsible for the development of Ethiopian education. As the report said:

> Perhaps the greatest challenge in implementing the recom-
> mendations of the Sector Review . . . would be the need to
> reorient the attitudes of the people. . . . The present system
> is structured at all levels primarily to provide on-going aca-
> demic education. By contrast, the recommended system
> would provide a self-contained program at each level that
> would be terminal for most students. *Its adoption would re-
> quire recognition and acceptance of this by pupils, parents,
> teachers, educational administrators, and people from all facets of
> Ethiopian society* [author's italics].[7]

The necessary reorientation would be facilitated by changes in examination procedures, by the reorganization of TTI curric-ula and instructional methods, and by the development of exten-sive in-service training programs for teachers. Reorganization of curricula, establishment of closer links between formal and non-formal systems, decentralization of administration, and the in-volvement of local authorities in planning would be included in its scope. The Ministry of Education would establish coordinat-ing bodies and integrate education into community and rural development plans. The conference stressed: *"Clearly it will be essential that the significance of these far-reaching changes be im-pressed on all levels of Ethiopian society, and it is urged that the implementation of new courses in Ethiopian education be accompanied by massive public information programs, supported and directed by the highest levels of the government* [author's italics]."[8]

In August 1972 the report was officially submitted to the

minister of education, who was to transmit it to the Council of Ministers and the emperor. Meanwhile, the massive volume of findings and recommendations was marked "restricted," and access was confined to review participants and to some high ministry officials. The mass media—newspapers, radio, and television—hardly mentioned the review. During the summer of 1973, some two thousand teachers, supervisors, and school directors attended a summer school at the national university where, despite their desire to know more about the report and to have their opinions considered, only a short briefing was given them by minor ministry officials.

In April 1973, the Council of Ministers was ready to accept the report, with only slight modifications. Although the ministry had decided to begin implementation in September, the final version of the Education Sector Review report was not made public until 8 February 1974.[9] Meanwhile, rumors were circulating in the country. Some people viewed aspects of the recommendations out of context. It was said that children would be taken out of school after the fourth grade, that only those with financial resources could proceed to the higher levels, and that teaching standards would be lowered. In all, the proposals were presented as a conspiracy against the people. Before the review was made public, the Teachers Association had decided to go on strike over the new salary scales, but some teachers misinformed their students as to the strike's purpose, emphasizing their objections to the Sector Review report. Naturally, the children passed these statements on to their parents.

Aware of the negative public opinion that was developing, and following the announcement of 8 February, the minister of education for the first time spoke on radio and television to explain the intentions of the review and the ministry's position. He was followed by the minister of state, but it was much too late. A whiplash reaction had already clouded the thinking of an otherwise receptive public. During the ensuing weeks a series of local and national strikes followed one after the other, some of them in direct opposition to the review. Opposition also came from the Addis Ababa branch of the Ethiopian University Teachers Association, which stated that the social, economic, and political situation of the country precluded the implementation of such far-reaching proposals in which millions of people were expected to participate. Reform of other sectors of the nation's economy and institutions would have to be undertaken before anything like the review's recommendations could be adopted. To this end they expressed solidarity with the strike of the Ethiopian Teachers Association.[10]

On 22 February, the government "suspended" implementation of the Sector Review recommendations until the essential institutions should be established and the understanding of the Ethiopian public gained.[11] On 27 February, following a series of strikes and disruptions involving members of the armed forces, the government resigned and a new prime minister was appointed. For the time being at least, implementation of the Education Sector Review report was abandoned, and with it the hopes of those who had labored long and hard to bring about meaningful and lasting change.

The report, far-reaching as it was, was concerned with only one sector, but such revolutionary changes in education were in fact predicated upon similar changes in other areas of the national life. Drastic alterations in the existing social, political, and administrative institutions and in agrarian land distribution were explicitly incorporated into the recommendations. It was also apparent that the old political order was neither willing nor able to initiate and carry out such radical reforms. There is no doubt that the Education Sector Review helped to expose the glaring weaknesses not only of the educational system but of the political order as well, and it may thus have contributed inadvertently to the speedy downfall of the regime. It is to be regretted, however, that the review's suggestions, which promised to pave the way toward universal meaningful education for the Ethiopian people, were never acted upon. Hope for that is now postponed indefinitely. When it is rekindled in the future, recommendations such as those of the Education Sector Review will have to be revived.

Conclusion

Given the nature of the society and its stage of economic development, Ethiopia found many of the issues that confronted her in the process of educational development complex and challenging. Even had good intentions and political will not been lacking, the limitation of available resources that should rightly have been appropriated for education were finite. There is no doubt, however, that even within existing limitations, more progress and fundamental change could have been achieved.

On the whole, as suggested above, the school system did not expand fast enough to supply the needs of the country for skilled manpower, nor was the cry from the people for more and better education satisfied. There are still acute shortages of qualified teachers, classrooms, equipment, and library facilities. Educational opportunity remains meager and of poor quality for rural children. Over 85 percent of primary school age children cannot find places in the school system; 90 percent of the adult population is still illiterate. In a culture that shunned most forms of non-farm-related manual labor, vocational education is still an outcast, and little effort has been made to change the public's attitude toward it. Education is still equated with promotion from one grade to the next, or with the passing of a series of national examinations. Encouraging children to understand that education is an introduction to life and a means to the solution of present and future problems has never been a strong feature of educational practice at any level. Although budgetary allocation to education has been relatively very large (third only to national defense and internal security), in terms of GNP it remains one of the lowest in Africa.

At all levels of the government machinery, excellence and merit have rarely been considered in the recruitment, placement, or promotion of personnel. Scouting for talent was never a concept in the minds of officialdom. Recruitment for high positions has been done on the basis of blood or marital relationship, depending more on loyalty to personalities than on competence per se. From the lowest to the highest office, personal ambition, nepotism, and dishonesty have long been the rule, so that many who were entrusted with high responsibilities in education were not equipped for the job. Furthermore, they did not have to prove themselves capable of carrying projects to successful completion because they were rewarded (or punished) not necessarily for accomplishment, but for pleasing their superiors. This, more than any other single fact, was the undoing of modern Ethiopia. A nation led by self-serving people who did not believe in excellence, competence, merit, and reward or even in popular participation was bound to be mediocre in achievement.

Following the February 1974 revolution that abolished a monarchy thirty centuries old, a number of reforms were initiated that were directly to affect the course of educational development. For a period of two years (1974 to 1976) education at the senior high, vocational, and university levels was discontinued for the express purpose of enabling young people and their teachers to travel throughout the country and to present to the peasantry the facts about literacy and the new political and social order. Private schools run for profit have been taken over by the government, and Haile Selassie I University has been reorganized under a new name, the University of Addis Ababa. The regional colleges have been granted autonomy. Directives have been sent out to make educational reforms conform to socialist ideals. There is also discussion about the passing of a law to make primary education universally available; the concepts of the Education Sector Review have been revived, alive under a new name. In the meantime, however, the country is engulfed by turmoil and political instabilities. The future form of the political and social orders is uncertain, and there has been no meaningful education beyond the primary level for the last four years.

Whatever form of government eventually emerges, however, it is to be hoped that it will be accompanied by freedom, equality of opportunity, and justice to all citizens, irrespective of religious affiliation, creed, or clan background. If the political and institutional changes are to mean a separation from the past, they will have to reflect the wishes of the majority of Ethiopians. The revolution must address itself to the proposition that ignorance, poverty, and injustice can be overcome only to the extent that the citizens have the will, as well as the intellectual and physical capacity, to overcome them. Educating the people for this objective will tax the resourcefulness of the best of leadership, but it is a venture worth the effort; without it, national development in the fullest sense of the term will be impossible.

Notes

Introduction

1. Ethiopia, Central Statistical Office, *Statistical Abstract 1970,* pp. 26–27.
2. Edward Ullendorff, *The Ethiopians: An Introduction to Country and People,* 2d ed. (London: Oxford University Press, 1965), pp. 47–48.
3. (Aba) Paulos Tzadua, "Organization of the Central Administration," in J. C. Paul and C. Clapham, *Ethiopian Constitutional Development,* vol. 1, pp. 315–16; Donald Levine, *Wax and Gold* (Chicago: University of Chicago Press, 1965), pp. 177–78.
4. Ullendorff, *The Ethiopians,* p. 79.
5. Paulos Tzadua, "Organization of the Central Administration," in Paul and Clapham, *Ethiopian Constitutional Development,* vol. 1, pp. 316–21; Ethiopia, Ministry of Pen, "Administrative Regulations (Amendment)," *Negarit Gazeta* (Addis Ababa, 28 June 1946).
6. (Blattengeta) Mahteme Sillase Welde Mesqel, *Zikre Neger* (Addis Ababa: Artistic Printers, 1962 E.C.), p. 490, n. 60.
7. Margery Perham, *The Government of Ethiopia,* pp. 60–61.
8. Paul and Clapham, *Ethiopian Constitutional Development,* vol. 1, pp. 340–41.
9. Demissie Wolde-Amanuel, *Constitution and Parliament of Ethiopia: A Historical Record,* translated by Stephen Wright (Addis Ababa: Berhaninna Selam Press, 1950 E.C.), quoted in Paul and Clapham, *Ethiopian Constitutional Development,* vol. 1, pp. 343–44.
10. George W. Baer, *The Coming of the Italian-Ethiopian War,* pp. 373–74.
11. Ibid., Preface.
12. Lord Rennell of Rodd, *British Military Administration of Occupied Territories in Africa* (London: H. M. Stationery Office, 1948), pp. 62–63, 71–73.
13. Ibid., Appendix I.
14. Ibid., p. 77.
15. Perham, *The Government of Ethiopia,* pp. 428–32.
16. Ibid., p. 97.
17. Paul and Clapham, *Ethiopian Constitutional Development,* vol. 1, pp. 393, 395.
18. Ibid., pp. 410–12.
19. Ibid., pp. 366, 372 ff.; Ethiopia, Ministry of Pen, "Order No. 27 of 1962," *Negarit Gazeta* (Addis Ababa, 15 November 1962).

Chapter 1

1. J. Spencer Trimingham, *Islam in Ethiopia,* p. 5.
2. Haile Gabriel Dagne, "Language in Ethiopia" (Unpublished paper; Addis Ababa, 1970), p. 1; Girma Amare, "Aims and Purposes of Church Education in Ethiopia," *Journal of Ethiopian Education,* no. 1 (June 1967), p. 1.
3. Haile Gabriel Dagne, "Language in Ethiopia," p. 1.
4. Richard Pankhurst, Introduction to *Traditional Ethiopian Church Education,* by (Alaka) Imbakom Kalewold (New York: Columbia University Teachers College, 1970), p. xiii.
5. *Revised Constitution of Ethiopia* (Addis Ababa: Berhaninna Selam Press, 1955); see also *Constitution of Ethiopia* (Addis Ababa, Berhaninna Selam Press, 1931).
6. Girma Amare, "Church Education in Ethiopia," p. 4, 11, 17.
7. Aymero Wondemagegnehu, ed., *A Short Introduction to the Ethiopian Orthodox Church* (Addis Ababa: Ethiopian Orthodox Mission, 1957 E.C.), p. 32.
8. Girma Amare, "Church Education in Ethiopia," p. 2; Haile Gabriel Dagne, "Language in Ethiopia," p. 1–2.
9. Maaza Bekele, "A Study of Modern Education in Ethiopia: Its Foundations, Its Developments, Its Future, with Emphasis on Primary Education," (Ph.D. dissertation, Columbia University Teachers College, 1966), p. 19; Mulugeta Wodajo, "Postwar Reform in Ethiopian Education," *Comparative Education Review* 2, no. 3 (1959), p. 18; Girma Amare, "Memorization in Ethiopian Schools," *Journal of Ethiopian Education* 1, no. 1 (January 1963), p. 28.
10. Maaza Bekele, "A Study of Modern Education in Ethiopia," pp. 19–21.
11. Imbakom Kalewold, *Traditional Ethiopian Church Education,* pp. 5–9.
12. Girma Amare, "Church Education in Ethiopia," pp. 1–11, 17; see also (Abba) Kidane Maryam Getahun, *Tintawiw YeQolo Temari* [Student of the traditional school] (Addis Ababa: Tinsae Zegbae Press, 1955 E.C.), pp. 39–40.
13. Imbakom Kalewold, *Traditional Ethiopian Church Education,* pp. 11–12.
14. E. A. Wallis Budge, *A History of Ethiopia, Nubia and Abyssinia,* pp. 570–71.
15. Girma Amare, "Church Education in Ethiopia," p. 3.
16. Imbakom Kalewold, *Traditional Ethiopian Church Education,* pp. 17–18, 21–23, 25–28; Kidane Maryam Getahun, *Tintawiw YeQolo Temari,* pp. 40–42.
17. Mulugeta Wodajo, "Ethiopia: Some Pressing Problems and the Role of Education in Their Resolution," *Journal of Negro Education* 30, no. 3 (1961), pp. 23–35.
18. Kidane Maryam Getahun, *Tintawiw YeQolo Temari,* pp. 44–46.
19. Imbakom Kalewold, *Traditional Ethiopian Church Education,* p. 31.
20. Budge, *A History of Ethiopia,* p. 574.
21. (Liqe Siltanat) Habte Maryam Werqneh, *Tintawiw Yeltyopya Timhirt* [Traditional school of Ethiopia] (Addis Ababa: Berhaninna Selam Press, 1963 E.C.), pp. 263–67.

22. Donald Levine, *Wax and Gold* (Chicago: University of Chicago Press, 1965), pp. 267–75.
23. Habte Maryam Werqneh, *Tintawiw Yeltyopya Timhirt*, pp. 270–75.
24. Ibid., p. 273. See also Assefa Liban, "Preparation of Parchment Manuscripts," University College of Addis Ababa, Ethnological Society Bulletin no. 8 (July 1958), pp. 5–22.
25. Habte Maryam Werqneh, *Tintawiw Yeltyopya Timhirt*, pp. 273–74.
26. Kidane Maryam Getahun, *Tintawiw YeQolo Temari*, pp. 37–38.
27. Imbakom Kalewold, *Traditional Ethiopian Church Education*, p. 9; C. H. Walker, *The Abyssinian at Home*, p. 12.
28. Habte Maryam Werqneh, *Tintawiw Yeltyopya Timhirt*, pp. 278–82.
29. Ibid., pp. 276, 282–83.
30. Imbakom Kalewold, *Traditional Ethiopian Church Education*, pp. 9–10.
31. E.C. stands for Ethiopian Calendar which corresponds to 1946–47 by the Georgian Calendar (G.C.).
32. Kidane Maryam Getahun, *Tintawiw YeQolo Temari*, p. 34.
33. Walker, *The Abyssinian at Home*, p. 13.
34. Levine, *Wax and Gold*, p. 267.
35. Girma Amare, "Church Education in Ethiopia," p. 4.

Chapter 2

1. Ethiopia, Ministry of Education and Fine Arts, *Education in Ethiopia: A Survey*, p. 4.
2. Richard Pankhurst, "The Foundations of Education, Printing, Newspapers, Book Production, Libraries and Literacy in Ethiopia," *Ethiopia Observer* 6, no. 3 (1962), p. 253.
3. Ibid., pp. 249–54.
4. Ibid., pp. 257–58.
5. R. P. Skinner, *Abyssinia of Today*, quoted in R. Pankhurst, "The Foundations of Education," p. 257.
6. R. Pankhurst, "The Foundations of Education," pp. 256–57.
7. Ibid., pp. 257–58.
8. C. F. Rey, *In the Country of the Blue Nile* (London: Duckworth, 1927), p. 208.
9. Kobes Jasperdean, "Modernization in Ethiopia, 1916–1966: Politics and Education" (M.A. thesis, Columbia University Teachers College, 1966), p. 62.
10. R. Pankhurst, "The Foundations of Education," pp. 254.
11. Ibid., pp. 254–56.
12. Ibid., pp. 258–59.
13. (Blattengeta) Mahteme Sillase Welde Mesqel, *Zikre Neger* (Addis Ababa: Artistic Printers, 1962 E.C.), pp. 600, 601.
14. R. Pankhurst, "The Foundations of Education," pp. 258–59.
15. Mahteme Sillase, *Zikre Neger*, pp. 526–27.
16. Ibid., pp. 53–54.
17. Ibid., p. 502.
18. Ibid., p. 60.

19. Teshome (Gebre Mikael) Wagaw, "Some Notes for the World of Work in Ethiopian Tradition," mimeographed, pp. 1–21.

20. Richard Pankhurst, *Economic History of Ethiopia, 1800–1935,* p. 43; for the Amharic version of this proclamation, see Mahteme Sillase, *Zikre Neger,* pp. 421–22.

21. Personal interview with Ato Yigzaw Goshu, Addis Ababa, April 1971.

22. Mahteme Sillase, *Zikre Neger,* p. 54.

23. Ibid., p. 621.

24. R. Pankhurst, "The Foundations of Education," p. 259; see also "Alliance Française in Ethiopia," *Ethiopia Observer* 4, no. 2 (January 1960), pp. 61–63.

25. J. I. Eadie, *An Amharic Reader* (Cambridge: Cambridge University Press, 1924), quoted in R. Pankhurst, "The Foundations of Education," p. 260.

26. Per Stjarne, "The Swedish Mission in Ethiopia," *Ethiopia Observer* 4, no. 3 (February 1960), pp. 37, 78.

27. Leonard Mosley, *Haile Selassie, The Conquering Lion,* p. 122.

28. Mahteme Sillase, *Zikre Neger,* pp. 608–12.

29. Mosley, *Haile Selassie,* pp. 44, 122.

30. E. Sylvia Pankhurst, *Ethiopia, a Cultural History,* pp. 534–35, 586–89.

31. *Berhaninna Selam,* 28 Ginbot 1917 E.C.; Stephen Wright's English translation in R. Pankhurst, "The Foundations of Education," pp. 266–67.

32. *Berhaninna Selam,* 6 Ginbot 1917 E.C., "Hakim Werqneh's speech delivered at the dedicatory service of the school established by H.I.H. The Crown Prince of Ethiopia."

33. Rey, *In the Country of the Blue Nile,* p. 209.

34. Ibid., p. 30.

35. R. Pankhurst, "The Foundations of Education," p. 267.

36. Rey, *In the Country of the Blue Nile,* p. 195.

37. *Berhaninna Selam,* 30 Sene 1919 E.C., pp. 213–15.

38. *Berhaninna Selam,* 5 Hamile 1920 E.C., "Student Prizes."

39. *Berhaninna Selam,* 21 Hamile 1919 E.C., "The Menelik II School Students Awarded Prizes for Excellence"; Stephen Wright's English translation in R. Pankhurst, "The Foundation of Education," pp. 268–69.

40. *Berhaninna Selam,* 18 Miyazya 1920 E.C.; 5 Hamile 1920 E.C., "Student Prizes."

41. *Berhaninna Selam,* 22 Meggabit 1919 E.C., "Better Education."

42. Teferma Belihu, "Response to the Misgivings Expressed Towards Those Who Study Foreign Languages," *Berhaninna Selam,* 21 Tir 1917 E.C.

43. Mahteme Sillase, *Zikre Neger,* pp. 604–7.

44. R. Pankhurst, "The Foundations of Education," pp. 271–79.

45. Ibid., p. 265.

46. Adrien Zervos, *L'Empire d'Ethiopie: Le Miroir de l'Ethiopie moderne, 1906–1935,* p. 223.

47. F. Ernest Work, "A Plan for Ethiopia's Educational System," *Journal of Negro Education* 3, no. 1 (January 1934), pp. 66–68; Maaza Bekele, "A Study of Modern Education in Ethiopia: Its Foundations, Its Developments, Its Future, with Emphasis on Primary Education," (Ph.D. dissertation, Columbia University Teachers College, 1966), pp. 281–84.

48. Zervos, *L'Empire d'Ethiopie*, pp. 229–30; R. Pankhurst, "The Foundations of Education," p. 279; E. S. Pankhurst, *Ethiopia, a Cultural History*, pp. 535–38.

49. Christine Sandford, *Ethiopia under Haile Selassie* (London: J. M. Dent and Sons, Ltd., 1946), p. 467.

50. Zervos, *L'Empire d'Ethiopie*, p. 230.

Chapter 3

1. A. H. M. Jones and Elizabeth Monroe, *A History of Ethiopia*, pp. 175–92; Roland R. De Marco, *The Italianization of African Natives: Government Native Education in the Italian Colonies, 1890–1937*, pp. 12–17; Leonard Mosley, *Haile Selassie, the Conquering Lion*, pp. 201–14.

2. De Marco, *The Italianization of African Natives*, p. 1.

3. Richard Pankhurst, "The Foundations of Education, Printing, Newspapers, Book Production, Libraries and Literacy in Ethiopia," *Ethiopia Observer* 6 no. 3 (1962), pp. 255–56.

4. Kobes Jasperdean, "Modernization in Ethiopia, 1916–1966: Politics and Education" (M.A. thesis, Columbia University Teachers College, 1966), pp. 43, 36.

5. De Marco, *The Italianization of African Natives*, pp. 46–47.

6. Ibid., p. 50.

7. Great Britain, Ministry of Information, *The First to be Freed: The Record of British Military Administration in Eritrea and Somalia, 1941–1943*, pp. 43–44, quoted in R. Pankhurst, "The Foundations of Education," p. 287.

8. De Marco, *The Italianization of African Natives*, pp. 4, 50–51.

9. Jasperdean, "Modernization in Ethiopia, 1916–1966," pp. 37–38.

10. Ibid., p. 5.

11. R. Pankhurst, "The Foundations of Education," p. 286.

12. De Marco, *The Italianization of African Natives*, pp. 51–52.

13. Ibid., p. 59.

14. Ibid., p. 54.

15. Ibid., pp. 51–59.

16. E. Sylvia Pankhurst and Richard Pankhurst, *Ethiopia and Eritrea: The Last Phase of the Reunion Struggle 1941–1952*, pp. 229–30; R. Pankhurst, "The Foundations of Education," p. 287.

17. G. B., Min. of Inf., *The First to be Freed*, p. 33, quoted in Richard Pankhurst, *Economic History of Ethiopia, 1800–1935*, p. 685.

18. E. Sylvia Pankhurst, *Ethiopia, a Cultural History*, pp. 694–95.

19. Jasperdean, "Modernization in Ethiopia," p. 43.

20. E. S. Pankhurst, *Ethiopia, a Cultural History*, p. 548; Maaza Bekele, "A Study of Modern Education in Ethiopia: Its Foundations, Its Developments, Its Future, with Emphasis on Primary Education," (Ph.D. dissertation, Columbia University Teachers College, 1966), p. 65.

21. Pankhurst and Pankhurst, *Ethiopia and Eritrea*, p. 302.

22. Maaza Bekele, "A Study of Modern Education in Ethiopia," pp. 542–48.

23. Ethiopia, Ministry of Justice, *Documents on Italian War Crimes*, vol. 1,

pp. 20–31; R. Pankhurst, "The Foundations of Education," pp. 274–75; see also *Ethiopia Observer* 3, no. 2 (1959), p. 356.

24. Mosley, *Haile Selassie,* p. 229; E. S. Pankhurst, *Ethiopia, a Cultural History,* p. 548.

25. De Marco, *The Italianization of African Natives,* p. 8.

26. Ibid., pp. 20-22, 51–59.

27. Quoted in E. S. Pankhurst, *Ethiopia, A Cultural History,* p. 692.

28. "La Civilisation Fasciste en Afrique Orientale Italienne," Centre d'Etudes de Droit et de Politique Coloniale Fasciste, L'Institut Nationale pour les Relations Culturelles avec l'Etranger (Rome, 1943), p. 32, quoted in E. S. Pankhurst, *Ethiopia, a Cultural History,* pp. 692–93.

29. Min. of Justice, *Documents on Italian War Crimes,* vol. 1 (1949), p. 30.

30. Ibid., p. 31.

31. De Marco, *The Italianization of African Natives,* pp. 36–37, 39.

32. Richard Pankhurst, "The Textbooks of Italian Colonial Africa," *Ethiopia Observer* 11, no. 4 (1967), pp. 330–31.

33. Ibid., pp. 331–32.

34. De Marco, *Italianization of African Natives,* p. 34.

35. Ibid., pp. 83–84.

36. *New Times and Ethiopian News,* 30 January 1937, in *Ethiopia Observer* 3, no. 11 (1959), p. 346.

37. *New Times and Ethiopian News,* 6 February 1937, in *Ethiopia Observer* 3, no. 11 (1959), p. 347.

38. Edouard Trudeau, "Higher Education in Ethiopia," (Ph.D. dissertation, Columbia University Teachers College, 1964), p. 6.

39. Margery Perham, *The Government of Ethiopia,* pp. 122–23.

40. Christine Sandford, *Ethiopia under Haile Selassie* (London: J. M. Dent and Sons, Ltd., 1946), pp. 95–96; R. Pankhurst, "The Foundations of Education, p. 267.

Chapter 4

1. Edward Ullendorff, *The Ethiopians: An Introduction to Country and People,* pp. 192–93.

2. Christine Sandford, *Ethiopia under Haile Selassie* (London: J. M. Dent and Sons, Ltd., 1946), p. 67.

3. Ethiopia, Ministry of Foreign Affairs, *Memoranda Presented by the Imperial Ethiopian Government to the Council of Foreign Ministers in London, September 1945* (Addis Ababa, 1955), p. 21.

4. Frank Klassen, "Teacher Education in Ethiopia," *School and Society* 91 (February 1963), p. 96.

5. Ethiopia, Ministry of Education and Fine Arts, *Elementary School Curriculum, Years I–VI, 1947–48,* pp. 13–14.

6. Kobes Jasperdean, "Modernization in Ethiopia, 1916–1966: Politics and Education" (M.A. thesis, Columbia University Teachers College, 1966), p. 61.

7. Ethiopia, Ministry of Education and Fine Arts, *Education in Ethiopia: A Survey,* p. 9; Ethiopia, Ministry of Education and Fine Arts, *A Ten-Year Plan for the Controlled Expansion of Ethiopian Education,* pp. 9–10.

8. Ethiopia, Ministry of Education and Fine Arts, *Yearbook 1940–41* E.C [1947–49 G.C.], p. 34.

9. Maaza Bekele, "A Study of Modern Education in Ethiopia: Its Foundations, Its Developments, Its Future, with Emphasis on Primary Education," (Ph.D. dissertation, Columbia University Teachers College, 1966), p. 86.

10. "Education in Ethiopia," *Ethiopian Herald,* 3 July 1943.

11. "Education for Citizenship," *Ethiopian Herald,* 24 July 1943.

12. H. G. Wells, "Constructive Education," *Ethiopian Herald,* 10 July 1943.

13. *Ethiopian Review,* 22 July 1946, in Margery Perham, *The Government of Ethiopia,* pp. 260–61.

14. Min. of Ed., *Yearbook 1940–41* E.C., p.18.

15. Girma Amare, "Government Education in Ethiopia," *Ethiopia Observer* 6, no. 4 (1963), p. 338.

16. Min. of Ed., *A Ten-Year Plan,* p. 92.

17. Taddesse Tereffe, "Progress, Problems and Prospects in Ethiopian Education," *Ethiopia Observer* 8, no. 1 (1964), p. 7.

18. Ethiopia, Ministry of Education and Fine Arts, *Yearbook 1942–43* E.C. [1949–51 G.C.], pp. 99–102, 106–9.

19. E. Sylvia Pankhurst, "Education in Ethiopia II: Secondary Education," *Ethiopia Observer* 2, no. 5 (1958), pp. 171–72.

20. Min. of Ed., *Yearbook 1942–43* E.C., pp. 100, 109–10.

21. E. S. Pankhurst, "Education in Ethiopia," pp. 172–75.

22. E. S. Pankhurst, "Education in Ethiopia," pp. 177–79.

23. Ibid., pp. 181–84; Min. of Ed., *Yearbook 1942–43* E.C., pp. 125–26.

24. Min. of Ed., *Yearbook 1942–43* E.C., pp. 147–52.

25. Min. of Ed., *Yearbook 1940–41* E.C., pp. 147–52.

26. Min. of Ed., *Education in Ethiopia: A Survey,* pp. 7–8.

27. Ibid., pp. 112–16; Min. of Ed., *Yearbook 1940–41* E.C., pp. 66–67.

28. Min. of Ed., *Yearbook 1940–41* E.C., pp.67–69; Min. of Ed., *Yearbook 1942–43* E.C. pp. 116–20.

29. Min. of Ed., *Yearbook 1940–41* E.C., pp. 69–70.

30. Min. of Ed., *Yearbook 1942–43* E.C., pp. 126–30.

31. Min. of Ed., *Yearbook 1942–43* E.C., pp. 126–31.

32. Min. of Ed., *Education in Ethiopia: A Survey,* p. 8; Ethiopia, Ministry of Education and Fine Arts, *The Development of Pre-Service Teacher Education, 1937–1963* E.C. [1944–1971 G.C.], pp. 1–3, passim.

33. Min. of Ed., *A Ten-Year Plan,* p. 76.

34. Min. of Ed., *Yearbook 1940–41* E.C., p. 3.

35. Min. of Ed., *Yearbook 1942–43* E.C., pp. 24–25, 27.

36. Min. of Ed., *The Development of Pre-Service Teacher Education,* pp. 4, 6, 24–25, 55.

37. Ibid., p. 4.

38. Ibid., pp. 28–29, 122–23; Min. of Ed., *Yearbook 1940–41* E.C., p. 26.

39. Min. of Ed., *Yearbook 1942–43* E.C., pp. 12–23; Edouard Trudeau, "Higher Education in Ethiopia," (Ph.D. dissertation, Columbia University Teachers College, 1964), pp. 32–42.

40. Edouard Trudeau, "Higher Education in Ethiopia," p. 34.

41. Min. of Ed., *Education in Ethiopia: A Survey*, pp. 6, 28.
42. Min. of Ed., *Yearbook 1942–43 E.C.*, p. 207.
43. Min. of Ed., *Yearbook 1940–41 E.C.*, pp. 97–99; Min. of Ed., *Yearbook 1942–43 E.C.*, pp. 198–201.
44. Senedu Gebru, "Girls' Education," *Ethiopia Observer* 1, no. 3 (1957), pp. 74–77.
45. Ibid., pp. 84–90.
46. "Empress Menen Handicraft School," *Ethiopia Observer* 1, no. 3 (1957), pp. 80–81.
47. Min. of Ed., *Yearbook 1940–41 E.C.*, p. 82.
48. Robert H. Beck, Walter W. Cook, and Nolan C. Kearney, *Curriculum in the Modern Elementary School*, pp. 1, 21.
49. Min. of Ed., *Elementary School Curriculum, Years I–VI, 1947–48*, p. 34; Ayalew Gebre Selassie, "Three Years' Experience in Education," *Ethiopia Observer* 8, no. 1 (1964), p. 19.
50. E. Sylvia Pankhurst, *Ethiopia, a Cultural History*, p. 566.
51. Min. of Ed., *Education in Ethiopia: A Survey*, p. 10.
52. Ibid.
53. Trudeau, "Higher Education in Ethiopia," p. 8; Germa Amare, "Government Education in Ethiopia," p. 336.
54. Trudeau, "Higher Education in Ethiopia," p. 8.
55. Min. of Ed., *A Ten-Year Plan*, p. 43.
56. Ibid.
57. Min. of Ed., *Elementary School Curriculum, Years I–VI, 1947–48*, pp. 139, 142, 148.
58. Min. of Ed., *Yearbook 1940–41 E.C.*, pp. 71–73.
59. Min. of Ed., *Elementary School Curriculum, Years I–VI, 1947–48*, p. 136.
60. Min. of Ed., *Yearbook 1940–41 E.C.*, p. 74.
61. Ibid., pp. 74–75.
62. Ibid., pp. 55–56.
63. Ibid., pp. 55–60; Min. of Ed., *Yearbook 1942–43 E.C.*, pp. 43–56; Min. of Ed., *Elementary School Curriculum, Years I–VI, 1947–48*, pp. 151–74.
64. E. S. Pankhurst, *Ethiopia, a Cultural History*, pp. 577–78.
65. Min. of Ed., *Yearbook 1940–41 E.C.*, p. 52.
66. Min. of Ed., *Yearbook 1942–43 E.C.*, p. 30; Min. of Ed., *Education in Ethiopia: A Survey*, pp. 32–33.
67. Min. of Ed., *Yearbook 1940–41 E.C.*, p. 87; Ethiopia, Ministry of Education and Fine Arts, *Yearbook 1951–53*, pp. 31–32; Min. of Ed., *Education in Ethiopia: A Survey*, p. 10.
68. Maaza Bekele, "A Study of Modern Education in Ethiopia," p. 75.
69. Min. of Ed., *Yearbook 1942–43 E.C.*, pp. 7, 62, 100, 108, 196.
70. Min. of Ed., *Yearbook 1940–41 E.C.*, p. 37.

Chapter 5

1. Ethiopia, Ministry of Education and Fine Arts, *A Ten-Year Plan for the Controlled Expansion of Ethiopian Education*, p. 62.
2. Ibid., pp. 62–63.

3. Ibid., p. 10.

4. Ibid., pp. x, 1, 33–35.

5. C. A. Ruckmick, "The Little White School-house in Ethiopia" (unpublished paper, 18 July 1950), in Ministry of Education files (p. 272), p. 3.

6. Kobes Jasperdean, "Modernization in Ethiopia, 1916–1966: Politics and Education" (M.A. thesis, Columbia University Teachers College, 1966), p. 62.

7. Margery Perham, *The Government of Ethiopia*, p. 14.

8. Richard Pankhurst, *Economic History of Ethiopia, 1800–1935,* p. 5.

9. Ibid., p. 24.

10. Ibid., p. 27. See also "The New Role of the Missionary," *Ethiopian Herald*, 9 March 1971.

11. Ethiopia, Ministry of Education and Fine Arts, *Yearbook 1951–53 E.C.,* pp. 110–12.

12. Perham, *The Government of Ethiopia*, p. 133.

13. Ethiopia, Ministry of Pen, "Decree No. 3 of 1944," *Negarit Gazeta* 3, no. 12; Ethiopia, Ministry of Education and Fine Arts, *Education in Ethiopia: A Survey,* Appendix I, p. 38.

14. Ruckmick, "The Little White School-house," p. 3.

15. Min. of Ed., *Yearbook 1951–53 E.C.,* pp. 113–15, 119–20.

16. Min. of Ed., *A Ten-Year Plan,* pp. 53–68.

17. Ethiopia, Ministry of Pen, "Decree No. 2 of 1942," *Negarit Gazeta* 2, no. 3; Perham, *The Government of Ethiopia,* pp. 128–31.

18. Perham, *The Government of Ethiopia,* p. 132; Ethiopia, Ministry of Education and Fine Arts, *Review* (Addis Ababa, June 1945), p. 7.

19. Ethiopia, Ministry of Pen, "Proclamation No. 93 of 1947," *Negarit Gazeta* (Addis Ababa, 30 November 1947); Min. of Ed., *Education in Ethiopia: A Survey,* p. 39.

20. Min. of Ed., *A Ten-Year Plan,* pp. 63–64; United States Operations Mission to Ethiopia, *Report on the Organization and Administration of the Ministry of Education and Fine Arts,* p. 8; Maaza Bekele, "A Study of Modern Education in Ethiopia: Its Foundations, Its Developments, Its Future, with Emphasis on Primary Education," (Ph.D. dissertation, Columbia University Teachers College, 1966), pp. 89–91. See also Minutes of the Board of Education, 28 Hidar 1943 E.C., filed in the Board's Secretariat.

21. Min. of Ed., *A Ten-Year Plan,* p. 64; Minutes of the Board of Education, 21–23 Tir 1943 E.C. See also File No. 0102 (Addis Ababa, Ministry of Education Library).

22. Maaza Bekele, "A Study of Modern Education in Ethiopia," p. 91.

23. Ethiopia, Ministry of Education and Fine Arts, *Yearbook 1940–41 E.C.,* pp. 26, 84; Min. of Ed., *A Ten-Year Plan,* pp. 66–67.

24. Min. of Ed., *A Ten-Year Plan,* p. 68.

25. Perham, *The Government of Ethiopia,* p. 396.

26. Girma Amare, "Government Education in Ethiopia," *Ethiopia Observer* 6, no. 4 (1963), p. 338.

27. Min. of Ed., *Yearbook 1940–41 E.C.,* p. 89.

28. Perham, *The Government of Ethiopia,* p. 257.

29. Million Neqniq et al., *Report on the Current Operation of the Education System in Ethiopia* (Addis Ababa, November 1966), p. 60.

30. Min. of Ed., *Yearbook 1940–41 E.C.,* p. 89.

31. Min. of Ed., *Yearbook 1951–53 E.C.,* pp. 34–35.

32. Maaza Bekele, "A Study of Modern Education in Ethiopia," p. 286.

33. Ethiopia, Ministry of Pen, "General Notice No. 1 of 1942," *Negarit Gazeta* 1, no. 1.

34. Ethiopia, Ministry of Pen, "Order No. 1 of 1943," *Negarit Gazeta* 2, no. 5, pp. 26–27. This law was amended by Order No. 44 of 1966 and Order No. 46 of 1966, but the essential points remained the same.

35. Ethiopia, Ministry of Pen, "Decree No. 3 of 1944," *Negarit Gazeta* 3, no. 12, pp. 125–28.

36. Ethiopia, Ministry of Pen, "Legal Notice No. 103 of 1947," *Negarit Gazeta* 6, no. 11.

37. Ethiopia, Ministry of Pen, "Legal Notice No. 153 of 1951," *Negarit Gazeta* 10, no. 8.

38. Ethiopia, Ministry of Pen, "Order No. 3 of 1947," *Negarit Gazeta* (Addis Ababa, 30 November 1947), p. 19.

39. Ethiopia, Ministry of Pen, "Proclamation No. 94 of 1947," *Negarit Gazeta* 7, no. 3, pp. 15–16.

40. Ibid., pp. 17–19.

41. Ethiopia, Ministry of Pen, "General Notice No. 135 of 1950," *Negarit Gazeta* (Addis Ababa, 28 July 1950), pp. 30–31.

42. Min. of Ed., *Yearbook 1940–41 E.C.* [1947–49 G.C.], p. 8.

43. Ibid., pp. 9–10.

44. Ibid., p. 11; Maaza Bekele, "A Study of Modern Education in Ethiopia," p. 72.

45. Ethiopia, Ministry of Pen, "General Notice No. 28 of 1944," *Negarit Gazeta* (Addis Ababa, 1 November 1944).

46. Ethiopia, Ministry of Pen, "General Notice No. 101 of 1947," *Negarit Gazeta* (Addis Ababa, 6 June 1947).

47. Min. of Ed., *Yearbook 1940–41 E.C.,* p. 11.

48. Ibid., p. 13.

49. Ibid., p. 14.

50. Ibid.

51. Ibid., pp. 14–15, 75–76.

52. Ibid., pp. 15–17, 76, 79; Ethiopia, Ministry of Education and Fine Arts, *Yearbook 1942–43 E.C.* [1949–51 G.C.], pp. 38–39.

53. Perham, *The Government of Ethiopia,* pp. 200–5; Ethiopia, Ministry of Pen, "Proclamation No. 76 of 1945," *Negarit Gazeta* (Addis Ababa, 29 May 1945); *Ethiopian Herald,* 13 May 1946.

54. Ernest W. Luther, *Ethiopia Today,* pp. 62, 65–68; Ethiopia, Ministry of Commerce and Industry, *Economic Handbook of Ethiopia,* p. 212.

55. Ethiopia, Ministry of Pen, "Proclamation No. 60 of 1944," *Negarit Gazeta* (Addis Ababa, 29 May 1944); Ethiopia, Ministry of Pen, "Proclamation No. 70 of 1944," *Negarit Gazeta* (Addis Ababa, 1 November 1944); Ethiopia, Ministry of Pen, "Proclamation No. 93 of 1947," *Negarit Gazeta* (Addis Ababa, 30 November 1947).

56. Min. of Pen, "Proclamation No. 94 of 1947," *Negarit Gazeta* (Addis Ababa, 30 November 1947).
57. Min. of Ed., *A Ten-Year Plan,* Appendix, pp. 1–2.
58. Ibid., p. 2; Ethiopia, Planning Board, *Five-Year Development Plan 1957–1961,* pp. 125–26.
59. "Education Report: Analysis of Development in Recent Years," *Ethiopia Observer* 5, no. 1 (1961), p. 71.
60. Min. of Ed., *Yearbook 1940–41 E.C.,* pp. 44–45; United States Operations Mission to Ethiopia, *Report on the Organization and Administration of the Ministry of Education and Fine Arts* (revised), p. 20.
61. Ruckmick, "The Little White School-house," p. 2.
62. Min. of Ed., *A Ten-Year Plan,* p. 51.
63. Min. of Ed., *Yearbook 1940–41 E.C.,* pp. 89, 107.
64. Ibid., opposite p. 50; David A. Talbot, *Ethiopia: Liberation Silver Jubilee* (Addis Ababa: Berhininna Selam Press, 1966), pp. 281–82.

Chapter 6

1. J. S. Trimingham, *The Christian Church and Missions in Ethiopia,* p. 16.
2. Sylvia Pankhurst and Richard Pankhurst, *Ethiopia and Eritrea: The Last Phase of the Reunion Struggle, 1941–1952,* pp. 226–27.
3. G. K. N. Trevaskis, *Eritrea: A Colony in Transition, 1941–52,* p. 33.
4. Ibid.
5. Pankhurst and Pankhurst, *Ethiopia and Eritrea,* pp. 229–30; Stephen H. Longrigg, *A Short History of Eritrea,* p. 137.
6. Trevaskis, *Eritrea,* pp. 134–35.
7. Ibid., p. 30.
8. Ibid., pp. 33–34.
9. Pankhurst and Pankhurst, *Ethiopia and Eritrea,* p. 304.
10. Trevaskis, *Eritrea,* pp. 34–40.
11. Pankhurst and Pankhurst, *Ethiopia and Eritrea,* pp. 98–99.
12. "Ethiopia's Young Navy," *Ethiopia Observer* 3, no. 9 (1959), pp. 279–80.
13. J. C. Paul and C. Clapham, *Ethiopian Constitutional Development: A Sourcebook,* p. 367.
14. Pankhurst and Pankhurst, *Ethiopia and Eritrea,* pp. 33–35.
15. Ethiopia, Ministry of Education and Fine Arts, *Education in Ethiopia: A Survey,* p. 36; Ethiopia, Ministry of Education and Fine Arts, *Yearbook 1951–53,* p. 121.
16. Information provided by Ato Alemu Begashaw, educational expert in Eritrea during part of the period of federation.
17. "Eritrea's First Secondary School," *Ethiopia Observer* 3, no. 7 (1959), p. 222.
18. Ibid., pp. 224–25.
19. Ibid., pp. 216–17.
20. Min. of Ed., *Yearbook 1951–53,* p. 121.
21. "The Emperor's Speech on the Reunion of Eritrea, November 15, 1962," *Ethiopia Observer* 6, no. 4 (1963), p. 311.

Chapter 7

1. United States Operations Mission to Ethiopia, *Progress Report: Point IV Cooperative Program in General Education,* pp. 5–7.
2. Edouard Trudeau, "Higher Education in Ethiopia" (Ph.D. dissertation, Columbia University Teachers College, 1964), pp. 8–9.
3. Ethiopia, Ministry of Education and Fine Arts, *A Ten-Year Plan for the Controlled Expansion of Ethiopian Education,* p. 11; other relevant sections: on community schools, pp. 90–107; on primary schools, pp. 53–61; on academic secondary schools, pp. 22–23; on middle schools, pp. 1–7; on technical education, pp. 128–36, 149–52; on financing the proposed plan, pp. 156–61.
4. Ibid., p. 15.
5. Ibid., pp. 91–92.
6. Ibid., pp. 92–93.
7. Ibid., p. 62.
8. Ibid., pp. 64–65.
9. Ibid., p. 73.
10. Ibid., p. 75.
11. Ibid., p. 79.
12. Ibid., p. 7.
13. Ibid., p. 21.
14. Ibid., pp. 4–6.
15. Ibid., pp. 42–43.
16. Ibid., p. 43.
17. Ethiopia, Planning Board, *Five-Year Development Plan, 1957–1961,* pp. 1–2.
18. Ibid.
19. Ibid., p. 123.
20. Ibid., p. 135.
21. Ibid., pp. 137–40.
22. Min. of Ed., *A Ten-Year Plan,* p. 107.
23. Ethiopia, Ministry of Education and Fine Arts, *The Development of Pre-Service Teaching Education, 1937–1963 E.C. [1944–1971 G.C.],* p. 8.
24. Ibid., p. 23.
25. Ibid., pp. 8–10. See also D. M. McLaren and I. M. McLaren, "The Tabasse Community Center, Ethiopia: An Experiment in Mass Education," *Overseas Education* 16, no. 2 (January 1945), p. 49; Ethiopia, Ministry of Education and Fine Arts, *Education in Ethiopia: A Survey,* pp. 11, 38–39; "Debre Berhan Community School," *Ethiopia Observer* 1, no. 7 (1957), pp. 232–35; and "Debre Berhan Community Training School," *Ethiopia Observer* 2, no. 10 (1958), pp. 330–43.
26. Min. of Ed., *The Development of Pre-Service Teacher Education, p. 24.*
27. Ethiopia, Ministry of Education and Fine Arts, Planning and Programming Office, "Report" (Addis Ababa, April 1973), pp. 1–2.
28. United States Operations Mission to Ethiopia, *Report on the Organization and Administration of the Ministry of Education and Fine Arts* (revised), pp. 1–2.

29. Ethiopia, Ministry of Education and Fine Arts, *Elementary Community School Curriculum, Years I–VI (Experimental)*, pp. 5–6.
30. Ibid., p. 2.
31. Ayalew Gebre Selassie, "Three Years' Experience in Education," *Ethiopia Observer* 8, no. 1 (1964), pp. 20–23.
32. Ibid., p. 23.
33. Girma Amare, "Government Education in Ethiopia," *Ethiopia Observer* 6, no. 4 (1963), pp. 339–41.
34. Marcel Cohen, "The Amharic Language," *Ethiopia Observer* 2, no. 3 (1958), p. 103.
35. Girma Amare, "Government Education in Ethiopia," pp. 339–40.
36. Ibid., pp. 341–42.
37. Ethiopia, Ministry of Education and Fine Arts, *Elementary School Curriculum, Years I–VI, 1947–48*, pp. 1–17.
38. Min. of Ed., *Elementary Community School Curriculum, Years I–VI (Experimental)*, pp. v–vi.
39. Ibid., p. vii.
40. Ibid.
41. Ibid., pp. vii–viii.
42. Ibid., p. ix.
43. Girma Amare, "Government Education in Ethiopia," p. 342.
44. Ethiopia, Ministry of Education and Fine Arts, *Yearbook 1951–53*, pp. 31, 121.
45. Million Neqniq, "The Most Urgent Needs in the Expansion of Ethiopian Education," *Ethiopia Observer* 2, no. 4 (1958), p. 138; Min. of Ed., *A Ten-Year Plan*, p. 28.
46. Ibid., p. 79.
47. Min. of Ed., *A Ten-Year Plan*, pp. 79–82.
48. Min. of Ed., *The Development of Pre-Service Teacher Education*, pp. 25, 34; Ethiopia, Ministry of Education and Fine Arts, *The Development of In-Service Teacher Education, 1957–1964 E.C. [1964–1972 G.C.]*, p. 4.
49. Aklilu Habte, "Brain Drain in the Elementary School: Why Teachers Leave the Profession," *Ethiopian Journal of Education*, no. 1 (1967), p. 35.
50. Ibid., p. 36.
51. Ibid.
52. Ibid., p. 33.
53. Min. of Ed., *A Ten-Year Plan*, pp. 34, 51.
54. Min. of Ed., *The Development of Pre-Service Teacher Education*, pp. 53–55; Min. of Ed., *The Development of In-Service Teacher Education*, pp. 2–3.
55. Beyene Negewo, "The Training of Elementary School Directors and Supervisors through an In-Service Programme in Ethiopia" (Addis Ababa: ISS/ECA Symposium on Educational Innovation in Africa, September 1971), pp. 5–6.
56. Ethiopia, Ministry of Education and Fine Arts, *School Census, 1960–1961*, p. 1.
57. Ibid.

58. The source does not indicate whether the figures include all grade levels or not. Here it is taken to include the primary and secondary grades.
59. Trudeau, "Higher Education in Ethiopia," p. 16.
60. Ibid., p. 18.
61. Teshome Wagaw, "Some Notes for the World of Work in Ethiopian Tradition," pp. 1–21.
62. Trudeau, "Higher Education in Ethiopia," p. 18.
63. Ibid., p. 19.
64. Ethiopia, Ministry of Education and Fine Arts, *Yearbook 1940–41 E.C.* [1947–49 G.C.], p. 82.
65. Min. of Ed., *Yearbook 1951–53,* pp. 32–33. See also Senedu Gebru, "Girls' Education," *Ethiopia Observer* 1, no. 3 (1957), pp. 74–107, and "Education in Ethiopia II: Secondary, Education," *Ethiopia Observer* 2, no. 5 (1958), p. 180.
66. Ethiopia, Ministry of Education and Fine Arts, *A Study of Student Wastage at Primary and Secondary Levels: Causes and Remedies,* pp. 9–11.
67. J. C. Paul and C. Clapham, *Ethiopian Constitutional Development: A Sourcebook,* vol. 1, p. 324.
68. Ibid., p. 387.
69. Min. of Ed., *Education in Ethiopia: A Survey,* p. 39.
70. Ernest W. Luther, *Ethiopia Today,* pp. 65–67.
71. "Point Four: Its Concept and Development," *Ethiopia Observer* 3, no. 1 (1959), p. 3.
72. Ibid., pp. 3–9; Min. of Ed., *Yearbook 1951–53,* pp. 21–23.
73. United States Operations Mission, *Report on the Organization and Administration of the Ministry of Education and Fine Arts* (revised), pp. 1–36. See also Min. of Ed., *Yearbook 1951–53,* p. 16.
74. Ibid., pp. 20–24, 33.
75. Min. of Ed., *A Ten-Year Plan,* Appendix, pp. 1–3.
76. "Education Report: Analysis of Developments in Recent Years," *Ethiopia Observer* 5, no. 1 (1961), p. 71.
77. Million Neqniq, "The Most Urgent Needs in the Expansion of Ethiopian Education," pp. 138–39.
78. Ibid., p. 139.
79. Maaza Bekele, "Some Thoughts on the Future," *Ethiopia Observer* 2, no. 4 (1958), p. 139.
80. Min. of Ed., *Education in Ethiopia: A Survey,* pp. 36–37.

Chapter 8

1. Haile Selassie I, "Inaugural Address," UNESCO-ECA, *Final Report* (UNESCO/E.D./181), 1961, p. 21.
2. Ibid., p. v.
3. Ibid., p. 3.
4. Teshome G. Wagaw, "A Follow-up Study of the 1961 Addis Ababa Education Conference of African States: Implications for Ethiopia," *Dialogue* 3, no. 2 (Addis Ababa, July 1971), pp. 19–34.
5. Ibid., pp. 19–21.

6. Ibid., pp. 21–23.
7. Ibid., pp. 23–24.
8. Edouard Trudeau, "Higher Education in Ethiopia," (Ph.D. dissertation, Columbia University Teachers College, 1964), pp. 21–22.
9. Ethiopia, Ministry of Education and Fine Arts, *Proposed Plan for the Development of Education in Ethiopia*, p. 14. See also Haddis Alemayehu, head of Ethiopian delegation at UNESCO conference, in *Addis Zemen*, 10 Ginbot 1953 E.C., pp. 1, 3.
10. Trudeau, "Higher Education in Ethiopia," p. 23.
11. Teshome G. Wagaw, "A Follow-up Study," pp. 25–33.
12. Ethiopia, Planning Board, *Second Five-Year Development Plan, 1963–1967*, p. 259.
13. Ibid., p. 52.
14. Trudeau, "Higher Education in Ethiopia," p. 23.
15. Ethiopia, Planning Board, *Second Five-Year Development Plan*, pp. 262–63.
16. Ethiopia, Ministry of Education and Fine Arts, *Project for the Expansion of Second Level Education in Ethiopia*, (1964), pp. 23–24.
17. Ibid., pp. 24–25.
18. Ethiopia, Ministry of Education and Fine Arts, *Elementary School Curriculum, Years I–VI*, pp. i–ii.
19. Ethiopia, Ministry of Education and Fine Arts, *The Current Operation of the Education System in Ethiopia*, p. 120.
20. Ibid., pp. 186–87.
21. Ibid., p. 123.
22. Ethiopia, Ministry of Education and Fine Arts, *Secondary School Curriculum, Book 1*, p. i.
23. Ibid., pp. vi–vii.
24. Ibid., p. ix.
25. Ibid., p. viii.
26. Ethiopia, Ministry of Education and Fine Arts, *Educational Projects Proposed for the Third Five-Year Plan*, pp. ii–iii.
27. Min. of Ed., *The Current Operation of the Education System*, pp. 126, 185.
28. Ibid., pp. 74, 77–78.
29. Ethiopia, Ministry of Education and Fine Arts, *Seminar of Junior and Senior Secondary School Directors*, p. 49.
30. Ibid., pp. 125, 126.
31. United Nations, untitled document presented to the Ministry of Education and Fine Arts (20 December 1969), pp. 5–6.
32. Ibid., p. 142; Min. of Ed., *Seminar of Junior and Senior Secondary School Directors*, p. 172.
33. Min. of Ed., *The Current Operation of the Education System*, p. 53.
34. Ibid., p. 9.
35. Beyene Negewo, "The Training of Elementary School Directors and Supervisors Through an In-Service Programme in Ethiopia" (Addis Ababa: ISS/ECA Symposium on Educational Innovation in Africa, September 1971), pp. 1–25.

36. Ethiopia, Ministry of Education and Fine Arts, *The Development of Pre-Service Teacher Education, 1937–1963 E.C.* [1944–1971 G.C.], pp. 12–13.
37. Ibid., pp. 27–28.
38. Ibid., pp. 34–37.
39. Ibid., pp. 48–53.
40. Min. of Ed., *The Current Operation of the Education System, pp. 46–48.*
41. Ibid., p. 52.
42. Min. of Ed., *The Development of Pre-Service Teacher Education,* p. 33.
43. Ibid., p. 38.
44. Min. of Ed., *The Current Operation of the Education System,* pp. 54–57.
45. Ibid., pp. 58–59.
46. Ibid., pp. 61–62.
47. Ibid., pp. 69–70.
48. Ibid., pp. 44, 46.
49. Min. of Ed., *The Development of Pre-Service Teacher Education,* p. 39.
50. Min. of Ed., *The Current Operation of the Education System,* p. 71.
51. Ethiopia, Ministry of Education and Fine Arts, *EBP/ESBU, 1965–1973* (Addis Ababa, July 1973), pp. 1–4.
52. Ethiopia, Ministry of Education and Fine Arts, *Report of the Evaluation Team on Elementary School Building Programme* (Addis Ababa, June 1973), pp. 50–65.
53. Min. of Ed., *The Current Operation of the Education System,* pp. 71–72; Min. of Ed., *Educational Projects Proposed for the Third Five-Year Plan,* p. 8.
54. Min. of Ed., *Project for the Expansion of Second Level Education,* pp. 3–5.
55. Min. of Ed., *The Current Operation of the Education System,* p. 72.
56. Ethiopia, Ministry of Education and Fine Arts, *Annual Report 1968–69* (Addis Ababa, July 1969), p. 14.
57. "Growth and Shortage," *Ethiopian Herald,* 3 April 1971.
58. Min. of Ed., *Annual Report 1968–69,* pp. 8–9.
59. Ibid., p. 26.
60. Ethiopia, Ministry of Education and Fine Arts, "Report on the Organization of Education in Ethiopia" (Paper prepared for the 34th session of the International Conference on Education, Geneva), (Addis Ababa, June 1973), pp. 10–12.
61. United Nations, "Ethiopian Education: General Situation and Policy," revised draft (Addis Ababa, 20 December 1969), pp. 15–16.
62. Ethiopia, Planning Commission, "Education Sector Report" (Addis Ababa, 1973), pp. 13–14.
63. Min. of Ed., *The Current Operation of the Education System,* p. 27.
64. Ibid., p. 101.
65. Min. of Ed., "Report on the Organization of Education in Ethiopia," pp. 22–23.
66. Min. of Ed., *The Current Operation of the Education System,* pp. 85–86.
67. Ethiopia, Ministry of Education and Fine Arts, *Annual Report 1970–71* (Addis Ababa, December 1973), p. 15.
68. Ibid., pp. 17–18; Min. of Ed., *The Current Operation of the Education System,* pp. 85–87.

69. Min. of Ed., *Annual Report 1968–69,* pp. 36–37; Min. of Ed., *Annual Report 1970–71,* pp. 13–14.
70. Min. of Ed., "Report on the Organization of Education in Ethiopia," p. 24.
71. Ethiopia, Ministry of Pen, "Proclamation No. 279 of 1970," *Negarit Gazeta* (Addis Ababa, 15 July 1970).
72. Ethiopia, Ministry of Pen, "Order No. 43 of 1966," *Negarit Gazeta* (Addis Ababa, 14 March 1966).
73. Ethiopia, Ministry of Pen, "Order No. 52 of 1968," *Negarit Gazeta.*
74. Min. of Pen, "Proclamation No. 279 of 1970," *Negarit Gazeta,* pp. 98–100.
75. Min. of Pen, "Order No. 43 of 1966," *Negarit Gazeta,* pp. 33–54.
76. Ethiopia, Ministry of Pen, "Order No. 55 of 1969," *Negarit Gazeta* (Addis Ababa, 31 January 1969), pp. 25–30.
77. International Bank for Reconstruction and Development (IBRD), *Recent Economic Performance and Future Prospects in Ethiopia,* vol. 1 (November 1972).
78. Ministry of Education and Fine Arts, "External Assistance for Education," Appendix II, p. 1.
79. Ethiopia, Ministry of Education and Fine Arts, "Financing Education: A Background Paper for Purposes of Drafting the Fourth Five-Year Plan," p. 18.
80. Min. of Ed., *The Current Operation of the Education System,* p. 39; Education Sector Review Conference, "Final Report—Financing of Education," pp. 27–32.
81. Mulugeta Wodajo, "The State of Educational Finance in Ethiopia: A Short Survey," *Ethiopian Journal of Education* 1, no. 1 (June 1967), pp. 21, 26.
82. Ed. Sector Rev. Conf., "Financing of Education," p. 43.
83. Ibid., p. 44.

Chapter 9

1. Ethiopia, Ministry of Education and Fine Arts, *Report of the Education Sector Review* (Addis Ababa, August 1972), p. I–2.
2. Ibid., p. I–3.
3. Ibid., p. I–7.
4. Ibid., p. II–1.
5. Ibid., pp. V–21 to V–22.
6. Ibid., Annex VI, p. 1.
7. Ibid., p. VII–5.
8. Ethiopia, Ministry of Education and Fine Arts, Planning Unit, "Summary of the Decisions of the Council of Ministers on the Education Sector Review Proposals" (Addis Ababa, April 1973), pp. 1–5.
9. "Notice given by the Ministry of Education and Fine Arts on the Education Sector Review," *Addis Zemen,* 1 Yekatit 1966 E.C. (8 February 1974), pp. 1, 3, 4.
10. Haile Selassie I University, Ethiopian University Teachers Association Circular, mimeographed (Addis Ababa: Haile Selassie I University, EUTA files, 1974).
11. "Government Notice," *Addis Zemen,* 15 Yekatit 1966 E.C. (22 February 1974), pp. 1–4.

Bibliography

Articles

Abebe Bekele. "Regional Cooperation in Education." *Ethiopian Journal of Education,* no. 3 (1969), p. 59.

Abir, Mordechai. "Education and National Unity in Ethiopia." *African Affairs* 69, no. 274 (London, 1970), pp. 44–59.

"The Addis Ababa African Summit Conference: Full Text of All Speeches, the African Charter and Resolutions (May 15–26, 1963)." *Ethiopia Observer* 7, no. 1 (1963), pp. 2–83.

Aklilu Habte [Aklilou Hapte]. "Brain Drain in the Elementary School: Why Teachers Leave the Profession." *Ethiopian Journal of Education,* no. 1 (1967), pp. 27–39.

———. "A Brief Review of the History of the University College of Addis Ababa." *University College Review* (Addis Ababa, Spring 1961), pp. 25–33.

———, Mengesha Gebre-Hiwet, and Monika Kehoe. "Higher Education in Ethiopia." *Journal of Ethiopian Studies* 1, no. 1 (1963), pp. 3–7.

Alemayehu Moges. "Language Teaching and Curricula in Traditional Education of the Ethiopian Orthodox Church." *Ethiopian Journal of Education* 6, no. 1 (1973), pp. 87–114.

"Alliance Française in Ethiopia." *Ethiopia Observer* 4, no. 2 (1960), pp. 61–63.

Andreas Eshete. "Some Principles of Ethiopian Education." *Challenge* (Journal of the Ethiopian Students Association in North America) 9, no. 1 (1968), pp. 6–21.

Asfaw Melaku. "A Survey of Text–Books for Teaching Amharic: Grades 1–12." *Ethiopian Journal of Education* 6, no. 1 (1973), pp. 28–42.

Assefa Bekele. "The Educational Framework of Economic Development in Ethiopia." *Ethiopia Observer* 11, no. 1 (1967), pp. 49–58.

Assefa Liban. "Preparation of Parchment Manuscripts." University College of Addis Ababa Ethnological Society Bulletin no. 8 (July 1958), pp. 5–21.

Ayalew Gebre Selassie. "Three Years' Experience in Education." *Ethiopia Observer* 8, no. 1 (1964), pp. 19–36.

Bairu Tafla. "Education of the Ethiopian Makwanent in the Nineteenth Century." *Ethiopian Journal of Education* 6, no. 1 (1973), pp. 18–27.

Barnes, Roger. "A Fitting Education." *Ethiopia in the World Press* (The Press and Information Department of His Imperial Majesty's Private Cabinet), no. 3 (1965), pp. 25–29.

Benveniste, Guy. "The Educational Technologies and the Developing Countries." In *World Yearbook of Education*. New York: Harcourt, Brace and World, 1967, pp. 375–81.

Brown, G. N. "Avoiding Europe's Mistakes." *West African Journal of Education* 7, no. 2 (1963), pp. 94–95.

Brown, Robert L., and Awad Abdallah. "Sociological Needs of Ethiopia." *Ethiopia Observer* 11, no. 3 (1967), pp. 178–200.

Callaway, Archibald. "Unemployment Among School Leavers in an African City." In *World Yearbook of Education*. New York: Harcourt, Brace and World, 1967, pp. 257–72.

Chojnacki, Stanislaw. "Alemayehu Bizuneh." *Ethiopia Observer* 14, no. 4 (1971), pp. 289–94.

Choudhury, S. K. Roy. "Curricular Courses Available in Addis Ababa." In *Educational Journal*. Addis Ababa Schools' Office, 1960, pp. 36–38.

———. "Kolo Tamari." *Yememhiran Dimts* 1, no. 1 (1965), pp. 34–35.

"College of Engineering and Technical School." *Ethiopia Observer* 1, no. 7 (1957), pp. 213–16.

"Communities Building Their Own School." *Menen* 9, no. 4 (1965), pp. 26–27.

"Conference on Elementary Education." *Menen* 9, no. 12 (1965), pp. 18–20.

Cox, David R. "The Adolescent in Ethiopia." *Ethiopian Journal of Education,* no. 1 (1967), pp. 50–56.

Damon, Philip. "The Metropolitan Volunteer." *Ethiopia Observer* 9, no. 1 (1965), pp. 24–25.

"Debre Berhan Community School." *Ethiopia Observer* 1, no. 7 (1957), pp. 232–35.

"The Development Decade and the Under–Developed World." *Ethiopian Economic Review,* no. 10 (January 1968), pp. 44–47.

Educational Journal Bulletin No. 1. Addis Ababa: The University College Education Students' Association (UCESA), 1954 E.C.

Educational Journal Bulletin No. 2. Addis Ababa: The University College Education Students' Association (UCESA), 1956 E.C.

Educational Journal Bulletin No. 3. Addis Ababa: The University College Education Students' Association (UCESA), 1958 E.C.

"Education and the Future." *Ethiopia Observer* 3, no. 1 (1958), pp. 5–9.

"Education Commission Appointed." *Addis Reporter* 1, no. 24 (1969), p. 10.

"Education for All." *Menen* 7, nos. 11 and 12 (1963), pp. 28–31.

"Education in British Somaliland." *Ethiopia Observer* 3, no. 3 (1959), pp. 97–98.

"Education in Ethiopia." *New Times and Ethiopian News,* 17 July 1937, pp. 3, 6.

"Education Report: Analysis of Developments in Recent Years." *Ethiopia Observer* 5, no. 1 (1961), pp. 61–73.

"The Emperor's Coronation Day Address of November 2, 1962." *Ethiopia Observer* 6, no. 4 (1963), pp. 297–301.

"The Emperor's Speech on the Reunion of Eritrea: November 15, 1962." *Ethiopia Observer* 6, no. 4 (1963), pp. 310–11.

Endalkatchew Makonnen. "Ethiopia's Role in Emergent Africa." *Ethiopia Observer* 5, no. 1 (1961), pp. 8–13.

Ephraim Isaac. "Social Structure of the Ethiopian Church." *Ethiopia Observer* 14, no. 4 (1971), pp. 240–88.

"The Ethiopian National Service." *Menen* 9, no. 10 (1965), pp. 14–15.

"Ethiopia's First Five-Year Plan." *Ethiopia Observer* 3, no. 4 (1959), pp. 106–35.

"Ethiopia's Second Five-Year Plan and Envisaged Land Reform: The Emperor's Speech." *Ethiopia Observer* 6, no. 4 (1963), pp. 294–97.

"Ethiopia's Young Navy." *Ethiopia Observer* 3, no. 9 (1959), pp. 281–90.

Evans, David R. "The Use of Graphical Analysis in Education Planning." *Comparative Education Review* 12, no. 2 (1968), pp. 139–48.

Festa, Andrea. "Presupposti e Fini dell'Azione Educativa nei Territori dell'A.O.I." *Atti del Terzo Congresso di Studi Coloniali* 6 (1937), pp. 126–36.

"Field Day at Debre Berhan." *Ethiopia Observer* 1, no. 10 (1957), p. 334.

"The First Ten Years of the Public Health College." *Menen* 9, no. 9 (1965), pp. 30–32.

"Foreign Community Schools." *Menen* 7, no. 7 (1963), p. 32.

"From Reports on the School Nutrition Activities." *Ethiopia Observer* 4, no. 4 (1960), pp. 110–12.

Gabrahewet Nebarai. "Eritrea School Nutrition and Gardening Programme." *Ethiopia Observer* 4, no. 4 (1960), pp. 108–9.

Garraud, R., and Ruth Imru. "Community Development Training at Majete." *Ethiopia Observer* 2, no. 9 (1958), pp. 301–3.

Gattegno, Caleb. "Ethiopia's Educational Problem." *Ethiopia Observer* 2, no. 4 (1958), p. 140.

Getachew Wolde Hanna. "School Nutrition and Gardening." *Ethiopia Observer* 4, no. 4 (1960), p. 106.

Gillett, Margaret. "Symposium on Africa: Western Academic Role Concepts in Ethiopian University." *Comparative Education Review* 7, no. 2 (1963), pp. 149–51.

Girma Amare [Germa Amare]. "Aims and Purposes of Church Education in Ethiopia." *Ethiopian Journal of Education,* no. 1 (June 1967), pp. 1–11.

———. "Government Education in Ethiopia." *Ethiopia Observer* 6, no. 4 (1963), pp. 335–42.

———. "Higher Education in Ethiopia: A Report on Haile Selassie I University. M. Kehoe, Reply." *Journal of Higher Education* 33, no. 7 (1963), pp. 398–400.

———. "Memorization in Ethiopian Schools." *Journal of Ethiopian Studies* 1, no. 1 (1963), pp. 27–31.

———. "Salary Scale for Ethiopian Teachers." In *The Educator.* Addis Ababa: The Teacher Training Institute, June 1967, pp. 10–16.

———. "Social Functions of African Education." In *Africa and the World.* Addis Ababa: Oxford University Press, 1970, pp. 193–204.

———. "Some Questions of Values in Nation Building: An Educational Perspective." *Ethiopian Journal of Education* 6, no. 1 (1973), pp. 1–17.

Grant, Michael. "Education in Ethiopia." *Times* (London), 4 August 1953, p. 4.

Greenfield, Richard David. "Afro-Ethiopia: A Note on the Current State of Higher Education and University Research in Ethiopia." *Mekerere Journal,* no. 8 (Kampala, 1963), pp. 1–15.

"Growth and Shortage." *Ethiopian Herald,* 3 April 1971, p. 2.

Guidi, Ignazio. "Qene o inni Abissini." *Rediconti della Reale Accademia dei Lincei* 9, nos. 7–8 (1900), pp. 463–510.

Gulavi, Stanley J. "The Development of Friendship Between Ethiopia and Her Southern Neighbors." *Ethiopia Observer* 3, no. 3 (1959), pp. 96–97.

Hagos Gebre Yesus. "Token Education in Ethiopia." *Africa Today* 13, no. 2 (1966), pp. 12–15.

Haile Fida. "Do We Need a University?" *UCESA Educational Journal* 2 (Addis Ababa, 1964), pp. 16–18.

Haile Gabriel Dagne. "Education Magic in Traditional Ethiopia." *Ethiopian Journal of Education* 4, no. 2 (1971), pp. 3–12.

———. "The Traditional Ethiopian Curriculum." *Ethiopian Journal of Education* 4, no. 2 (1971), pp. 79–80.

Haile Mariam Goshu. "Unique Assistance and Response." *Addis Reporter,* 19 September 1969, pp. 7–10.

———. "War Against Ignorance." *Addis Reporter,* 1 August 1969, pp. 13–16.

Haile Selassie I, Emperor. "Address to the Ethiopian Parliament, November 2, 1958." *Ethiopia Observer* 3, no. 3 (1959), pp. 66–69.

———. "Ethiopia's Achievements and Objectives: Coronation Speech, November 3, 1960." *Ethiopia Observer* 5, no. 1 (1961), pp. 3–7.

Haile Wolde Mikael. "Problems in Philosophy of Education." *Dialogue* 3, no. 1 (1970), pp. 23–32.

Hammerschmidt, Ernst. "A Brief History of German Contributions to the Study of Ethiopia." *Journal of Ethiopian Studies* 1, no. 2 (1963), pp. 30–48.

Han, Lee–Min. "A Historical Sketch of the Public Health College and Training Center, Gondar." *Ethiopia Observer* 10, no. 3 (1966), pp. 199–203.

"A Helping Hand." *Ethiopian Herald,* 13 May 1971, p. 2.

Hunter, Guy. "Primary Education and Employment in the Rural Economy with Special Reference to East Africa." In *World Yearbook of Education.* New York: Harcourt, Brace and World, 1967, pp. 242–56.

Jacobson, Gene S. "The Organization and Administration of the Public School in Ethiopia." *Ethiopian Journal of Education,* no. 1 (1967), pp. 12–17.

Jager, Otto A. "Ethiopian Manuscript Paintings." *Ethiopia Observer* 4, no. 11 (1960), pp. 353–91.

James, S. R. "Amharic as the Medium of Instruction in the Ethiopian Elementary Schools." *Yememhiran Dimts* 1, no. 1 (1965), pp. 26–33.

Jandy, Edward C. "The New Ethiopia and Socioeducational Problems." *Sociology and Social Research* 33, no. 2 (1948), pp. 113–24.

Johnstone, Quintin. "Fifth Annual Report of the Dean 1967–1968 (1960 E.C.)." *Journal of Ethiopian Law* 5, no. 1 (1968), pp. 15–21.

———. "Sixth Annual Report of the Dean 1968–1969 (1961 E.C.)." *Journal of Ethiopian Law* 6, no. 1 (1969), pp. 15–24.

Karugu, F. T. "A Kenya African Comes to Study in Addis." *Ethiopia Observer* 3, no. 3 (1959), pp. 86–87.

Kehoe, Monika. "Higher Education in Ethiopia: A Report on Haile Selassie I University." *Higher Education* 33 (December 1962), pp. 475–78.

Klassen, Frank. "Teacher Education in Ethiopia." *School and Society* 91 (February 1963), pp. 96–98.

Knowles, L., Jr. "History of the Peace Corps at the Business College of Haile Selassie I University." *Ethiopia Observer* 9, no. 1 (1965), pp. 42–45.

Kramer, Roberta C. "Teacher Training in Ethiopia." *Ethiopia Observer* 9, no. 1 (1965), pp. 37–38.

Krzeczunowicz, Jerzy. "The Ethiopian Civil Code: Its Usefulness, Relation to Custom and Applicability." *Journal of African Law* 7, no. 3 (London, 1963), pp. 172–77.

————. "Ethiopian Legal Education: Retrospection and Prospects." *Journal of Ethiopian Studies* 1, no. 1 (1963), pp. 68–74.

Last, Geoffrey C. "The Aims and Purposes of Geography Teaching." *Ethiopia Observer* 2, no. 5 (1958), pp. 190–91.

Leslau, Wolf. "The Black Jews of Ethiopia: An Expedition to the Felashas." *Commentary* 7 (1949), pp. 216–24.

Le Thank, Khoi. "Problems of Educational Planning in Africa." In *World Yearbook of Education*. New York: Harcourt, Brace and World, 1963.

"Liberation Day Address by Ethiopian Prime Minister and Emperor's Reply. An Exchange of Speeches on May 5, 1964." *Ethiopia Observer* 8, no. 1 (1964), pp. 2–6.

Lilliefelt, Theodor C. P. "United Nations' Technical Assistance." *Ethiopia Observer* 2, no. 9 (1958), pp. 290–95.

Lord, Edith. "Education—What For?" *Ethiopia Observer* 2, no. 4 (1958), p. 141.

Maaza Bekele. "Ethiopian Education: Challenge of the 70's." *Educational Leadership,* March 1968, pp. 511–17.

————. "Some Thoughts on the Future." *Ethiopia Observer* 2, no. 4 (1958), pp. 139–40.

Madsen, Harold S. "The Curriculum—ESLC Seminar of 1967." *Ethiopian Journal of Education* 2, no. 1 (1968), pp. 2–10.

(Balambaras) Mahteme Selassie Wolde Maskal. "The Land System of Ethiopia." *Ethiopia Observer* 1, no. 9 (1957), pp. 283–301.

Mairegu Bezabih. "Focus on Swedish Assistance to Ethiopia." *Ethiopian Herald,* 19 November 1968, pp. 3, 5.

Megeletcha: Magazine for Teachers 1, nos. 1–4 (1965–66); 2, nos. 1–3 (1966–67). The Laboratory School, Haile Selassie I University.

Menghistu Lemma. "Technical Aspects of Amharic Versification." *Journal of Ethiopian Studies* 1, no. 2 (1963), pp. 133–51.

Miles, Richard. "Training Agriculturists." *Addis Reporter,* 15 August 1969, p. 21.

Million Bemedhin. "Gross Cultural Distortion." *Ethiopian Herald,* 23 January 1963, p. 2.

————. "How Promising is the Tempo of Ethiopianization?" *Ethiopian Herald,* 15 November 1962, p. 2.

Million Neqniq. "The Most Urgent Needs in the Expansion of Ethiopian Education." *Ethiopia Observer* 2, no. 4 (1958), pp. 138–39.

"Missionaries and the Law." *Ethiopia Observer* 4, no. 2 (1960), pp. 62–63.

"Mission Schools in Ethiopia." *Menen* 7, no. 4 (1963), p. 32.

Mondon-Vidailhet, François Marie Casimir. "La Musique Ethiopienne." In *Encyclopedie de la Musique et Dictionnaire du Conservatoire*. Paris, 1922, pp. 3179–98.

Mulugeta Eteffa. "Knowledge of Priorities in Education." *Dialogue* 2, no. 2 (1969), pp. 27–35.

Mulugeta Wodajo. "Ethiopia: Some Pressing Problems and the Role of Education in their Resolution." *Journal of Negro Education* 30 (Summer 1961),
pp. 232–40.

———. "Post–War Reform in Ethiopian Education." *Comparative Education Review* 2, no. 3 (1959), pp. 24–28.

———. "Secondary Education and Man–Power Requirements of the Second
Five-Year Plan." *UCESA Educational Journal,* no. 2 (Addis Ababa, 1964),
pp. 19–23.

———. "The State of Educational Finance in Ethiopia: A Short Survey." *Ethiopian Journal of Education,* no. 1 (1967), pp. 18–26.

Muthusami, I. J. "Balanced Education." *Yememhiran Dimts* 1, no. 1 (1965),
pp. 30–33.

"The New Faculty of Law." *Menen* 8, no. 1 (1963), pp. 23–24.

Ocbaselassie Ghebremedhin. "Educational Standards in Ethiopia." *UCESA Educational Journal,* no. 3 (1966), pp. 18–20.

O'Donovan, Katherine. "Women's Status Under the Civil Law." *Ethiopian Herald,* 6 June 1972, pp. 2, 4.

Ouko, Robert J. "Kenya Education and the African District Council." *Ethiopia
Observer* 3, no. 3 (1959), pp. 92–94.

Pankhurst, E. Sylvia. "Ambo Agricultural School." *Ethiopia Observer* 1, no. 40
(1957), pp. 309–11.

———. "Bishoftu Agricultural Research Station." *Ethiopia Observer* 1, no. 10
(1957), pp. 330–34.

———. "Community Development Training at Majete." *Ethiopia Observer* 2,
no. 9 (1958), pp. 301–3.

———. "Debre Berhan Community Training School." *Ethiopia Observer* 2, no.
10 (1958), pp. 330–35.

———. "Education in Ethiopia: A Remarkable Achievement." *New Times and
Ethiopian News,* 13 April 1946, p. 2.

———. "Education in Ethiopia II: Secondary Education." *Ethiopia Observer* 2,
no. 5 (1958), pp. 162–64.

———. "History of Ethiopian Schools." *Ethiopia Observer* 2, no. 4 (1958),
pp. 130–32.

———. "Imperial College of Agriculture and Mechanical Arts." *Ethiopia Observer* 1, no. 10 (1957), pp. 312–17.

———. "The Institute of Building Technology." *Ethiopia Observer* 1, no. 11
(1957), pp. 370–71.

———. "Jimma Agricultural School." *Ethiopia Observer* 1, no. 10 (1957),
pp. 318–24.

Pankhurst, Richard. "Ethiopia and the African Personality." *Ethiopia Observer* 3,
no. 3 (1959), pp. 70–72.

———. "Ethiopia in the Nineteenth Century." *Ethiopia Observer* 7, no. 1
(1963), pp. 84–96.

———. "Ethiopia's First Students Abroad." *Addis Reporter,* 4 July 1969, pp. 22–
24.

———. "The Foundations of Education, Printing, Newspapers, Book Production, Libraries and Literacy in Ethiopia." *Ethiopia Observer* 6, no. 3 (1962), pp. 241–90.

————. "Some Schools of Addis Ababa." *The Educational Magazine* 9, no. 2 (1952), pp. 92–96.

————. "Two Forgotten Ethiopian Scholars of the Late Eighteenth and Early Nineteenth Centuries: Abu Rumi and Liq Atsqu." *Ethiopia Observer* 12, no. 2 (1969), p. 140.

————, and Andreas Eshete. "Self-Help in Ethiopia." *Ethiopia Observer* 2, no. 11 (1958), pp. 354–64.

Paul, J. C. N. "Fourth Annual Report from the Dean, 1966–1967 (1959 E.C.)." *Journal of Ethiopian Law* 4, no. 1 (1967), pp. 21–31.

Pennisi, Pesquale. "La Scuola Fascista per L'Italia Africana." *Rassegna Sociale dell' Africa Italiana* 3, no. 2 (1940), pp. 85–90.

Phillips, H. M. "Trends in Educational Expansion in Developing Countries." In *World Yearbook of Education.* New York: Harcourt, Brace and World, 1967, pp. 382–89.

Point IV (USAID). "Special Technical Education, and Arts and Crafts Training." *Point IV News,* November–December 1954, pp. 11–12.

"Post-Secondary Vacation Course for Teachers." *Educational Torch* 1, no. 1 (1951 E.C.), p. 41.

"Prince Makonnen School, Massawa." *Ethiopia Observer* 3, no. 9 (1959), pp. 279–80.

"Radio as an Effective Medium of Education." *Menen* 9, no. 7 (1965), pp. 22–23, 32.

Rado, Emil R. "Manpower Planning in East Africa." In *World Yearbook of Education.* New York: Harcourt, Brace and World, 1967, pp. 273–93.

"Recent Developments in Ethiopian Education." *Ethiopian Economic Review,* no. 6 (1963), pp. 67–69.

"Regular and Advanced Vacation Courses for Teachers." *Educational Torch* 1, no. 1 (1951 E.C.), p. 21.

"Results of a Family Budget Study of 106 Households in Addis Ababa." *Ethiopian Economic Review,* no. 3 (1960), pp. 7–15.

"Review of Current Economic Conditions in Ethiopia." *Ethiopian Economic Review,* no. 9 (1966), p. 7.

"Review of Social Development Trends and Policies of Ethiopia." *Ethiopian Economic Review,* no. 8 (1964), pp. 7–15.

Robertson, Jean E. "Some Administrative Problems Associated With Literacy Work in Ethiopia." *Alberta Journal of Educational Research* 6, no. 3 (1960), pp. 153–62.

Rud, Oljira. "School Drop-outs in Ethiopia." *UCESA Educational Journal,* no. 3 (1966), pp. 13–16.

"School of Home Economics, Addis Ababa." *Ethiopia Observer* 4, no. 4 (1960), pp. 113–14.

"Schools." *Ethiopia Observer* 2, no. 2 (1958), pp. 81–88.

Schwab, Peter. "Education in Ethiopia: A Brief Survey." *Acta Africana: Geneva Africa* 8, no. 2 (1969), pp. 1–3.

Senedu Gebru. "Girls' Education." *Ethiopia Observer* 1, no. 3 (1957), pp. 76–80, 93.

Shack, William A. "Organization and Problems of Education in Ethiopia." *Journal of Negro Education,* no. 28 (1959), pp. 405–20.

"Short Review of Economic Conditions in Ethiopia." *Ethiopian Economic Review,* no. 3 (1960), pp. 16–21.

Solomon Inquai. "Adult Literacy in Ethiopia—A Profile." *Journal of Ethiopian Studies* 7, no. 1 (1969), pp. 55–63.

———. "What Kind of a University?" *Dialogue* 1, no. 2 (1968), pp. 35–39.

"Statistical Study Showing Progress in Education in Addis Ababa Since 1955 E.C." In *Educational Journal.* Addis Ababa Schools' Office, 1960, pp. 82–87.

"Summer Courses in Addis Ababa." In *Educational Journal.* Addis Ababa Schools Office, 1960, pp. 74–79.

Taddesse Tereffe. "Progress, Problems, and Prospects in Ethiopian Education." *Ethiopia Observer* 8, no. 1 (1964), pp. 6–18.

"Teachers in Ethiopia." *Time,* 7 August 1944, p. 50.

Teferra Wolde Semait. "Economic Development and Education." *Economic Journal* 1, no. 1 (1964), pp. 60–65.

Tereffe Asrat. "VOS: The British Peace Corps." *Addis Reporter,* 9 May 1969, pp. 18–19.

Tesfaye Kabtihimar. "Higher Education in Ethiopia." *Ethiopia Mirror* 2, nos. 2–3 (1963), p. 5.

Tesfaye Shewaye. "An Introduction to the Development of Ethiopian Education." *UCESA Educational Journal,* no. 3 (1966), pp. 10–12.

Teshager Wube. "The Wandering Student." *University College of Addis Ababa Ethnological Society Bulletin,* no. 9 (July–December 1959), pp. 52–60.

Teshome G. Wagaw. "Access to Haile Selassie I University." *Ethiopia Observer* 14, no. 1 (1971), pp. 31–46.

———. "A Follow-up Study of the 1961 Addis Ababa Education Conference of African States: Implications for Ethiopia." *Dialogue* 3, no. 2 (1971), pp. 41–56.

———, and Darge Wole. "Teachers and Directors Speak Out About School Problems." *Ethiopian Journal of Education* 4, no. 2 (1971), pp. 43–67.

Tickaher Hailu. "Is the Junior College Idea Useful for Ethiopia?" *Dialogue* 2, no. 1 (1968), pp. 37–40.

———. "Two Major Educational Problems in Developing Countries." *Yememhiran Dimts* 1, no. 1 (1965), pp. 19–21.

Tilahun Gamta. "That Education at All Levels is the Basis for Any Country's Development." *UCESA Educational Journal,* no. 2 (1964), pp. 3–8.

"The University College of Addis Ababa." *Ethiopia Observer* 2, no. 6 (1958), pp. 195–207, 210–13.

"University College of Addis Ababa Examination Papers." *Ethiopia Observer* 2, no. 6 (1958), pp. 213–14.

Vagliani, Pierluigi. "Literacy—A Lever for Ethiopia's Development." *New Africa* 10, no. 5–6 (1968), pp. 14–15.

Vestal, Theodore M. "The Peace Corps in Ethiopia: An Overall View." *Ethiopia Observer* 9, no. 1 (1965), pp. 11–24.

"The Vocational Building School." *Ethiopia Observer* 1, no. 7 (1957), pp. 221–24.

"Voluntary Social Work in Ethiopia." *Ethiopia Observer* 4, no. 2 (1960), pp. 44–45.

"What Modern Ethiopia Achieved For Herself." *New Times and Ethiopian News,* 5 March 1938, pp. 1–4.

Work, F. Ernest. "A Plan for Ethiopia's Educational System." *Journal of Negro Education* 3 (1934), pp. 66–68.

Workaferahu Kebede. "Volunteers in Ethiopia." *Addis Reporter,* 21 August 1969, pp. 18–22.

"World Bank Issues Sector Pamphlets." *Ethiopian Herald,* 11 August 1972, p. 3.

Wright, Stephen. "Book and Manuscript Collections in Ethiopia." *Journal of Ethiopian Studies* 2, no. 1 (1964), pp. 11–24.

Zaudneh Yimtatu. "Director's Review." *Educator,* June 1967, pp. 17–20.

Books and Monographs

Abebe Ambachew. "The Influence of Higher Education on the American Society and its Implications for the Role of Higher Education in Ethiopia." Ph.D. dissertation, Ohio State University, 1962.

Abebe Bekele. *Some Major Problems in the Curricular Offering in the Elementary Schools of Ethiopia.* Mimeographed. Addis Ababa: Haile Selassie I University, Faculty of Education, 1971.

Abraham Demoz. "The Problem of Quality in Higher Education: A Case Study." Mimeographed. Paper presented at the Conference on the Role of a University in a Developing Country. Addis Ababa, 1967.

Adams, Don, and Bjork, Robert M. *Education in Developing Areas.* New York: David Mackay Co., 1969.

Agadew Redie, and Jacobson, Martin. *Educational Opportunities in Ethiopia for High School Teachers and Students.* Addis Ababa: Ministry of Education and Fine Arts, Department of Educational Operations, 1970.

Aklilu Gebre Heywot. "Ethiopian Church Education." Mimeographed. Addis Ababa: Haile Selassie I University, Institute of Ethiopian Studies, 1965.

Aklilu Habte. "Brief Remarks on the Historical Development of the Department of Education." In *Final Report of the Conference on Secondary Education in Ethiopia.* Mimeographed. Addis Ababa: Haile Selassie I University, 1962.

———. "Education and Development." Mimeographed. Addis Ababa: Haile Selassie I University, Faculty of Arts, 1968.

———. "Educational Reform in Ethiopia: The Challenge of the Century." Mimeographed. Addis Ababa, 1967.

———. "Factors Affecting the Development of Universities in Africa: A Case of Ethiopia." Mimeographed. Paper presented at the Conference on the Role of a University in a Developing Country. Addis Ababa, 1967.

———. "The Production and Retention of Elementary School Teachers in Ethiopia." Mimeographed. Addis Ababa: Haile Selassie I University, 1967.

———, and Trudeau, Edouard. "Project for a School or Institute of Education of University College of Addis Ababa." Mimeographed. Addis Ababa: Haile Selassie I University, 1962.

Alemu Begashaw. *Where Are You Going to School?: Orientation and Guidance for Eighth Grade Students in Ethiopian Schools.* 2d ed. Addis Ababa: Ministry of Education and United States Operations Mission to Ethiopia, Cooperative Education Program Press, 1955.

Almond, Gabriel A., and Coleman, James S., eds. *The Politics of the Developing Areas.* Princeton: Princeton University Press, 1960.

Alvares, Francisco. *The Prester John of the Indies. Narrative of the Portuguese Embassy to Ethiopia in 1520.* Translated by Lord Stanley of Alderley, 1881. 2 Vols. Revised and edited by C. F. Beckingham and G. W. B. Huntingford. Cambridge: The Hakluyt Society, Cambridge University Press, 1961.

Amberber Mengesha, comp. "Legal Provisions with Reference to Youth and School Activities," pt.1. Mimeographed. Addis Ababa, 1969.

American Assembly. *The United States and Africa: Background Papers . . . and the Final Report of the Thirteenth American Assembly.* Harriman, N.Y.: Arden House, Harriman Campus of Columbia University, 1958.

Ashby, Eric. *African Universities and Western Tradition.* Cambridge: Harvard University Press, 1964.

———. "Investment in Education. A Report of the Commission on Post–School Certificate and Higher Education in Africa." Mimeographed. Lagos: The Government Printers, 1960.

———, and Anderson, Mary. *Universities: British, Indian, African: A Study in the Ecology of Higher Education.* Cambridge: Harvard University Press, 1966.

Asher, Robert E., et al. *Development of the Emerging Countries: An Agenda for Research.* Washington, D.C.: The Brookings Institution, 1962.

Assazenew Baysa. "Ethiopia." In *The Recruitment and Training of University Teachers.* Ghent: International Association of University Professors and Lecturers, 1967.

Atnafu Makonnen, comp. *Ethiopia Today.* Tokyo: Radiopress, 1960.

Austen, Ralph A. *Northwest Tanzania Under German and British Rule: Colonial Policy and Tribal Politics, 1889–1939.* New Haven: Yale University Press, 1968.

Ayars, Albert L. *Administering the People's Schools.* New York: McGraw-Hill, 1957.

Badoglio, Pietro. *The War in Abyssinia.* London: Methuen, 1937.

Baer, George W. *The Coming of the Italian-Ethiopian War.* Cambridge: Harvard University Press, 1967.

Barker, A. J. *Eritrea 1941.* London: Faber and Faber, 1966.

Barnett, Homer Garner. *Innovation: The Basis of Cultural Change.* New York: McGraw-Hill, 1953.

Beck, Robert H.; Cook, Walter W.; and Kearney, Nolan C. *Curriculum in the Modern Elementary School.* New York: Prentice-Hall, 1953.

Beeby, Clarence E. *The Quality of Education in Developing Countries.* Cambridge: Harvard University Press, 1966.

Bekele Getahun. "Working Paper on Teacher Education." Mimeographed. Addis Ababa, 1969.

Benson, Charles S. *The Economics of Public Education.* Boston: Houghton-Mifflin, 1961.

Bent, Rudyard K., and Kronenberg, Henry H. *Principles of Secondary Education.* 3d ed. New York: McGraw-Hill, 1955.

Bentwich, Norman. *Ethiopia at the Paris Peace Conference.* London: Abyssinia (Ethiopia) Association, 1946.

———. *Ethiopia, Eritrea and Somaliland.* London: Victor Gollancz, 1945.

Beyene Negewo. "The Training of Elementary School Directors and Supervisors through an In-service Programme in Ethiopia." Mimeographed. Paper presented at Symposium on Educational Innovation in Africa, Addis Ababa, 1–10 September 1971. Addis Ababa, 1971.

Bjeren, Gunilla. "Makelle (Ethiopia) Elementary School Drop-Out 1967; Research Report No. 5." Mimeographed. Uppsala: The Scandinavian Institute of African Studies, 1969.

Bjerkan, Ole-Christian. "Plans, Targets and Trends in Ethiopian Education." Ph.D. dissertation, University of Maryland, 1970.

Bowers, John, and Langmur, Charles R. "Individual Intelligence Testing of Pre-school Ethiopian Children." Mimeographed. Addis Ababa: Haile Selassie I University, University Testing Center, 1967.

Branson, Bruce W., et al. "Report of Visiting Committee for the Faculty of Medicine, HSIU." Mimeographed. Addis Ababa, 1966.

Brembeck, Cole S., and John, Keith P. *Education in Emerging Africa: A Select and Annotated Bibliography.* East Lansing: Michigan State University, n.d.

Broberg, Bertram, et al. "Report on Technical Education for Haile Selassie I University." Mimeographed. Addis Ababa, 1969.

Brooks, Kenneth G. "The Campaign Against Illiteracy in Ethiopia." Report prepared for UNESCO. Mimeographed. Addis Ababa, 1966.

Brown, Robert Lane. "A Resume on Attitudes of Ethiopian Students." Mimeographed. Addis Ababa: Haile Selassie I University, Faculty of Arts, 1968.

Bruce, James. *Bruce's Travels and Adventures in Abyssinia.* Edited by J. Morison Clingan. Edinburgh: Adam and Charles Black, 1860.

Bruner, Jerome S. *The Process of Education.* Cambridge: Harvard University Press, 1960.

Budge, E. A. Wallis. *The Book of the Saints of the Ethiopian Church: A Translation of the Ethiopic Synaxarium.* Cambridge: Cambridge University Press, 1928.

———. *A History of Ethiopia, Nubia and Abyssinia.* 2 vols. London: Methuen and Co., 1928.

———. *The Queen of Sheba and Her Only Son Menelik . . . .* London: Martin Hopkinson, 1922.

Buell, Raymond Leslie. *The Native Problem in Africa.* Hamden, Conn.: Archon Books, 1928.

Burns, Donald G. *African Education: An Introductory Survey of Education in Commonwealth Countries.* London: Oxford University Press, 1965.

Burns, Emile. *Ethiopia and Italy.* New York: International Publishers, 1935.

Butts, Robert F. *American Education in International Development.* New York: Harper and Row, 1963.

Carr-Saunders, Sir Alexander M. *Staffing African Universities.* London: Overseas Development Institute, 1963.

Castle, Edgar B. *Growing Up in East Africa.* London: Oxford University Press, 1966.

Cecchi, Antonio. *Da Zeila alle Frontiere del Kaffa.* Edited by E. Siracusa Cabrini. Turin: C. B. Paravia and Co., 1930.

Cerulli, Enrico. *Storia della Letteratura Etiopica.* Milan: Nuova Accademia Editrice, 1956.

Cerych, Ladislav. *Problems of Aid to Education in Developing Countries.* Translated and edited by Noël Lindsay et al. New York: Frederick A. Praeger, 1965.

Chaine, Marius. *La Chronologie des Temps Chrétiens de l'Égypte et de l'Éthiopie . . . .* Paris: P. Geuthner, 1925.

Chojnacki, Stanislaw, and Pankhurst, Richard K. P., eds. "Register of Current Research on Ethiopia and the Horn of Africa." Addis Ababa: Haile Selassie I University, Institute of Ethiopian Studies, 1964.

Clapham, Christopher S. *Haile Selassie's Government.* New York: Frederick A. Praeger, 1969.

Clignet, Remi, and Foster, Philip. *The Fortunate Few: A Study of Secondary Schools and Students in the Ivory Coast.* Evanston, Ill.: Northwestern University Press, 1966.

Coleman, James S., ed. *Education and Political Development.* Princeton: Princeton University Press, 1965.

Coleman, James S., and Roseberg, Carl G., eds. *Political Parties and National Integration in Tropical Africa.* Berkeley: University of California Press, 1964.

Conzelman, William E. *Chronique de Gelawdewos (Claudius), Roi d'Éthiopie.* É.'Bouillon, 1895.

Coulbeaux, Jean Baptiste. *Histoire Politique et Religieuse d'Abyssinie.* 3 vols. Paris: P. Geuthner, 1929.

Cowan, Laing Gray, et al., eds. *Education and Nation-Building in Africa.* New York: Frederick A. Praeger, 1965.

Cox, David R. "Principles of Learning for Teachers." Addis Ababa: Artistic Printers, 1968.

Cramer, John Francis, and Browne, George S. *Contemporary Education: A Comparative Study of National Systems.* New York: Harcourt, Brace, and Co., 1956.

Crawford, Osbert G. S. *Ethiopian Itineraries, circa 1400–1524.* Cambridge: Cambridge University Press, 1958.

Culbertson, Jack A.; Jacobson, Paul B.; and Reller, Theodore L. *Administrative Relationships: A Case Book.* Englewood, N.J.: Prentice-Hall, 1960.

Curle, Adam. *Educational Strategy for Developing Societies: A Study of Educational Social Factors in Relation to Economic Growth.* London: Tavistock Publications, 1963.

Currie, Lauchlin B. *Obstacles to Development.* East Lansing: Michigan State University Press, 1967.

Davis, Jackson; Campbell, Thomas M.; and Wrong, Margaret. *Africa Advancing: A Study of Rural Education and Agriculture in West Africa and the Belgian Congo.* New York: The Friendship Press; London: The Internal Committee on Christian Literature for Africa, 1945.

Davis, Russell G. *Planning Human Resource Development: Educational Models and Schemata.* Chicago: Rand-McNally, 1966.

del Boca, Angelo. *The Ethiopian War 1935–1941.* Translated by P. D. Cummins. Chicago: University of Chicago Press, 1969.

De Marco, Roland R., *The Italianization of the African Natives: Government Native Education in the Italian Colonies, 1890–1937.* New York: Columbia University Teachers College, 1943.

de Vries, Egbert. *Man in Rapid Social Change.* Garden City, N.Y.: Doubleday, 1961.

Dewey, John. *Experience and Education.* New York: Collier Books, 1963.

Dolan, Eleanor F. *Higher Education in Africa South of the Sahara: Selected Bibliographies, 1945–1961.* Washington, D.C.: American Association of University Writers Educational Foundation, 1961.

Doresse, Jean. *Ethiopia: Ancient Cities and Temples.* Translated by Elsa Coult. London: Elek Books; New York: Putnam, 1959.

Dower, Kenneth G. *Abyssinian Patchwork: An Anthology.* London: Frederick Muller, 1949.

Drake, Howard. *A Bibliography of African Education South of the Sahara.* Aberdeen: Aberdeen University, 1942.

Duesenberry, James S. *Income, Saving and the Theory of Consumer Behavior.* Cambridge: Harvard University Press, 1949.

Eby, Frederick. *The Development of Modern Education in Theory, Organization, and Practice.* 2d ed. New York: Prentice–Hall, 1952.

Education Sector Review Conference. "Final Report—Agricultural Education." In *Collected Papers,* vol. 3. Addis Ababa, 1972.

———. "Final Report—Aspects of Higher Education." In *Collected Papers,* vol. 3. Addis Ababa, 1972.

———. "Final Report—Distribution of Educational Opportunities." In *Collected Papers,* vol. 1. Addis Ababa, 1972.

———. "Final Report—Education for Development." In *Collected Papers,* vol. 2. Addis Ababa, 1972.

———. "Final Report—Education for National Integration." In *Collected Papers,* vol. 2. Addis Ababa, 1972.

———. "Final Report—Education Objectives." In *Collected Papers,* vol. 1. Addis Ababa, 1972.

———. "Final Report—Educational Research." In *Collected Papers,* vol. 3. Addis Ababa, 1972.

———. "Final Report—Educational Technology." In *Collected Papers,* vol. 3. Addis Ababa, 1972.

———. "Final Report—Financing of Education." In *Collected Papers,* vol. 2. Addis Ababa, 1972.

———. "Final Report—Guidance, Counselling and Social Control." In *Collected Papers,* vol. 3. Addis Ababa, 1972.

———. "Final Report—Health Education." In *Collected Papers,* vol. 3. Addis Ababa, 1972.

———. "Final Report—Manpower." In *Collected Papers,* vol. 1. Addis Ababa, 1972.

———. "Final Report—Non-Government Schools." In *Collected Papers,* vol. 3. Addis Ababa, 1972.

————. "Final Report—Organization and Management." In *Collected Papers,* vol. 2. Addis Ababa, 1972.

————. "Final Report—Pre-School Education in Ethiopia." In *Collected Papers,* vol. 3. Addis Ababa, 1972.

————. "Symposium—Summary of the Discussions Held in Africa Hall from January 16–19, 1972." In *Collected Papers,* vol. 2. Addis Ababa, 1972.

Ellenwood, James Lee. *One Generation After Another.* New York: Charles Scribner and Sons, 1953.

Elliott, Dean A. "Role of Agricultural Education in the Development of Agriculture in Ethiopia." Ph.D. dissertation, Iowa State University, 1957.

Enbakom Kalewold [Imbakom Kalewold]. "Ethiopian Church Education." Mimeographed. Addis Ababa: Haile Selassie I University, Institute of Ethiopian Studies, 1965.

Eshetu Chole, and Assefa Bekele. "Taxation and Economic Development in Ethiopia." Mimeographed. Addis Ababa: Haile Selassie I University, 1966.

Ethio-Swedish Institute of Building Technology. *Annual Report: 1959–1960.* Addis Ababa, 1960.

Ethiopian Women's Welfare Association. *Princess Tenagné Worq School for Women.* [Cover Title—*Prospectus.*] Addis Ababa: Central Printing Press, 1960.

Firth, Raymond W. *Elements of Social Organization.* 3d ed. London: Watts, 1963.

Forbes, Rosita T. *From Red Sea To Blue Nile: Abyssinian Adventures.* London: Cassell and Company, 1925.

Foster, Philip J. *Education and Social Change in Ghana.* London: Routledge and Kegan Paul, 1965.

Fournet, J. D. *Mission in Ethiopia (1903–1909).* 2 vols. Paris: Masson et Cie., 1908–9.

Galbraith, John Kenneth. *Economic Development.* Cambridge: Harvard University Press, 1964.

Gardner, John W. *Self-Renewal: The Individual and the Innovative Society.* New York: Harper and Row, 1964.

Gattegno, Caleb. "Ethiopian Problems of Education." Mimeographed. Addis Ababa, 1957.

Geiger, Theodore. *Trans-World Airline's Services to Ethiopia.* Washington, D.C.: National Planning Association, 1959.

Ginsberg, Norton S. *Atlas of Economic Development.* Chicago: University of Chicago Press, 1961.

Ginzberg, Eli, ed. *Technology and Social Change.* New York: Columbia University Press, 1965.

Ginzberg, Eli, and Smith, Herbert A. *Manpower Strategy for Developing Countries: Lessons from Ethiopia.* New York: Columbia University Press, 1967.

Girma Amare [Germa Amare]. "Education and the Conflict of Values in Ethiopia. A Study of the Socio-Moral Problems Arising out of the Introduction of Modern Education in Ethiopia." Ph.D. dissertation, Southern Illinois University, 1964.

————. "A Review of a University in the Making: Past Experiences and Future Expectations." Paper presented at the Conference on the Role of a University in a Developing Country. Addis Ababa, 1967.

Gobat, Samuel. *Journal of a Three Years' Residence in Abyssinia.* London: Hatchard and Son, Seeley and Sons, 1834.

Goldschmidt, Walter R., ed. *The United States and Africa.* Rev. ed. New York: Frederick A. Praeger, 1963.

Greenfield, Richard D. *Ethiopia: A New Political History.* New York: Frederick A. Praeger, 1968.

Griaule, Marcel. *Le livre de recettes d'un Dabtara abyssin.* Paris: Institut d'ethnologie, Université de Paris, 1930.

Grove, H. M. *Education and Economic Growth.* Washington, D.C.: National Education Association, 1961.

Groves, Charles P. *The Planting of Christianity in Africa.* 4 vols. London: Lutterworth Press, 1948–58.

Guèbrè Selassié. *Chronique du règne de Ménélik II, roi des rois d'Éthiopie.* Translated from Amharic by Tesfa Selassié, published and annotated by Maurice de Coppet. 2 vols. Paris: Maisonneuve Frères, 1930–32.

Guidi, Ignazio. *"Fetha Nagast"* or *"Legistazione dei re; codice e civile di Abissinia."* Naples: R. Instituto Orientale, 1936.

Gwynn, John Minor. *Theory and Practice of Supervision.* New York: Dodd, Mead, 1961.

Hagen, Everett E. *On the Theory of Social Change: How Economic Growth Begins.* Homewood, Ill.: Dorsey Press, 1962.

Haile Gabriel Dagne. "The Entoto Speech on Church School Training." Mimeographed. Addis Ababa: Haile Selassie I University, 1967.

———. "Versuch einer Erziehungxreform in Äthiopien von 1896 bis 1936." Ph.D. dissertation, Die Philosophische Facuiltat der Freien Universität, Berlin, 1971.

Hailer, Harold H., et al. *Secondary School Curriculum.* Edited by John R. Wright, Columbus: Charles E. Merrill, 1963.

Haile Selassie I. "Address by His Imperial Majesty, Chancellor, on the Occasion of the Graduation of 1969, College of Agriculture." Mimeographed. Alemaya, 1969.

Haile Selassie Belay. "A Comparative Analysis of Higher Education in Agriculture and a Proposed Plan for Further Developing the System in Ethiopia." Ph.D. dissertation, Cornell University, 1964.

Haile Selassie I University. "Consolidated Legislation of the Faculty Council of the Haile Selassie I University." Mimeographed. Addis Ababa, 1967.

———. "Consolidated Legislation of the Faculty Council—Revised to July 1, 1968, except for Title V." Mimeographed. Addis Ababa, 1968.

———. "Convocation Celebrating the Founding of Haile Selassie I University, Monday, December 18, 1961." Addis Ababa: Artistic Printing Press, 1965.

———. *A Forward Look, A Special Report from the President.* Addis Ababa: Commercial Printing Press, 1969.

———. *Haile Selassie I University, The Last Decade.* Addis Ababa: Artistic Printers, 1972.

———. "Interim Report of the Development Committee to the Faculty Council, December 1965." Mimeographed. Addis Ababa, n.d.

———. "Outline Guide to the Central Business and Financial Administration and Planning Services." Mimeographed. Addis Ababa: Haile Selassie I University, Office of the Vice-President for Business and Development, 1969.

———. "A Preliminary Study of Certain Aspects of Haile Selassie I University." Mimeographed. Addis Ababa, 1964.

———. "The President's Annual Report 1968–69 and Faculty Reports." Mimeographed. Addis Ababa, 1968–69.

———. "Statute on Academic Rank, Tenure, Salaries and Academic Responsibility and Freedom." Mimeographed. Addis Ababa, 1964.

———. *Twentieth Anniversary of Higher Education in Ethiopia.* Addis Ababa: Artistic Printers, 1971.

———. "University Policies and Procedures." Mimeographed. Addis Ababa, 1966.

———. "University Procedures and Academic Regulation 1970–71." Mimeographed. Addis Ababa, 1968.

———, Advisory Committee on Higher Education. *First Report of the Advisory Committee on Higher Education to His Imperial Majesty Haile Selassie I Chancellor of the University.* Addis Ababa: Commercial Printing Press, 1966.

———, Advisory Committee on Higher Education. *Second Report of the Advisory Committee on Higher Education to His Imperial Majesty Haile Selassie I, Chancellor of the University.* Addis Ababa: Commercial Printing Press, 1971.

———, Extension. "Information Bulletin, 1962." Mimeographed. Addis Ababa, 1962.

———, Faculty of Education. "Annual Report of the Dean of the Faculty of Education." Mimeographed. Addis Ababa, 1967.

———, Faculty of Education. "Conference on Elementary School Administration, 29 August–4 September 1965." Mimeographed. Addis Ababa, 1965.

———, Faculty of Education. "Expansion Project for Faculty of Education Haile Selassie I University, Secondary School Teachers Training Programme." Mimeographed. Addis Ababa, 1964.

———, Faculty of Education. "Innovation in Teacher Education." Report of the Addis Ababa Conference of African Teachers Education Association, 25 March–1 April 1972. Mimeographed. Addis Ababa, 1972.

———, Faculty of Law. "Report of the Dean for the Year 1956 E.C. [1963–64 G.C.]." Mimeographed. Addis Ababa, 1964.

———, Faculty of Law. "Report of the Dean of the Faculty of Law for the Academic Year 1964–65 [1957 E.C.]." Mimeographed. Addis Ababa, 1965.

———, Faculty of Law. "Report of the Dean of the Faculty of Law to the President for 1958 E.C. [1966–67 G.C.]." Mimeographed. Addis Ababa, 1966.

———, Faculty of Medicine. "Present State of the Faculty of Medicine, 11 October 1965." Mimeographed. Addis Ababa, 1965.

———, Faculty of Science. "Faculty of Science Bulletin 1967–68." Mimeographed. Addis Ababa, 1967.

———, Faculty of Science. "School of Pharmacy 1965–66." Mimeographed. Addis Ababa, 1965.

———, Faculty of Science. "Statistical Training Centre: Prospectus." Mimeographed. Addis Ababa, 1966.

————, Laboratory School. "Director's Report, Prince Bede Mariam Laboratory School, 1969–70, HSIU." Mimeographed. Addis Ababa, 1970.

————, Office of the Academic Vice-President. "HSIU Leadership Seminar: A Summary of Proceedings." Mimeographed. Nazareth (Ethiopia), 1971.

————, Office of the Academic Vice-President. "Annual Report 1969–70." Mimeographed. Addis Ababa, n.d.

————, Office of the Dean of Students. "Report on Student Support, presented to Dr. Aklilu Habte, President of HSIU, by Office of the Dean of Students." Mimeographed. Addis Ababa, 9 May 1969.

————, Office of Public Relations. "The Ethiopian University Service." Mimeographed. Addis Ababa, 1973.

————, Office of Public Relations. "Ethiopian University Service Handbook." Mimeographed. Addis Ababa, 1966.

————, Office of Public Relations. "Ethiopian University Service: Student Manual." Mimeographed. Addis Ababa, 1970.

————, Office of Public Relations. *This Is Haile Selassie I University.* Addis Ababa: Artistic Printing Press, 1964.

————, Office of the Registrar. "Enrollment Statistics of Haile Selassie I University, 1963–69." Mimeographed. Addis Ababa: 1969.

————, Office of the Registrar. "Number of Graduates from Haile Selassie I University by Country and Field of Studies to Date." Mimeographed. Addis Ababa, n.d.

————, Office of the Registrar. "Number of Other African Students Enrolled in Institutions of Higher Learning in Ethiopia between 1958–68." Mimeographed. Addis Ababa, n.d.

————, Presidential Commission on Planning, Reorganization and Consolidation of Academic Programs of the University. "Final Report." Mimeographed. Addis Ababa, 1968.

————, Theological College. "Report of a Consultation on Theological Education, January 16–17, 1970." Mimeographed. Addis Ababa, 1970.

————, Theological College. "Seminar on Theological College." Collected Papers. Mimeographed. Addis Ababa, 6 January 1970.

————, and Ministry of Education. "Educational Administration Conference: Final Report. 15 July–22 July 1963." Mimeographed. Addis Ababa, 1963.

Haile Wolde Mikael. "The Problems of Admission to the University Through School Leaving Certificate Examination." Mimeographed. Addis Ababa: Haile Selassie I University, Faculty of Education, 1969.

————. "Social Dependency in Ethiopia and its Consequences for Learning." Mimeographed. Addis Ababa: Haile Selassie I University, Faculty of Education, 1968.

————. "Some Problems Facing the Ethiopian System of Education." Mimeographed. Addis Ababa, 1969.

Haile Yesus Abedjie. "Summary Report: Some Elementary School Problems and Some Suggested Solutions." Mimeographed. Addis Ababa: Ministry of Education, 1963.

Hailey, William Malcolm. *An African Survey: A Study of Problems Arising in Africa South of the Sahara.* London: Oxford University Press, 1957.

Hambidge, Gove, ed. *Dynamics of Development: An International Development Reader.* New York: Frederick A. Praeger, 1964.

Hampton, David R.; Summer, Charles E.; and Webber, Ross A., comps. *Organizational Behavior and the Practice of Management.* Glenview, Ill.: Scott, Foresman, 1968.

Hans, Nicholas A. *Comparative Education: A Study of Educational Factors and Traditions.* 3d ed., rev. London: Routledge and Kegan Paul, 1958.

Hanson, Herbert M., and Hanson, Della. *For God and Emperor.* Mountain View, Calif.: Pacific Press Publishing Association, 1958.

Hanson, John Wagner. *Secondary Level Teachers: Supply and Demand in Ethiopia.* East Lansing: Institute for International Studies in Education and African Studies Center, Michigan State University, 1970.

————, and Gibson, Geoffrey W. *African Education and Development since 1960: A Select and Annotated Bibliography.* East Lansing: Institute for International Studies in Education and African Studies Center, Michigan State University, 1966.

Harbison, Frederick A., and Meyers, Charles A. *Education, Manpower, and Economic Growth: Strategies of Human Resource Development.* New York: McGraw-Hill, 1964.

————. *Manpower and Education: Country Studies in Economic Development.* New York: McGraw-Hill, 1965.

Harris, Seymour E. *More Resources for Education.* New York: Harper and Brothers, 1960.

Havighurst, Robert J., and Neugarten, Bernice L. *Society and Education.* 2d ed. Boston: Allyn and Bacon, 1962.

Henderson, Algo D. *Policies and Practices in Higher Education.* New York: Harper and Row, 1960.

Herskovits, Melville J. *The Human Factor in Changing Africa.* New York: Alfred A. Knopf, 1962.

Hodgkinson, Harold L. *Education in Social and Cultural Perspectives.* Englewood Cliffs, N.J.: Prentice-Hall, 1962.

Howard, William E. H. *Public Administration in Ethiopia: A Study in Retrospect and Prospect.* Groningen: J. B. Wolters, 1955.

Hu, Ch'ang-tu. *Politics and Economics in Chinese Education: Educational Investment in the Pacific Community.* Fifth Annual Conference Report on International Understanding. Washington, D.C.: American Association of Colleges for Teacher Education, 1963.

Huebner, Dwayne. "Curriculum as a Field of Study." In *Precedents and Promise in the Curriculum Field,* edited by Helen F. Robinson. New York: Bureau of Publications, Columbia University Teachers College, 1966.

Hunter, Guy. *Education for a Developing Region: A Study of East Africa.* London: George Allen and Unwin, 1963.

Hyatt, Herry M. *The Church of Abyssinia.* London: Luzac and Co., 1928.

International Seminar on Inter-University Co-operation in West Africa (Freetown, Sierra Leone, 1961). *The West African Intellectual Community: Papers and Discussions.* Ibadan, Nigeria: Ibadan University Press, 1967.

Isenberg, Karl William, and Krapf, Ludwig. *Journals*. London: Seeley, Burnside, and Seeley, 1843.

Jacobsen, Gene S. "The Organization and Administration of the Public Schools in Ethiopia." Mimeographed. Addis Ababa: Haile Selassie I University, Faculty of Arts, 1967.

Jesman, Czeslaw. *The Ethiopian Paradox*. London: Oxford University Press, 1963.

Jones, Arnold H. M., and Monroe, Elizabeth. *A History of Ethiopia*. 2d ed. Oxford: Clarendon Press, 1955.

Jones, Thomas Jesse. *Education in Africa. A Study of West, South and Equatorial Africa by the African Education Commission Under Auspices of the Phelps-Stokes Fund and Foreign Mission Societies of North America and Europe*. New York: Phelps-Stokes Fund, 1922.

————. *Education in East Africa*. New York: Phelps-Stokes Fund, 1926.

Kammerer, Albert. *La Mer rouge, l'Abyssinie depuis l'antiquité*. Cairo: Société Royale de Geographie d'Egypte, 1929.

Kandel, Isaac L. *Comparative Education*. Boston: Houghton-Mifflin, 1933.

Kautsky, John H., ed. *Political Change in Underdeveloped Countries*. New York: John Wiley and Sons, 1962.

Kaypaghian, Fiammetta Prota. "A Study of Elementary School Girl Dropouts and Nondropouts in Addis Ababa, Ethiopia." Ph.D. dissertation, Harvard University, 1960.

Kimble, George H. T. *Tropical Africa*. New York: Twentieth Century Fund, 1960.

Kindleberger, Charles P. *Economic Development*. New York: McGraw-Hill, 1958.

Klausmeier, Herbert J., and Goodwin, William. *Learning and Human Abilities: Educational Psychology*. 2d ed. New York: Harper and Row, 1966.

Koehn, Peter H. "Political Socialization and Political Integration: The Impact of the Faculty of Arts, HSIU." Mimeographed. Paper prepared for the Interdisciplinary Seminar of the Faculties of Arts and Education. Addis Ababa: Haile Selassie I University, 1972.

Korten, David C., and Korten, Frances. "A Novel Educational Program for Development: Ethiopia's Use of National University Students in a Year of Rural Service." Mimeographed. Addis Ababa, 1965.

————, "Proposal for Revision of the Curriculum of the College of Business Administration." Addis Ababa: Haile Selassie I University, 1964.

Krapf, Ludwig. *Travels, Researches, and Missionary Labours*. London: Trübner and Co., 1860.

Kulick, Gilbert. "The Rise and Fall of the Eritrea-Ethiopia Federation 1941–1962." Mimeographed. Foreign Service Institute, 1969.

Lagos Matus, Gustavo. *International Stratification and Underdeveloped Countries*. Chapel Hill: University of North Carolina Press, 1963.

Last, G. C. "Survey of the Secondary School System 1962. Interim Report of Text Books." Mimeographed. Addis Ababa: Ministry of Education and Fine Arts, 1962.

Lerner, Daniel. *The Passing of Traditional Society: Modernizing the Middle East.* Glencoe, Ill.: Free Press, 1958.

Leroy, Jules. *La Pittura Etiopica durante il Medioevo e Sotto la Dinastia di Gondar.* Milan: Electa Editrice, 1964.

Leslau, Wolf. *Ethiopians Speak: Studies in Cultural Background: 1 Harari.* Berkeley and Los Angeles: University of California Press, 1965.

Levine, Donald N. *Wax and Gold: Tradition and Innovation in Ethiopian Culture.* Chicago: University of Chicago Press, 1965.

Lewis, Arthur J. "AID and Secondary Education in Nigeria." Mimeographed. Paper prepared for the Committee on Education and Human Resources Development of Education and World Affairs. New York: Education and World Affairs, 1966.

Lewis, Leonard J. *Education and Political Independence in Africa, and Other Essays.* Edinburgh: Thomas Nelson Sons, 1962.

———. *Phelps-Stokes Reports on Education in Africa.* London, New York: Oxford University Press, 1962.

Lewis, William Arthur. *The Theory of Economic Growth.* Homewood, Ill.: Richard D. Irwin, 1955.

Lipsky, George A. *Ethiopia: Its People, Its Society, Its Culture.* New Haven: Human Relations Area Files Press, 1962.

Lister, D. G. "A Five-Year Study of Enrollment at All Levels in the 12 Provinces, Addis Ababa and Eritrea Government Schools." Mimeographed. Addis Ababa, 1960.

Little, Everett. "Two Years of Education in Ethiopia. End of Tour of Duty Report." Mimeographed. Addis Ababa: Ethiopian-United States Cooperative Education Program, 1958.

Littmann, Enno. *Publications of the Princeton Expedition to Abyssinia.* 4 vols. Leyden: E. J. Brill, 1910–15.

Longrigg, Stephen H. *A Short History of Eritrea.* Oxford: Clarendon Press, 1945.

Lord, Edith. *Cultural Patterns in Ethiopia.* Rev. ed. Washington, D.C.: Agency for International Development, 1963.

———. "The Impact of Education on Non-Scientific Beliefs in Ethiopia." Mimeographed. Addis Ababa, 1958.

Lovegrove, N. S. "Working Draft: Objectives in Education, 1961–1970 E.C." Mimeographed. Addis Ababa: Ministry of Education and Fine Arts, 1967.

Ludolf, Hiob. *Historiam Aethiopicam. A Source of Historical Material on the Ethiopian Church, Written in Conjunction with Abba Gregorius in Geez and Latin.* Frankfurt: J. D. Zunner, 1691.

Ludolphus, Job. *A New History of Ethiopia.* London: S. Smith, 1682.

Luther, Ernest W. *Ethiopia Today.* Stanford: Stanford University Press, 1958.

Lyons, Raymond F. *Problems and Strategies of Educational Planning: Lessons from Latin America.* Paris: UNESCO, International Institute for Educational Planning, 1965.

Maaza Bekele. *Report on the Experimental Programme for Elementary and Secondary Education E.C. 1949–1953.* Addis Ababa: Department of Research and Curriculum Development, 1961.

———. "A Study of Modern Education in Ethiopia: its Foundations, its Development, its Future, with Emphasis on Primary Education." Ph.D. dissertation, Columbia University Teachers College, 1966.

Macartney, Maxwell H., and Cremona, Paul. *Italy's Foreign and Colonial Policy 1914–37*. 1938. Reprint. New York: Oxford University Press, 1973.

McCrindle, J. W., trans. *The Christian Topography of Cosmas, an Egyptian Monk*. London: Hakluyt Society, 1897.

MacDonald, James B. "The Person in the Curriculum." In *Precedents and Promise in the Curriculum Field,* edited by Helen F. Robinson. New York: Bureau of Publications, Columbia University Teachers College, 1964.

Mair, Lucy P. *New Nations*. Chicago: University of Chicago Press, 1963.

Malinowski, Bronislaw. *The Dynamics of Culture Change: An Inquiry into Race Relations in Africa*. New Haven: Yale University Press, 1961.

Mannheim, Karl. *Diagnosis of Our Time: Wartime Essays of a Sociologist*. London: Routledge and Kegan Paul, 1966.

Marein, Nathan. *The Judicial System and the Laws of Ethiopia*. Rev. ed. Rotterdam: Royal Netherlands Printing and Lithographing Co., 1951.

Mathew, David. *Ethiopia, the Study of a Polity, 1540–1935*. London: Eyre and Spottiswoode, 1947.

Matte, Lucien. "Projet de Collège. A Report Given to the Vice-Minister of Education." Mimeographed. Addis Ababa: Haile Selassie I University, 1949.

Mead, Margaret, ed. *Cultural Patterns and Technical Change*. New York: New American Library, Mentor Books, 1955.

Mengesha Gebre-Hiwet. "A Study of Mass Literacy Programs with Special Emphasis on a Proposal for the Development of a Mass Literacy Program in Ethiopia." Ph.D. dissertation, Ohio State University, 1956.

Mexune, Lawrence E. *National Compendium of Televised Education*. East Lansing: Michigan State University Continuing Education Service, 1963.

Miles, Matthew B., ed. *Innovation in Education*. New York: Bureau of Publication, Teachers College, Columbia University, 1964.

Millikan, Max F., and Blackmer, Donald L. M., eds. *The Emerging Nations: Their Growth and United States Policy*. Boston: Little, Brown, 1961.

Million Neqniq, and Tilaye Kassaye. "Report of the Visit in the South East Asian Countries (Philippines, Taiwan, S. Korea, Japan, Thailand, Ceylon)." Mimeographed. Addis Ababa: Ministry of Education and Fine Arts, 1969.

Moorehead, Alan. *The Blue Nile*. New York: Harper and Row, 1962.

Mosley, Leonard O. *Haile Selassie, The Conquering Lion*. Englewood Cliffs, N.J.: Prentice-Hall, 1964.

Moussa, Pierre. *The Underprivileged Nations*. Translated by Alan Braley. Boston: Beacon Press, Beacon Paperbacks, 1963.

Mulugeta Wodajo. "Government and University Relationship and its Implication to University Autonomy." Paper presented at the Conference on the Role of a University in a Developing Country. Addis Ababa, 1967.

———. "The Schools in Ethiopia: Where Do We Go From Here?" Mimeographed. Paper prepared for the second Koka Conference on Education. Addis Ababa: Haile Selassie I University, Faculty of Education, 1969.

Nduka, Otonti. *Western Education and the Nigerian Cultural Background*. Ibadan, Nigeria: Oxford University Press, 1964.

Nilson, K., and Taddesse Mengesha. "Report on a Survey for Educational Development in Northern Shoa (Tegulet and Bulga, Yifat and Timuga and Menz and Gishie Awrajas)." Mimeographed. Addis Ababa: Ministry of Education and Fine Arts, 1969.

North, William Haven. "Education in Ethiopia." Mimeographed. Addis Ababa, 1952.

Nurkse, Ragnar. *Problems of Capital Formation in Underdeveloped Countries.* New York: Oxford University Press, 1953.

Nyerere, Julius K. "After the Arusha Declaration." In *Freedom and Socialism.* pp. 385–409. Dar es Salaam: Oxford University Press, 1968.

————. *Education for Self-Reliance.* Dar es Salaam: Government Printers, 1967.

O'Hanlon, Douglas. *Features of the Abyssinian Church.* London: Society for Promoting Christian Knowledge, 1946.

Oklahoma State University. "Oklahoma State University in Ethiopia: Terminal Report, 1952–1968." Stillwater, Oklahoma: Oklahoma State University, 1969.

O'Leary, De Lacy E. *The Ethiopian Church: Historical Notes on the Church of Abyssinia.* London: Society for Promoting Christian Knowledge, 1936.

Oliver, Roland A. *The Missionary Factor in East Africa.* London: Longmans, Green, 1952.

Ottenberg, Simon, and Ottenberg, Phoebe, eds. *Cultures and Societies of Africa.* New York: Random House, 1960.

Overseas Development Institute. *Aid in Uganda. Part 2: Education.* London: Overseas Development Institute, 1966.

————. *Aid to Education: An Anglo-American Appraisal.* London: Overseas Development Institute and Ditehley Foundation, 1965.

Ozanic, Ivanka. "Ethiopian Schools of Nurses." In *Nursing in Ethiopia.* Addis Ababa: Ethiopian Nurses Association, 1961, pp. 24–28.

Páez, Pedro. *História da Etiópia.* 3 vols. Portugal: Livraria Civilizacao, 1945–46.

Palmer, Alice H. "A Textbook Program for Ethiopia, 1962–1967." Mimeographed. Addis Ababa: USAID Education, 1962.

Pankhurst, E. Sylvia. *Eritrea on the Eve: The Past and Future of Italy's First-Born Colony, Ethiopia's Ancient Sea Province.* Woodford Green, Essex: New Times and Ethiopia News Books, 1952.

————. *Ethiopia, A Cultural History.* Essex: Lalibela House, 1955.

————, and Pankhurst, Richard. *Ethiopia and Eritrea: The Last Phase of the Reunion Struggle 1941–1952.* Essex: Lalibela House, 1953.

Pankhurst, Richard K. P. *Economic History of Ethiopia, 1800–1935.* Addis Ababa: Haile Selassie I University Press, 1968.

————, ed. *The Ethiopian Royal Chronicles.* Addis Ababa: Oxford University Press, 1967.

————. *An Introduction to the Economic History of Ethiopia, from Early Times to 1800.* London: Lalibela House, 1961.

————. "Language and Education in Ethiopia: Historical Background to the Post-War Period." Mimeographed. Addis Ababa: Haile Selassie I University, 1969.

Parkyns, Mansfield. *Life in Abyssinia: Being Notes Collected During Three Years' Residence and Travels in That Country.* London: John Murray, 1853.

Paul, J. C., and Clapham, C. *Ethiopian Constitutional Development: A Sourcebook.* Addis Ababa: Haile Selassie I University, Faculty of Law, in association with Oxford University Press, 1967.

Pearce, Nathaniel. *The Life and Adventures of Nathaniel Pearce.* London: Henry Colburn and Richard Bentley, 1831.

Perham, Margery F. *The Government of Ethiopia.* 2d ed. London: Faber and Faber, 1969.

Perkins, James. "Report of the Chairman." In *International Conference on World Crisis in Education.* Edited by ———. New York: Oxford University Press, 1969.

Peter, Yehuda. "Engineering Education in Ethiopia." Mimeographed. Addis Ababa: Haile Selassie I University, Engineering College, 1967.

Piccioli, Angelo. "Le Instituzioni educative nell 'Africa Orientale Italiana." In *L'Africa Orientale Italiana e il Conflitto Italo-Etiopica.* Edited by T. Sillani. Rome, 1936.

Plowden, Walter C. *Travels in Abyssinia and the Galla Country, with an Account of a Mission to Ras Ali in 1848.* London: Longmans, Green, and Co., 1868.

Pollera, Alberto. *Lo Stato Etiopico e la Sua Chiesa.* Rome, Milan: Società editrice d'arta Illustrata, 1926.

Powne, Michael. *Ethiopian Music: An Introduction; A Survey of Ecclesiastical and Secular Ethiopian Music and Instruments.* London: Oxford University Press, 1968.

Quaranta Di San Severino, Ferdinardo. *Ethiopia: An Empire in the Making.* London: P. S. King and Son, 1939.

Rey, Charles F. *Unconquered Abyssinia as It Is Today.* Philadelphia: J. B. Lippincott Co.; London: Seely, Service, and Co., 1924.

Rhoades, Margaret M., comp. *Research Center on the Developing Areas.* Washington, D.C.: Department of State, Bureau of Intelligence and Research, 1964.

Robinson, Edward A. G., and Vaizey, J. E., eds. *The Economics of Education: Proceedings of a Conference Held by the International Economic Association.* London: Macmillan; New York: St. Martin's Press, 1966.

Rogers, Everett M. *Diffusion of Innovations.* New York: Free Press of Glencoe, 1924.

Rosen, Sam. *National Income: Its Measurement, Determination, and Relation to Public Policy.* New York: Holt, Rinehart, and Winston, 1963.

Rostow, Walt W. *The States of Economic Growth: A Non-Communist Manifesto.* New York: Cambridge University Press, 1960.

Royal Institute of International Affairs. *Abyssinia and Italy.* New York: Oxford University Press, 1935.

Rubenson, Sven. *Wichale XVII: The Attempt to Establish a Protectorate Over Ethiopia.* Addis Ababa: Artistic Printing Press, 1964.

Sasnett, Martena, and Sepmeyer, Inez. *Educational Systems of Africa: Interpretations for Use in the Evaluation of Academic Credentials.* Berkeley: University of California Press, 1966.

Scanlon, David G., ed. *Traditions of African Education.* New York: Bureau of Publications, Teachers College, Columbia University Press, 1964.

Schramm, Wilbur L. *Mass Media and National Development: The Role of Information in the Developing Countries.* Stanford: Stanford University Press, 1964.

Selznick, Philip. *Leadership in Administration: A Sociological Interpretation.* Evanston, Ill.: Row, Peterson, 1957.

Shack, William A. *The Gurage: A People of the Ensete Culture.* London: Oxford University Press, 1966.

Shibberu Wolde Mariam. "Science and Technology: The Missing Links in the Development of Ethiopia." Mimeographed. Paper presented at the first National Conference of Engineers and Architects. Addis Ababa: Haile Selassie I University, Faculty of Science, n.d.

Simmons, Frederick J. *Northwest Ethiopia: Peoples and Economy.* Madison: University of Wisconsin Press, 1960.

Skinner, Robert P. *Abyssinia of Today: An Account of the First Mission Sent by the American Government to the Court of the King of 1903–04.* London: E. Arnold; New York: Longmans, Green, and Co., 1906.

Sloan, Ruth, comp., and Kitchen, Helen, ed. *The Educated African.* New York: Frederick A. Praeger, 1962.

Solomon Inquai. "The Application of Radio in Community Education in Ethiopia." Ph.D. dissertation, Ohio State University, 1963.

Standford, Christine L. *Ethiopia Under Haile Selassie.* London: L. M. Dent and Sons, 1946.

Steer, George L. *Caesar in Abyssinia.* Boston: Little, Brown, and Co., 1937.

———. *Sealed and Delivered: A Book on the Abyssinian Campaign.* London: Hodder and Stoughton, 1942.

Stenlake, Ron. "The Establishment of Schools Radio in Ethiopia." Mimeographed. Addis Ababa, 1968.

Stern, Henry A. *Wanderings Among the Falashas in Abyssinia; Together With a Description of the Country and its Various Inhabitants.* London: Wertheim, Macintosh, and Hunt, 1862.

Summerskill, John. "Haile Selassie I University: A Blueprint for Development." Mimeographed. Addis Ababa: The Ford Foundation, 1970.

Svennilson, Ingvar; Edding, Frederick; and Elvin, Lionel. *Targets for Education in Europe in 1970. Vol. 2, Policy Conference on Economic Growth and Investment in Education.* Paris: Organization for Economic Cooperation and Development, 1962.

Taba, Hilda. *Curriculum Development: Theory and Practice.* New York: Harcourt, Brace, and World, 1962.

Taddesse Mengesha. "National Survey of School Dropouts at the Primary and Secondary Levels." Mimeographed. Addis Ababa: Ministry of Education and Fine Arts, 1969.

Taddesse Tamrat. "Education in Fifteenth Century Ethiopia: A Brief Note." Mimeographed. Addis Ababa: Haile Selassie I University, 1970.

Talbot, David A. *Contemporary Ethiopia.* New York: Philosophical Library, 1952.

———. *Ethiopia: Liberation Silver Jubilee.* Addis Ababa: Berhaninna Selam Press, 1966.

———. *Haile Selassie I: Silver Jubilee.* The Hague: W. P. van Stockum, 1965.

Teachers' Association of Ethiopia. "Code of Ethics for Teachers in Ethiopia." Mimeographed. Addis Ababa, n.d.

Teferra Wolde Semait. "Education as a Basic Factor in Ethiopia's Economic

Development." Mimeographed. Addis Ababa: Haile Selassie I University, Department of Economics, 1964.

Teshome G. Wagaw. "A Call for the Establishment of Guidance and Counseling, Employment, and Research Department at HSIU." Mimeographed. Addis Ababa: Haile Selassie I University, Faculty of Education, 1968.

———. "An Evaluation Survey of High-Level Manpower Output and Development to Meet Critical Needs in Social Development." Mimeographed. Addis Ababa: Haile Selassie I University, Faculty of Education, 1970.

———. "High-Level Manpower Development and Utilization in U.A.R." Mimeographed. Addis Ababa: Haile Selassie I University, Faculty of Education, 1970.

———. "High-Level Manpower Output Utilization in Ethiopia." Mimeographed. Addis Ababa: Haile Selassie I University, Faculty of Education, 1970.

———. "Multiplicity of Holidays in Ethiopia: Their Possible Effects on the Psycho–socioeconomic Development of the Country." Mimeographed. Paper prepared for the Interdisciplinary Seminar of the Faculties of Arts and Education. Addis Ababa: Haile Selassie I University, Faculty of Education, 1971.

———. "Some Notes for the World of Work in Ethiopian Tradition." Paper presented to the annual Historical Society of Ethiopia Conference. Mimeographed. Addis Ababa, 1971.

Tibebu Abebe. "Major Problems in Spreading Education in Tegulet and Bulga Awraja." Mimeographed. Addis Ababa: Haile Selassie I University, Faculty of Education, June 1970.

Tickaher Hailu. "Improved Staff Utilization as a Remedy for the Teacher Shortage in Ethiopia." Ph.D. dissertation, University of Colorado, 1968.

Tinbergen, Jan. *Shaping the World Economy: Suggestions for an International Economic Policy.* New York: Twentieth Century Fund, 1962.

Toppenberg, Vlademar E. *Africa Has My Heart.* Mountain View, Calif.: Pacific Press Co., 1958.

Toure, Sekou. "Education and Social Progress." In *Education and Nation-Building in Africa.* Edited by L. Gray Cowan; James O'Connell; and David G. Scanlon. London: Pall Mall Press, 1965.

Toynbee, Arnold J. *Between Niger and Nile.* London: Oxford University Press, 1965.

Travers, Robert M. W. *Essentials of Learning: An Overview for Students of Education.* 2d ed. New York: Macmillan, 1967.

Trevaskis, G. K. N. *Eritrea: A Colony in Transition, 1941–52.* London: Oxford University Press, 1960.

Trimingham, John S. *The Christian Church and Missions in Ethiopia (Including Eritrea and the Somalilands).* London, New York: World Dominion Press, 1950.

———. *Islam in Ethiopia.* London: Oxford University Press, 1952.

Trudeau, Edouard. "Education in Ethiopia: Policies and Practices in Education in Modern Ethiopia." Mimeographed. Montreal, 1964.

———. "Higher Education in Ethiopia." Ph.D. dissertation, Columbia University Teachers College, 1964.

Turner, John D. *Educational Problems of Technological Africa.* Natal: University of Natal Press, 1967.

Ullendorff, Edward. *The Ethiopians: An Introduction to Country and People.* London: Oxford University Press, 1960.

――――. *The Ethiopians: An Introduction to Country and People.* 2d ed. London: Oxford University Press, 1965.

――――. "The Obelisk of Matara." In Appendix to *Exploration and Study of Abyssinia.* Asmara, Ethiopia, 1945.

University of Utah Survey Team. *Higher Education in Ethiopia: Survey Report and Recommendations.* Salt Lake City: University of Utah, 1959–60.

Vare, H. E. Daniele, and D'Zmunzio, Ugo V. *Italy, Great Britain and the League in the Italo-Ethiopian Conflict.* New York: Unione Italiana d'America, n.d.

Vignon, Louis. *L'Exploitation de notre Empire Colonial: Les Questions Indigenes.* Paris: Librarie Plon, 1919.

Walker, Craven H. *The Abyssinian at Home.* London: Sheldon Press, 1933.

Wallenstein, W. *The Emergence of Two West-African Nations.* New York: Columbia University Press, 1959.

Walshe, Philip. *Rural Science and Crop Husbandry (Horticulture): Structure and Content.* Addis Ababa: Ministry of Education and Fine Arts, 1965.

Ward, William Ernest Frank. *Educating Young Nations.* London: George Allan and Unwin, 1959.

Wasserman, William. *Education Price and Quantity Indexes.* Syracuse: Syracuse University Press, 1963.

Weeks, Sheldon. *Divergence in Education Development: The Case of Kenya and Uganda.* New York: Columbia University Press, 1967.

Wilcox, Ray T. *Effective Teaching in Ethiopian Schools.* Addis Ababa: Artistic Printers, 1969.

Williamson, Edmund G. *Student Personnel Services in Colleges and Universities.* New York: McGraw-Hill, 1961.

Willoughby, W. C. *Race Problems in the New Africa.* Oxford: Clarendon Press, 1923.

Wilson, John. *Education and Changing West African Culture.* New York: Bureau of Publications, Teachers College, Columbia University, 1963.

Work, Ernest. *Ethiopia: A Pawn in European Diplomacy.* New York: Macmillan Co., 1936.

World Confederation of Organizations of the Teaching Profession. *Field Report on the Survey of the Status of the Teaching Profession in Africa.* Paper prepared for the WCOTP Commission on Educational Policy for Africa (CEPA) Study of Recruitment and Retention of Teachers, Washington, D.C., 1963.

Wright, W. *Catalogue of the Ethiopic Manuscripts in the British Museum Acquired Since the Year 1847.* London: Longmans and Co., 1877.

Wrinkle, William L. "The Improvement and Expansion of Ethiopian Teacher Education." Mimeographed. Addis Ababa: Ministry of Education and Fine Arts, 1953.

Wylde, Augustus B. *Modern Abyssinia.* London: Methuen and Co., 1901.

Yoloye, E. Ayotunde. "Evaluation for Innovation: African Primary Science Programme Evaluation Report." Mimeographed. Accra, 1971.

Zartman, I. William. *Government and Politics in Northern Africa: Morocco, Algeria, Tunisia, Libya, Egypt, Sudan, Ethiopia, Somalia.* New York, London: Frederick A. Praeger, 1963.

Zervos, Adrien. *L'Empire d'Ethiopie: Le Miroir de L'Ethiopie moderne, 1906–1935.* Alexandria, Egypt: Impr. de l'Ecole Professionnelle des Frères, 1936.

Government Publications

Ethiopia, Central Statistical Office. *Statistical Abstract 1963.* Addis Ababa: Commercial Printing Press, 1963.

———. *Statistical Abstract 1964.* Addis Ababa, 1964.

———. *Statistical Abstract 1965.* Addis Ababa, 1965.

———. *Statistical Abstract 1966.* Addis Ababa, 1966.

———. *Statistical Abstract 1967 and 1968.* Addis Ababa, 1968.

———. *Statistical Abstract 1969.* Addis Ababa, 1969.

———. *Statistical Abstract 1970.* Addis Ababa, 1970.

———. *Statistical Abstract 1971.* Addis Ababa, 1971.

———. *Survey of Major Towns in Ethiopia.* Addis Ababa, 1968.

Ethiopia, Ethiopia Chamber of Commerce. *Guide Book of Ethiopia.* Addis Ababa, 1954.

Ethiopia, Imperial Air Force. "The Training in IEAF: The Technical Schools." In *Join the Air Force.* Addis Ababa: Berhaninna Selam Printing Press, 1967.

Ethiopia, Imperial Ethiopian Government/United Nations. *School of Social Work: Bulletin 1961–1962.* Addis Ababa: Artistic Printers, 1961.

Ethiopia, Ministry of Commerce and Industry. *Economic Handbook of Ethiopia.* Addis Ababa: Berhaninna Selam Printing Press, 1951.

Ethiopia, Ministry of Education and Fine Arts. *An Administrative Handbook for Schools.* Addis Ababa, 1962.

———. *Administrative Handbook for Asfa Wossen Comprehensive Secondary School.* Addis Ababa, 1961 E.C..

———. *Adult Education (Literacy and Further Education), A Survey.* Addis Ababa, 1964.

———. *Adult Literacy Project in Ethiopia.* Addis Ababa: Division of Elementary and Community Education, 1965.

———. *Assessment Report of the Effectiveness of the Sixteen United States Aid for International Development Assisted General Secondary Schools in Ethiopia.* Addis Ababa: Division of Secondary Education, 1970.

———. *Basic Recommendations for the Reorganizations and Development of Education in Ethiopia.* Addis Ababa: Long-Term Planning Committee, 1955.

———. *Brief Report on Educational Development in Ethiopia During 1968–1969.* Addis Ababa, 1969.

———. *A Catalogue of Text-Books available for the 1963 E.C. Academic Year.* Addis Ababa, 1971.

———. *The Current Operation of the Education System in Ethiopia.* Addis Ababa, 1966.

————. *Curriculum Policies and Standards: Teacher Training Institutes.* Addis Ababa: Division of Secondary Education, 1965.

————. *The Development of In-Service Teacher Education, 1957–1964 E.C.* Addis Ababa: Teacher Education Division, Department of Instruction, 1972.

————. *The Development of Pre-Service Teacher Education 1937–1963 E.C.* Addis Ababa: Teacher Education Division, Department of Instruction, 1972.

————. *Directors' Report 1937.* Addis Ababa, 1945.

————. *Draft Report: Report of the Education Sector Review.* Symposium and Conference, Addis Ababa, 1972.

————. *Education and the First Second-Level Statistical Summary.* Addis Ababa: Office of Educational Planning and Statistics, 1968.

————. *Education in Ethiopia.* Addis Ababa, 1960.

————. *Education in Ethiopia.* Bk. I. Addis Ababa: Commercial Printing Press, 1964.

————. *Education in Ethiopia: A Survey Issued by the Ministry of Education and Fine Arts.* Addis Ababa, 1961.

————. *Educational Projects Proposed for the Third Five-Year Plan.* Addis Ababa, 1967.

————. *Elementary Community School Curriculum, Years I–VI (Experimental).* Addis Ababa: Cooperative Education Press, 1959.

————. *Elementary School Curriculum, Years I–VI, 1947–48.* Addis Ababa, 1947–48.

————. *Elementary School Curriculum, Years I–VI.* Addis Ababa, 1964.

————. *Ethiopia: Community Development and Training Project 1966–67.* Addis Ababa, 1966.

————. *Ethiopian Primary School Teachers Survey.* Addis Ababa: Bureau of Educational Research and Statistics, 1962

————. *Ethiopia: Primary Teacher Training 1966–67 (Third Year).* Addis Ababa, 1965.

————. *The Ethiopian School Leaving Certificate Examination and the Content of Second Level Education.* Addis Ababa, n.d.

————. "Ethiopian School Leaving Certificate Examination, Official Results." Mimeographed. Addis Ababa, 1970.

————. "Ethiopian School Leaving Certificate Examination, 1969, Registration Figures." Mimeographed. Addis Ababa, 1969.

————. "Ethiopian School Leaving Certificate Examination Report." Mimeographed. Addis Ababa, 1965.

————. "Ethiopian School Leaving Certificate Examination Report." Mimeographed. Addis Ababa, 1966.

————. "Ethiopian School Leaving Certificate Examination Report, 1967." Mimeographed. Addis Ababa, 1967.

————. *An Explanation of the New Salary Schedule for Ethiopian Teachers of the Ministry of Education and Fine Arts.* Addis Ababa, 1955.

————. "External Assistance for Education." Addis Ababa, n.d.

————. "Financing Education: A Background Paper for Purposes of Drafting the Fourth Five-Year Plan." Addis Ababa: Planning and Programming Office, 1973.

————. *Financing the Proposed Ten-Year Plan for the Expansion of the Ethiopian Education System,* prepared by M. Molkup. Addis Ababa, 1955.

————. *First Annual Review of School Enrollments and Recurrent Costs as Forecast in the Third Five-Year Plan and in the IDA Project of December 1968.* Addis Ababa: Research Department, 1969.

————. *First Five-Year Plan of Economic Development—1957–1961.* Addis Ababa: Education Section, 1965.

————. *First Report of the Long-Term Planning Committee.* Addis Ababa, 1954.

————. *Flow Chart of Current Ethiopian Education Sequence 1955–1956.* Addis Ababa: Education and Statistical Information Service, 1956.

————. *Foreword to the Educational Plan for the Third Five-Year Planning Period.* Addis Ababa, 1963.

————. *General Information on Educational Policy, Legislation and Administration.* Addis Ababa: Department of Programme, Planning, and Research, 1968.

————. *General Secondary Education Administration Handbook (Draft).* Pt. 2, Appendixes. Addis Ababa, 1965.

————. *General Secondary School Curriculum.* 3 vols. Addis Ababa: Curriculum Material Development Division, 1963.

————. *A Glance at Elementary Education, by Awrajas.* Addis Ababa, 1968–69.

————. *Government, Mission and Private School Census for the Year 1958.* Addis Ababa: Ethiopian-United States Cooperative Education Program, 1958.

————. *Government, Mission, Private, Community and Church Schools, 1959–1960.* Addis Ababa, 1961.

————. *Government School Census: 1952–1959 E.C.* Addis Ababa, 1967.

————. *Haile Selassie I University Committee Report: Technical and Agricultural Education.* Addis Ababa, 1952.

————. *Handbook for Elementary Schools.* Prepared by the Department of Elementary and Adult Education. Addis Ababa, 1964.

————. *The Harar Teacher Training School Bulletin, 1954 E.C.* Dire Dawa: St. Lazare Printing Press, 1962.

————. *Implementing the Second Five-Year Plan. First Report of the Planning Group, Government Schools.* Addis Ababa: Division of Programme and Planning, 1963.

————. *Junior Secondary School Curriculum Years 7–8. Experimental.* Addis Ababa, 1961.

————. *Major Tasks and Responsibilities During the Third Five-Year Plan Period 1961–1965 E.C.* Addis Ababa: Curriculum Division, 1968–69.

————. *Minutes of the Meeting of the Committee on Technical Training and the Proposed Imperial College of Engineering, 28 March 1950.* Addis Ababa, 1950.

————. *National Awraja Survey for Educational Development.* Addis Ababa, 1969.

————. *New Insights and the Curriculum Yearbook 1963.* Edited by Alexander Fraizer, Washington, D.C., 1963.

————. *Organizational Structure.* Addis Ababa, 1967.

————. *Organization Handbook.* Addis Ababa, 1965.

————. *Personnel Policy for Professional Employees of the Ministry of Education and Fine Arts.* Addis Ababa, 1963.

————. *Personnel Regulations.* Addis Ababa, 1960.

————. "Plan for Technical Education for Ethiopia," prepared by Mikael Mesgenna. Addis Ababa, 1965.

————. *Plan of Operations for a Primary Teachers' Emergency Training Project in Ethiopia.* E/ICEF/P/L 466. Addis Ababa, 1965.

————. *Preliminary Teachers Survey in Government Primary and Secondary Schools, 1960 E.C.* Addis Ababa: Office of Educational Planning and Statistics, 1969.

————. *Primary, Secondary and Teacher Education Project Based on the Report of the United Nations Educational, Scientific, and Cultural Organization Educational Investment Mission to Ethiopia.* Addis Ababa: Division of Programme and Planning, 1963.

————. *Project for the Expansion of Second Level Education in Ethiopia.* 5 vols. Addis Ababa, 1964.

————. *Project for the Expansion of Second Level Education in Ethiopia.* Addis Ababa, 1965.

————. *Proposal for Expenditure of Budget for General Supplies, Books and Equipment for All Grades in 1953 for 1954* [1960–61 for 1961–62 G.C.]. Addis Ababa: Department of Research and Curriculum Development, 1960.

————. *Proposed Organizational Changes in the Ministry of Education and Fine Arts.* Addis Ababa, 1954.

————. *Proposed Plan for the Development of Education in Ethiopia.* Mimeographed. Addis Ababa: Board of Education Study Committee, 1961.

————. *Proposed Reorganization and Regulations Governing the Ministry of Education and Fine Arts.* Addis Ababa, 1961.

————. *Protestant and Catholic Mission Schools and Clinics in Ethiopia, by Province.* Addis Ababa, 1969.

————. *Provincial Education Project.* Addis Ababa: Ethiopian-United States Cooperative Education Programme, 1958.

————. *Recommendations Made by the Conference on Teacher Training Education Held at the Ministry of Education and Fine Arts on 21–23 March, 1963.* Addis Ababa, 1963.

————. *Reconnaissance Survey of the Records, Archives and Paperwork Needs of the Ministry of Education and Fine Arts.* Addis Ababa, n.d.

————. *Report of the Conference of Directors of Teacher Training Institutions Held at the University College of Addis Ababa in July 1961.* Addis Ababa, 1961.

————. *Report of the Conference of Primary and Secondary School Directors.* Addis Ababa: Haile Selassie I University, 1963.

————. *Report on the Current Operation of the Education System in Ethiopia, with Special Reference to Secondary Education and the Twelfth Grade Examination.* Addis Ababa, 1966.

————. *Report on Educational Development in 1966–1967.* Paper presented at the thirtieth session of the Conference on Public Education, Geneva, July 1967. Addis Ababa, 1967.

————. *Report on Educational Development in 1967–1968.* Paper presented at the thirty-first session of the Conference on Public Education, Geneva, July 1968. Addis Ababa, 1968.

————. *Report on Educational Progress in 1958–1959.* Paper presented at the twenty-second International Conference on Public Education, Geneva, July 1959. Addis Ababa, 1959.

————. *Report on Educational Progress 1959–1960.* Paper presented at the twenty-third International Conference of Public Education, Geneva, July 1960. Addis Ababa, 1960.

————. *Report on 1959 E.C. Grade 6, 8 National Examination.* Addis Ababa: Division of Tests and Measurements, 1959.

————. *Review.* Addis Ababa, 1952.

————. *Rules and Regulations Governing Private Schools.* Addis Ababa, 1969.

————. *Rules of General Administration of the Schools.* Addis Ababa, 1966 or 1967.

————. *Rural Science: Animal Husbandry, General.* Addis Ababa, 1964.

————. *Rural Science: Basic Lessons, Connected Lessons, and Practical Applications.* Addis Ababa, 1964.

————. *Rural Science: Basic Science Syllabus and Six Year Courses.* Addis Ababa, 1965.

————. *School Census, 1958–1959.* Addis Ababa: Bureau of Educational Research and Statistics, 1959.

————. *School Census, 1959–1960.* Addis Ababa: Bureau of Educational Research and Statistics, 1960.

————. *School Census for Ethiopia, 1960–1961.* Addis Ababa, 1962.

————. *School Census for Ethiopia, 1961–1962.* Addis Ababa, 1963.

————. *School Census for Ethiopia, 1962–1963.* Addis Ababa, 1964.

————. *School Census for Ethiopia, 1963–1964.* Addis Ababa, 1965.

————. *School Census for Ethiopia 1961–1962, 1962–1963, 1963–1964, 1964–1965, 1965–1966, 1966–1967 E.C.* Addis Ababa, 1967.

————. *School Census for Ethiopia, 1967–1968. Pt. 1.* Addis Ababa: Office of Educational Planning and Statistics, 1968.

————. *School Census for Ethiopia, 1967–1968. Pt. 2.* Addis Ababa: Office of Educational Planning and Statistics, 1968.

————. *School Census for Ethiopia, 1968–1969. Pt. 1.* Addis Ababa: Office of Educational Planning and Statistics, 1969.

————. *School Census Parts I and II, Shoa Province, 1962 E.C.* Preliminary Table. Addis Ababa: Educational Office of Shoa Statistics, Tests and Measurements, 1971.

————. *School Census Part II, 1964 E.C. (1971–1972 G.C.).* Addis Ababa: Educational Office of Shoa Province, Statistics Department, 1973.

————. *School Construction Program for Ethiopia: Study and Proposal.* 3 vols. Addis Ababa, 1965.

————. *Secondary Education in Ethiopia, General and Vocational.* Addis Ababa, 1960.

————. *Secondary School Curriculum.* Bk. I. 2d ed. Addis Ababa: Division of Curriculum and Teaching Materials, 1967.

————. *Secondary School Curriculum.* Bks. 1, 2, and 3. Addis Ababa, Material Development Division, 1963.

————. *Secondary School Training Project.* Paper prepared for the UNDP/UNESCO Review Mission. Addis Ababa, 1968.

————. *Second Level Education in the Third Five-Year Plan: A Review of Current Development in Relation to Investment Requirements.* Addis Ababa, 1969.

————. *Seminar of Junior and Senior Secondary School Directors.* Addis Ababa, 1971.

————. *The 6–3–3 Pattern of Education: Its Adaptability for Ethiopia,* prepared by Tadesse Tereffe. Addis Ababa, 1964.

————. *Some Elementary School Problems and Some Recommendations.* Summary Report No. 2. Addis Ababa: Elementary Division, 1964.

————. *Standard List of Textbooks for 1962 E.C.* Addis Ababa, 1962.

————. *A Study of Student Wastage at Primary and Secondary Levels: Causes and Remedies.* Addis Ababa: Department of Programme, Planning, and Research, 1969.

————. *Suggested Content of the Basic School Programme: The Second Report of the Long-Term Planning Committee for Ethiopian Education.* Addis Ababa, 1954.

————. *Summary Evaluation Charts Indicating Qualitative Achievements During the Third Five-Year Plan.* Addis Ababa: Planning Office, 1972.

————. *Supervisors' Handbook.* Addis Ababa, 1963.

————. *Teacher Education in Ethiopia.* Addis Ababa: Department of Teacher Education, 1965.

————. *Teachers' Salary Schedule for Ethiopian Elementary and Secondary Teachers.* Addis Ababa, 1960.

————. *Teacher Training Institutes.* Addis Ababa, n.d.

————. *Technical and Vocational Education in Ethiopia.* Addis Ababa: Division of Technical and Vocational Education, 1966.

————. *A Ten-Year Plan for the Controlled Expansion of Ethiopian Education.* Addis Ababa: Long-Term Planning Committee, 1955.

————. *Textbook Production Programme 1948–1952 E.C.* Addis Ababa: Cooperative Education Press, 1956.

————. *That All Will Learn.* Addis Ababa, 1969.

————. *Training Manual.* Addis Ababa: Department of Adult Education and Literacy Project, UNESCO Work Oriented Adult Literacy Project, Training Section, 1971.

————. *Vocational and Technical Education Today and Tomorrow.* Addis Ababa: Department of Vocational and Technical Education, 1964.

————. *Yearbook 1940–1941 E.C.* Addis Ababa, 1950.

————. *Yearbook 1942–1943 E.C.* [1949–1951 G.C.]. Addis Ababa, 1952.

————. *Yearbook 1944–1945 E.C.* Addis Ababa, 1954.

————. *Yearbook 1947–1949.* Addis Ababa, n.d.

————. *Yearbook 1949–1951.* Addis Ababa, 1952.

————. *Yearbook 1951–1953.* Addis Ababa, 1954.

————, and Haile Selassie I University. *Conference on Teacher Education.* Addis Ababa, 1969.

Ethiopia, Ministry of Information. *Agriculture in Ethiopia.* Addis Ababa: Publications and Foreign Languages Press Department, 1964.

————. *Ethiopia, Liberation Silver Jubilee, 1941–1966.* Addis Ababa: Publication and Foreign Languages Press Department, 1966.

————. *Facts Sheets of Ethiopia.* 6 pamphlets. Addis Ababa, 1967.

————. *Image of Ethiopia*. Addis Ababa, 1962.

————. *Our Land, Ethiopia*. Addis Ababa: Publications and Foreign Languages Press Department, 1963.

————. *Patterns of Progress: Education in Ethiopia*. Bk. I, rev. Addis Ababa: Publications and Foreign Languages Press Department, 1967.

————. *Patterns of Progress: Government in Ethiopia*. Addis Ababa: Publications and Foreign Languages Press Department, 1966.

Ethiopia, Ministry of Justice. *Documents on Italian War Crimes*. 2 vols. Documents submitted to the United Nations War Crimes Commission. Addis Ababa, 1949–50.

Ethiopia, Ministry of Pen. *Negarit Gazeta* 1, no. 1 (1942). General Notice No. 1. Notice of Appointment of a Minister of Education.

————. *Negarit Gazeta* 2, no. 3 (1942). Decree No. 2. Regulations for the Administration of All Church Lands.

————. *Negarit Gazeta* 2, no. 5 (1943). Order No. 1. An Order to Define the Powers and Duties of Our Ministers.

————. *Negarit Gazeta* 3, no. 12 (1944). Decree No. 3 of 1944. Regulations Concerning the Establishment of Missions.

————. *Negarit Gazeta* 6, no. 11 (1947). Legal Notice No. 103 of 1947, Item No. 350. Import-Export Tariff Regulations, Earmarking Funds for Education and Public Health.

————. *Negarit Gazeta* 7, no. 3 (1947). Proclamation No. 94. A Proclamation to Provide for Education Expenditure.

————. *Negarit Gazeta* 10, no. 8 (1951). Legal Notice No. 153. The Customs Revised Import and Export Duties Proclamation.

————. *Negarit Gazeta* 11, no. 8 (1952). Legal Notice No. 162. Revised Import and Export Tariff (Amendment No. 1).

————. *Negarit Gazeta* 13, no. 13 (1954). General Notice No. 185. Charter of the University College of Addis Ababa.

————. *Negarit Gazeta* 20, no. 8 (1961). General Notice No. 284. Haile Selassie I University Charter.

————. *Negarit Gazeta* 27, no. 19 (1968). Order No. 52. University of Asmara Charter.

————. *Negarit Gazeta* 28, no. 18 (1969). Order No. 57. National Commission for Education Order.

Ethiopia, National Literacy Campaign Organization. *National Literacy Campaign in Ethiopia*. Addis Ababa: Berhaninna Selam Printing Press, 1965.

Ethiopia, Planning Board. *Five-Year Development Plan, 1957–1961*. Addis Ababa, 1969.

————. *Second Five-Year Development Plan, 1963–1967*. Addis Ababa: Berhaninna Selam Printing Press, 1963.

Ethiopia, Press and Information Department. "Ethiopian Education." In *Ethiopian Background Information*. Revised. Addis Ababa: Commercial Printing Press, 1958.

Ethiopian-United States Cooperative Education Program. *Brief Analysis of the Ethiopian-United States Government Education Program*. Addis Ababa, 1959.

Ethio-Swedish Building Union. *Low Cost Elementary Schools*. Addis Ababa, 1964.

Great Britain, Advisory Committee on Education in the Colonies. "Mass Education in African Society." Mimeographed. London: His Majesty's Stationery Office, 1944.

Great Britain, Advisory Committee on Native Education in the British Tropical African Dependencies. "Education in British Tropical Africa." Mimeographed. London: His Majesty's Stationery Office, 1925.

Great Britain, Ministry of Information. *Abyssinian Campaigns: The Official Story of the Conquest of Italian East Africa.* London: His Majesty's Stationery Office, 1942.

————. *The First to be Freed: The Record of British Military Administration in Eritrea and Somalia, 1941–1943.* London: His Majesty's Stationery Office, 1944.

International Bank for Reconstruction and Development. "Ethiopia: A Preliminary Economic Survey," prepared by J. H. Collier. Mimeographed. Washington, D.C., 1950.

Italy, Italian Library of Information, New York. Development of Italian East Africa. New York, 1940.

Netherland's Economic Institute. *The Financing of Higher Education in Africa.* Report prepared for the Conference on the Development of Higher Education in Africa. Paris: UNESCO, 1962.

Nigeria, Ministry of Education, Western Region. *Triennial Report on Education (1955–1958).* Ibadan: Government of Nigeria, 1959.

Purdy, Ralph D. *Education Sector Evaluation USAID/Ethiopia.* Addis Ababa, 1969.

Tanzania African National Union. *The Arusha Declaration and Tanzania African National Union's Policy on Socialism and Self-Reliance.* Dar es Salaam: TANU Publicity Section, 1967.

United Nations. *Africa's Strategy for Development in the 1970's.* Tunis, 1971.

United Nations, Department of Public Information. *Shaping a People's Destiny: The Story of Eritrea and the United Nations.* New York, 1953.

United Nations, Economic and Social Council. *United Nations Children's Emergency Fund. Recommendation of the Executive Director for an Allocation.* Ethiopia, Basic Health Services Continuation, 1965–1966, Addis Ababa, 1966.

United Nations, Economic Commission for Africa. *Final Report: Conference of African States on Development of Education in Africa, Addis Ababa, 15–25 May 1961.* UNESCO/ED/181. Paris, 1961.

————. *Educational Development in Africa: Costing and Financing.* Paris, 1968.

————. *Educational Development in Africa: Integration and Administration.* Paris, 1967.

————. *Educational Development in Africa: The Planning Process.* Paris, 1967.

————. *Final Report of the 1962 Paris Conference.* Paris, 1962.

————. *Report of an Evaluation Survey of University Level Manpower Supply and Demand in Selected African Countries.* Addis Ababa, 1970.

United Nations, Educational Scientific, and Cultural Organization. *Current Educational Budgeting in Relation to the Goals of Addis Ababa.* UNESCO/ED/MIN/IV. Paris, 1962.

————. *The Development of Higher Education in Africa.* Paris: UNESCO, 1963.

————. *Final Report. Ethiopia.* Report of meeting of ministers of education of

African countries participating in the implementation of the Addis Ababa Plan. Paris: UNESCO, 1962.

———. *Methods of Analyzing Educational Outlay,* prepared by F. Edding. Paris, 1966.

———. *Outline of a Plan for African Educational Development. Conference of African States on the Development of Education in Africa, Addis Ababa, 15–25 May 1961.* UNESCO/ED/180. Paris, 1961.

———. *Report on Investment in Education in Ethiopia.* Educational Programming Investment Mission, September to November 1962. Paris: UNESCO, 1963.

———. *The Role of Education in Economic Development in OECD Mediterranean Region Project.* Paris, 1963.

———. *World Survey of Education.* Vol. I, *Handbook of Educational Organization and Statistics.* ED/54. D.64. Paris: UNESCO, 1955.

———. *World Survey of Education.* ED.63/IX.4/A. Paris, 1966.

———. *World Yearbook of Education.* Pt. II. ED.57/IX/2A. Paris, 1958.

———, and Organization of African Unity. */Cesta/Ref. 1-6.* Papers prepared for the Nairobi conference. Paris, n.d.

———. */Cesta/2-7.* Papers prepared for the Nairobi conference. Paris, n.d.

———. *Final Report of the Lagos Conference.* Lagos, 1964.

———. *The Nairobi July 1968 Conference, Final Report.* Nairobi, 1968.

United Nations, Office of the Resident Representative. *United Nations in Ethiopia, 1951–1966.* Addis Ababa: Berhanenna Selam Printing Press, 1966.

United Nations, Work Oriented Adult Literacy Project, Ethiopia. *Experience Survey (National Literacy Efforts),* prepared by Dr. B. N. Singh and Abraha Gebrezion. Addis Ababa, 1969.

———. *Work Oriented Adult Literacy Project.* Addis Ababa, 1968.

United States, Agency for International Development. *The University of Utah Project in Ethiopia.* Logan: University of Utah Printing Service, 1967.

United States, Library of Congress, General Reference and Bibliography Division. *Africa South of the Sahara: A Selected, Annotated List of Writing,* compiled by Helen F. Conover. Washington, D.C., 1963.

———. *Agricultural Development Schemes in Sub-Saharan Africa: A Bibliography.* Washington, D.C., 1963.

———, Office of Education, Division of International Studies and Services. *Information on Education Around the World.* Recommendations of the twenty-fifth International Conference on Public Education sponsored by UNESCO and the International Bureau of Education. Geneva, July 1962.

United States Operations Mission to Ethiopia. *Point IV Report to Ethiopia on Ten Years of Joint Technical and Economic Cooperation Between the United States and the Imperial Ethiopian Government.* Addis Ababa: Communications Media Center, 1961.

———. *Progress Report: Point IV Cooperative Program in General Education.* Addis Ababa, 1953.

———. *Report on the Organization and Administration of the Ministry of Education and Fine Arts.* 2d ed., rev. Addis Ababa: Cooperative Education Program Press, 1954.

Index

Abidjan Conference, 151
Adwa, Battle of, 41–42
Afan Oromo, 25, 39
African Ministers of Education, Conference of, 151
African States, Conference of, 139, 149–51
Ahmed ibn Ibrahim, 3
Aklilu Habte, 128
Aklilu Habte Wold, 38
Aksum, 2–3, 10
Amharic, 1, 121, 155–56
Anglo-Ethiopian Agreements, 7, 91–92; Treaty, 7
Aqwaqwam, 13, 14, 16
Arat-Ayna, 16
Awraja, 160, 177

Badoglio, Pietro, 42, 48, 49, 51
Ballabat school. *See* Medhane Alem School
Bey, Hanna Saleh, 29, 30
Boy Scouts, 58, 89

Calligraphy, 17
Christianity, 10
Commissions, education: Education Sector Review, 184–95, 197; Long-Term Planning, 105–14, 118, 126, 139; National, 177–78, 184; Secondary Education, 155–58, 159, 162
Committee on Secondary Education, 155–58, 159, 162
Conferences, education (international): Abidjan, 151; African Ministers of Education, 151; African States, 139, 149–51; Nairobi, 151–52; Tananarive, 151
Confessions of Faith, 11
Council of Ministers, 7
Crafts, native, 73–74, 105
Cushitics, 2

Debre Berhan Community and Teacher Training Schools, 116–17, 141
Debtera, 10
Dervishes, 28
Development Plans, education: Five-Year, 114–16, 147, 153–55, 170; Long-Term, 105–14, 135
Digwa, 13

Education, attitudes toward: of nobility, 31, 36, 37; of public, 31, 38, 118, 193, 196; for women, 135–36, 169
Education, government: adult, 66–67, 105, 173, 175–76; community, 116, 124, 187–88, 192; curriculum, 69–70, 71–75, 104–5, 121, 123–25, 146, 155–57; evaluation of, 103–5, 118, 145–46, 152–53, 181–82, 183–84, 195–96; expenditure, 89, 92–93, 120, 144, 178–82, 196; finance, 39, 60, 84, 89, 92–93, 108, 143, 151, 167–68, 176–77, 178–80; higher, 64–66, 70, 77–78, 136, 151; legislation, 29, 32, 88–89, 138–39, 176–77; mandatory, 29, 32, 38; and mass

Education, government (*cont.*)
media, 173–75; and nobility, 28, 31, 36, 37; objectives of, 56, 119–20, 146, 154, 156–57, 169, 183, 186–89; physical, 75; provincial, 59–60, 91, 94, 125, 143, 159–60, 169–71, 177, 192; secondary, 57–59, 71, 76–77, 80, 112, 133–35, 156–58, 166–67, 171–72; and study abroad, 23–27, 38, 65–66, 78, 87; and women, 23, 38, 67–69, 135–36

Education, nongovernment: Ethiopian Orthodox Church, 10, 22, 29–30, 83–84, 108; missions, 22–23, 27–28, 33–34, 38–39, 80–82, 88, 96, 136; Moslem, 53, 80–81; private, 82–83, 197; and school enrollment, 108, 119, 168–69; and traditional church education, 10–21

Education Sector Review, 184–95, 197

Employment. *See* Manpower

Empress Menen School for Girls. *See* Itegue Menen School

Eritrea: education in, 38, 95–102; and Ethiopian relations, 8, 98, 102

Ethiopia: constitutions of, 5, 7, 8, 11, 138–39; economy of, 91–92, 114, 140, 180, 186; geography of, 1, 2; government of, 5–6, 7–9, 197; population of, 1–2; religion of, 10; revolution of, 9, 195, 197; settlement of, 2–4

Ethiopianization: of curriculum, 71, 122–23; and teachers, 104, 134, 165

Ethiopian Orthodox Church. *See* Education, nongovernment

Examinations, 77–78, 119, 136–37, 146

Ezana, 2–3

Fasiladas, 3–4
Felasha, 23, 81
Fitha Negest, 16
Flad, Martin, 22, 23

Foreign relations (aid): with African nations, 149; with France, 42; with Great Britain, 6–7, 42, 54–55, 70, 85, 91–92, 175; with Italy, 6, 41–42; with Russia, 85; with Sweden, 85–86, 165–66; with the United States, 85–86, 92, 105–6, 140–41

Gebru Desta, 23–24
Ge'ez, 2, 19, 47
General Wingate Secondary School, 57–58
Germa Amare (Girma Amare), 16, 21
Gondar, 11, 14
Gran. *See* Ahmed ibn Ibrahim
Graziani, Viceroy, 48, 51
Great Britain, 6–7, 42, 54–55, 70, 85, 91–92, 95, 175
Gubae Qanna, 15

Habte Maryam, Liqe Siltanat, 17
Haile Selassie I, 5, 22, 27, 34, 56–57, 59, 81–82, 83, 139
Haile Selassie I Secondary School, 57, 85, 86
Health, 75–76

International Development Association, 167, 184
Islam, 3, 10, 53
Israelite Universelle, Alliance, 27
Italian Occupation: and education, 42–53; and employment, 28, 45, 50; and Eritrea, 28, 42–46, 95–97; and Ethiopia, 6, 42, 54; massacre, 47–48, 55; and racism, 46, 49–50
Italy, 6, 41–42, 44, 95–96
Itegue Menen School, 38, 40, 58, 68, 73–74, 86
Iyasu I, 4, 11

Jasperdean, Kobes, 44
Judaism, 10. *See also* Felasha

Labor, 30
Languages of Instruction, 40, 70, 72,

88, 120, 155, 187; and Ethiopian-
ization, 39, 121–23; and Italian
Occupation, 43, 47, 52
League of Nations, 5, 27, 42
Lij Iyasu, 4–5, 31–32
Literacy, 40, 116, 139, 174, 175–76,
197
Literature, 17–18
Long-Term Planning Committee,
105–14, 118, 126, 139

Maaza Bekele, 84, 145–46
Mahdere Qal, 23
Manpower, 56–57, 77, 112, 115
Martin, Charles. See Werqneh Ishete
Matewos, Abun, 4, 29–30
Matte, Lucien, 64
Medhane Alem School, 58–59
Mekonnen Desta, 88, 90
Menelik II, 4, 22, 26, 27, 28–32, 34, 81
Menelik II School, 31, 34, 40, 86
Mercha Werqu, 23
Metsahift Bet, 16, 19–20
Ministry of Education: establishment
of, 4, 39, 88, 139; functions of, 88,
89–90, 98, 119, 135, 142; and
nongovernment schools, 84, 119;
organization of, 89–91, 128, 142–
43, 159, 177, 192; and teachers,
109–10, 128–30, 164
Missions. See Education, nongovern-
ment
Mulugeta Wodajo, 179
Music, 74–75
Mussolini, Benito, 6, 42, 47, 49, 51

Nairobi Conference, 151–52
National Commission for Education,
177–78, 184

Oromos, 3–4

Paganism, 10
Painting, 17–18
Pankhurst, Richard, 43, 96
Pankhurst, Sylvia, 24, 47, 75–76, 96,
97

Parliament, 5–6, 7, 8
Point IV, 100–102, 105, 140–41

Qine, 14–16, 19, 21
Queen of Sheba, 2

Racism. See Italian Occupation
Ras Tafari Makonnen. See Haile
Selassie I
Roman Catholicism, 31, 52–53

Sabeans, 2
Schools: community, 116–18, 124,
145; enrollment in, 108–9, 130–
33, 153, 168–71, 190; facilities in,
87, 97, 103, 125; preschools, 69;
promotion in, 76–78, 111, 119,
124, 136–38, 154–55, 157, 173;
technical-vocational, 59, 60–62,
100, 102, 112–14
Sweden, 85–86, 165–66

Taddesse Tereffe, 57
Tafari Makonnen Lyceum, 34–37,
40, 58
Tananarive Conference, 151
Teachers: attrition rates of, 128–29,
162, 164; and church teaching 19–
20; foreign personnel as, 69, 71–
72, 85–87, 129, 134; qualifications
of, 109, 125–27, 129–30, 162,
163–65; and Reconstruction, 69,
84–85; training of, 62–64, 110,
116–17, 127–28, 130, 141, 159,
160–65, 192
Technical Cooperation Program. See
Point IV
Tekle Hawaryat, 26
Tewodros II, 4, 22, 23
Textbooks, 158; during Italian Occupation, 47, 51–52; during Reconstruction, 70, 72
Tselat, 20

UNESCO, 116–17, 141, 147, 149,
151, 175–76, 177, 236
United Nations, 8, 98, 141, 149

United States, 85–86, 92, 140–41
University College, 65, 87, 105, 118–19

Werqneh Ishete, 25, 35
Weyzero Zewditu, 5, 32, 139
Women: education of, 23, 38, 67–69, 135–36, 164–65, 168–69; and

marriage, 67; and politics, 38, 67–68
World War II, 54, 55

Yared, 13
Yohannes IV, 4, 24

Zara Yakob, 3, 11
Zema, 13–15, 19